RAILWAY LAW

IN

ILLINOIS.

THE RELATIONS OF RAILROADS TO THE PEOPLE, AS SET FORTH IN THE CONSTITUTION, THE STATUTES AND THE DECISIONS OF ILLINOIS; TOGETHER WITH THE DECISIONS OF OTHER STATES AND THE FEDERAL COURTS UPON THE CONSTITUTIONAL QUESTIONS INVOLVED.

WITH AN

INTRODUCTION BY HON. JOHN M. PALMER,

AND AN APPENDIX SHOWING THE CONDITION OF ALL THE RAILWAYS IN THE STATE, AND THE TARIFF SCHEDULE PREPARED IN ACCORDANCE WITH LAW.

BY FRANK GILBERT.

"A Corporation holds its Rights and Franchises Subordinate to the General Welfare of Society."—*Supreme Court of Illinois.*

CHICAGO:
CALLAGHAN AND COMPANY
1873.

PREFACE.

All who give special attention to the subject of railroads in their relations to the public, are intently watching Illinois. This is alike true, whether railways are considered from a legal, an economic or a political point of view. The present constitution and recent railway legislation of the State, together with the decision of the Supreme Court based thereon, explain and abundantly justify this prominence. It is obvious that while, in its leading features, the common carrier law is substantially the same as administered in the different States, yet there are many points of diversity, as the result both of legislation and judicial decision. Those special features in this State are of such a nature as to make Illinois the pathfinder in the present effort to readjust the carrying trade of the country.

This treatise is largely the result of investigations prosecuted with no thought of book-making. The writer has constant occasion, in the performance of his daily work, to state some phase of railway law, and has often found it necessary to consult many authorities in ascertaining positively the correct answer to what might seem to be a very simple question. Throughout these pages scrupulous care has been taken to avoid blending mere personal opinions with the authoritative utterances of the judiciary, and the exact limitations of the written law. Great caution has been observed to prevent errors. The author's object will have been attained and his labors abundantly rewarded if the result shall prove of service in lessening the work of determining with exactitude what is railway law in Illinois, and contribute in some degree to a better understanding and adjustment of the relations which the railroads of the country sustain in law, and should sustain in fact, to the people.

F. G.

CHICAGO, Oct. 15, 1873.

TABLE OF CASES.

THE FIGURES REFER TO THE PAGES.

A.

B.

C.

D.

E.

F.

I.

P.

R.

S.

CONTENTS.

THE REFERENCES ARE TO THE SECTIONS.

CHAPTER I.

THE RAILWAY SITUATION.

CHAPTER II.

RAILROAD CORPORATIONS.

I.

II.

III.

CHAPTER V.

RAILWAY CONSTRUCTION.

I.

CHAPTER VI.

RAILWAY LIABILITIES.

I.

III.

INTRODUCTION,*

BY HON. JOHN M. PALMER.

THE COMMON LAW OF RAILWAYS.

So much has been said about vested rights, and such unwarrantable claims have been based upon them, that we have become the victims of delusions created by ourselves. But the railroads exist. They are part of our social and business system, and if they inflicted double the wrongs upon us that they do now, they themselves are fixed, and will never be disturbed. It is not necessary for me to engage in the discussion of any of the controverted theories which have been advanced in respect to the nature or extent of the powers of railroad corporations under what are called their charters.

I admit the law to be as decided by the Supreme Court of the United States in the case of "The Trustees of Dartmouth College against Woodward." I have no doubt that the Supreme Court held correctly, that the charter granted by the British Crown to the Trustees of Dartmouth College, in the year 1769, is a contract, within the meaning of that clause of the

* This subject was elaborately discussed by Ex-Governor Palmer, in an address, delivered and published when this treatise was nearly ready for the press. The author at once requested the Governor to furnish a preliminary paper, for use in this connection, which he kindly consented to do.

Constitution of the United States which declares that no State shall make any law impairing the obligation of contracts, and I am quite as clear, upon principles that are well understood and eminently just, that the acts of the General Assembly of New Hampshire by which it was proposed to change the name and essentially modify the powers of that corporation, and also to seize the property and usurp the government of the institution, were in violation of the Constitution, and I am prepared also to assent to the doctrine of the Supreme Court of Illinois, that the charters of private corporations are contracts which are inviolable, and as decided by the same court in the cases of "Neustadt and others against the Illinois Central Railroad Company," and of the "Illinois Central Railroad Company against the County of McLean," that the act incorporating the Illinois Central Railroad Company, which declares certain exemptions of the property of the Company from taxation is a contract between the State and the Company, which cannot be changed or amended without the consent of both parties. Indeed, I concede it to be too well established to be shaken or questioned that the State cannot, by the action of any of the departments of its government, impair the charters of private corporations in any material respect.

Having made these concessions, no one will expect me either to attack the claim of corporations to vested rights, or to complain of those decisions of the courts that recognize such rights and vindicate them against every attempt to impair them. Many persons who are under the influence of the delusions for which the representatives of corporate pretensions are responsible, observing that I admit all that has been decided by the Courts in respect to the nature and inviolability of the rights of corporations will be ready to conclude that I have, by my concessions, already defined the rights and obligations of railway carriers, and that I have abandoned the only grounds upon which the correction of the abuses which are known to exist in the railway carrying system can be demanded; but I hope to demonstrate that the principles which recognize the inviolability of contracts between the State and the railway corporations, so far from justifying the pretensions of railway carriers to be "a law unto themselves," afford support to theories I will hereafter present and maintain in regard to the legal extent of their duties and obligations.

Carriers are among the earliest agencies of the intercourse of mankind. One of the earliest records of the human race preserves the fact that "Jonah went down to Joppa, and found a ship going to Tarshish, *and paid the fare thereof*, and went down into it to go with them to Tarshish." Accounts equally ancient refer to the freighting of ships with the products of the industry and skill of the oldest of the nations. In all ages the office or employment of carrier has borne an important relation to the commerce and business of the world, and their obligations and liabilities, as well as their duties and powers are defined in the commercial codes of all civilized nations.

All over the world their business is treated as a public office or employment, and their rights and duties are held to result from the relation they voluntarily assume to the public. Wherever the English language is spoken they are called "common carriers," a term which indicates the general nature of their business, and at the same time describe the extent of their legal obligations. The distinguishing feature of the office or employment implied in the term "Common Carrier" is, that its obligations and liabilities are not dependent upon the contract, but are imposed by law. I will only enumerate, in this connection, a few of the duties and obligations which the law has imposed upon common carriers, and I will confine myself to those which are least disputed, and interest the public most. "They must furnish reasonable and ordinary facilities for transportation, such as will meet the ordinary demands of the public."

They are obliged by law to undertake the charge of transportation indifferently for all, without partiality or improper discrimination, and for a reasonable compensation. These obligations are implied in the very nature of the office, for a common carrier, in the language of the courts of highest authority, is one who holds himself out to the world as ready to undertake to carry all persons, or for all persons, indifferently for hire, as a business. He engages to receive at all reasonable times, according to the nature of the business, all passengers, if a carrier of passengers, or, if a carrier of freights, all property which is of a character suited to his means of transportation, in the order in which it is offered, and to transport with safety and reasonable dispatch, and to discharge or deliver, at the place or to the persons expressed or implied in his undertaking, and by the very nature of his employment he undertakes to discharge all the ordinary duties he assumes for a reasonable reward, and as these are duties and obligations imposed upon common carriers by law, they cannot release themselves from them except by the consent of every person who may call upon them to perform them. Railway corporations, and all natural persons who undertake the duties which I have described as pertaining to that office or employment, are common carriers.

The Supreme Court of our own State, in one of the cases before it, speaking through Justice Breese, a venerable name in jurisprudence, uses the following language: "We suppose that it is not necessary that the charters should provide, in so many words, that the railroad companies created by them shall be common carriers. The authorities are numerous to the point, that such companies using cars for the purpose of conveying goods for all persons indifferently for hire, and whose custom and uniform practice is to do so, are common carriers, and are liable as such. There needs no legislative declaration to make them such; they are so in virtue of their uniform business, and are subject to the provisions of the common law which are applicable to carriers." And the same Court said in another case: "It is admitted by respondent's counsel that railway companies are common carriers. Regarded merely as common carriers at common law, and independently of any obligations imposed by the acceptance of its charter, it would owe important duties to the public, from which it could not release itself except with the consent of every person who might call upon it to perform them. These obligations grow out of the relation voluntarily assumed by the carrier to the public. But railway companies may well be regarded as under higher obligations, if that were possible, than those imposed by the common law, to discharge their duties to the public as common carriers fairly and impartially. As has been said by other courts, the State has endowed them with a portion of its sovereignty in giving them the right of eminent domain. By virtue of this power they take the lands of the citizen against his will, and can, if need be, demolish his house. Is it supposed these great powers were granted merely for the private gain of the corporations? On the contrary, we all know the companies were created for the public good. The object of the Legislature was to add to the means of travel and commerce." And the Supreme Court maintains that railway corporations are common carriers, and subject to all the obligations imposed upon common carriers at common law, both upon the ground that the Legislature so intended in creating the corporations, and that the corporators contracted to be common carriers when they accepted the charters.

The Court, in the cases from which I quote, concede that the charters of railway corporations are contracts between the corporators and the State, which neither party can annul or change without the consent of the other, and that such contracts impose reciprocal obligations. In one case the Court say: "We hold simply that it [meaning a railway corporation] must perform all those duties of a common carrier to which it knew it would be liable when it sought and obtained its charter." "The company can make such rules and contracts as it pleases, not inconsistent with its duties as common carrier, but it can go no farther; and any general language its charter may contain must necessarily be construed with that limitation." "But the charter was granted to promote the convenience of commerce, and it is the constant duty of the respondent to adopt its agencies to that end. It can be permitted to establish no custom inconsistent with its charter." And, in a late case, the Court said: "Can any one suppose it was merely to enrich and aggrandize the stockholders and the officers of these companies that the people through their representatives, have granted such liberal charters. On the contrary, we all know that the grant of such powers were conferred to advance the public interest as the first and great object. But to accomplish this great purpose, it was found necessary to enlist private enterprise and capital. And to call it forth for the accomplishment of the end, rights, privileges, and immunities had to be conferred and secured to those who would embark in the construction and operation of these roads. Hence in these charters the rights and duties of the companies are expressed or implied. When created bodies corporate, they became invested with the right to construct and use their roads to transport both persons and property over their lines and to receive compensation for the same. And when these bodies accept their charters, it is with the implied understanding that they will fairly perform the duties of public common carriers of both persons and property. These are duties they owe to the public and it was in consideration that they would be performed that this charter was granted."

These decisions cover the whole ground of the controvrsy between the people and the railway carriers, and they define "the legal rights and legal duties of persons whose business and employment it is to receive, transport, and discharge passengers and freight on and by railways," to be the rights and duties of common carriers at common law, and they maintain the vested rights of the public under the charter contracts between the railroad companies and the State, to insist that such companies shall be held to a complete performance of all the obligations which the law has attached to that relation.

I have referred to some of the rules of the common law relating to the duties of common carriers, and will add that the common law is but "the body of principles and usages and rules the product of wisdom, counsel, experience and observation of many ages of wise and observing men." And it materially adds to the value of these principles, usages and rules, that they rest for their support upon reason and justice, that they are not limited in their operation to any one or more of the States, but are in force wherever reason rules and justice are regarded. They defy power and spurn corruption. They may be disregarded, but cannot be destroyed or changed. They regulate the carrying trade of the ocean and the great lakes and rivers, and in their application will be found the solution of what is aptly called the "railway problem."

RAILWAY LAW IN ILLINOIS.

CHAPTER I.

THE RAILWAY SITUATION.

§ 1. Illinois has something over six thousand miles of railroad, which is more than any other state in the Union has. Their cost, with equipments, was about two hundred and forty million dollars. The collection into one volume of the laws relating to an interest so vast is a matter of great convenience and greater importance. Those laws are scattered through the legislation of a quarter century, and the decisions, not only of this state, but of other states and the United States, covering a wide range of legal literature.

§ 2. Before entering upon a detailed analysis of the subject in hand it will be of interest to take a general survey of the field. Facts and law are so intertwined that such a survey is indispensible.

§ 3. Although the railroads themselves are novel, and all legislation in regard to them essentially experimental, the great body of laws applicable to them are as old as well regulated commerce. The equitable principles which govern the relations of a common carrier to the public form a cardinal feature of what might fitly be termed the code of civilization. A clear understanding of the whole subject would require thorough study of the history and laws of commerce in all times and lands. Our historical inquiry must necessarily be cursory, and strictly confined to the one method of carrying on traffic between different places, which has come into existence within the memory of many, and has already attained overshadowing proportions.

§ 4. Delving among the rubbish of the past could unearth no railway relic half a century old. If some of the ancients had tramways with groved vehicles they had no knowledge of steam as a motive power. The Appian way of Rome was doubtless the best road of any considerable length ever built prior to the railroad constructed in England in the year 1829. That date marks an era second in importance only to the discovery of movable types.

§ 5. The railway system of the United States dates from 1830. The honor of seniority is claimed by the Boston and Lowell railroad, also by the Baltimore and Ohio. The whistle of the locomotive was first heard in Illinois eight years later, at the insignificant town of Meredosia. The state was then in the twentieth year of its age. The track-laying on that pioneer line began May 9, 1838. The first locomotive arrived in September, and on the eighth of November eight miles of that long since abandoned and almost forgotten Northern Cross railroad was in operation. That was the first railroad of the Mississippi Valley.

§ 6. At the time Illinois entered the field of railway construction there was in the entire country 1,913 miles of railway in operation. At the beginning of 1873 there were 67,104 miles of road in actual use. The increase for the latter year was 6,427 miles, or about the same as the total mileage of road in Illinois. It was not until ten years after the pioneer railroad of the state had been built that railway operations fairly began here. Until 1848 the total extent of railroads in the state was only twenty-two miles. Since then the growth has been steady, and reasonably proportioned to the needs of the people. The total cost of the railroads of the country is estimated at $3,159,423,057, and the net earnings at 5.20 per cent. of the cost. The cost of the British railroads was $2,763,400,535, and the earnings are 4.65 per cent. The per cent. of net earnings to cost in Illinois is 6.2.

§ 7. Railway construction has been in part the result of private enterprise and in part of public gifts of one kind or another. In the list of public donations should be included individual aid afforded without any expectation of direct return. The amount of aid afforded by personal contributions cannot be stated, even approximately. Neither can the aid afforded by states, counties, cities and towns be given. We only know that quite a large per centage of the actual cost of building railroads was borne by the public. It is equally true that as a rule the original builders did not realized upon their investments, and through mortgage foreclosures, or sales at a great reduction, the property has generally passed into other hands. The Chicago and Alton railroad, for example, now one of the most profitable lines in the country, was projected by a New York banker, who sunk over a million dollars in the enterprise, and finally went into bankruptcy. The experience of Mr. Dwight was that of a great many others, although usually on a smaller scale. The actual cost of the railroads of the country to their present owners was vastly less than the actual cost of construction. Consequently the average net earnings of the roads are very considerably greater then appears upon the surface.

§ 8. Congress has issued bonds in aid of six railroad enterprises, viz.: the Union Pacific; the Central Pacific; the Kansas Pacific; the Central Branch Union Pacific; the Western Pacific, and the Sioux City and Pacific. The principal on these bonds foots up $64,623,512, all bearing interest at six per cent., payable semi-annually. The acts authorizing these bonds were passed in July, 1862, and July, 1864. The principal will fall due thirty years from the date of issue. In *theory* these bonds are a loan of the national credit to the companies named, but in reality they are a donation.

§ 9. The chief aid extended to railway projects by the General Government was in the nature of gifts from the public domain. The past tense is used because while many land grant bills were introduced in the forty-second congress, and will doubtless be revived in the forty-third, popular sentiment is so strongly and unitedly against railway subsidies of every kind that it is safe to predict that no such measure will hereafter become a law. The land grant policy, so far as concerns railroads, dates back to 1850, and in this respect, also, Illinois was the pioneer state. As the honor of projecting a railroad across the continent to the Pacific fairly belongs to Hon. SIDNEY BREESE, Chief Justice of Illinois, and formerly member of the United States senate from this state, so Hon. STEPHEN A. DOUGLAS might justly be called the Father of Subsidy. On the twentieth of September, 1850, congress granted 2,595,053.00 acres to the Illinois Central, and the Mobile and Chicago railroads, practically one enterprise. The method adopted and ever since adhered to was to grant the *odd* sections. The appreciation of the *even* sections in consequence of the facilities for communication afforded by the roads was such that the price was raised from $1.25 to $2.50 per acre.[1] No other railway enterprise in Illinois has ever been aided by congress.

§ 10. The legal mode of operation has been always to vest the title to the land in the state. Usually, the state legislature has unconditionally turned the

[1] See Poor's Railroad Manual, 1873–74, 696.

grant over to the railroad, or railroads. Illinois exacted of the Illinois Central payment into the state treasury of seven per cent. of its gross earnings, at the same time exempting the property of the road from ordinary taxation. This contract has since been hedged about by special constitutional enactment, and from it there could be no deviation through legislative action. The annual revenue of the state from this source is about half a million, and steadily increasing.

§ 11. In estimating the grants of public land in aid of railroad projects, a distinction must be made between the amount granted and the amount certified. In Illinois, the whole grant has been certified; but this is not true in any other state. The total number of acres granted to aid works of improvement, is 198,-165,794$\frac{67}{100}$, or about 300,000 square miles.[1] This area is greater than that of the six New England states, with New York, Pennsylvania, Illinois, Indiana, Ohio, and New Jersey combined. It includes 4,405,986 acres granted in aid of canals, also, 3,857,-213$\frac{27}{100}$ acres recently donated in aid of wagon roads. Deducting the grants made but not certified, and the quantity is still enormous. "The amount," says Poor, "yet to be made in the several states will probably reach 35,000,000 or 40,000,000 of acres. In Iowa, for example, the grants made call for 7,207,837$\frac{98}{100}$ acres. Of these, 3,511,149$\frac{60}{100}$ acres have been certified, there not having been an amount of government lands of *odd* sections within the limits of the grants at the time they were made equalling the nominal

[1] Poor's Manual, 700.

amounts of the same." The same authority estimates the total extent of railroads constructed and to be constructed on the strength of these land grants at 15,000 miles of line.

§ 12. The states which have thus been made the agents of the General Government in carrying out the subsidy policy are Iowa, Michigan, Illinois, Minnesota, Alabama, Missouri, Arkansas, Florida, Wisconsin, Mississippi, California, Oregon and Louisiana. From the standpoint of aggregate grants, certified and uncertified, Minnesota is the first in the list, and Kansas second.

§ 13. There has been an appalling amount of corruption in connection with the subsidy policy, and it is a matter of rejoicing that both political parties are agreed in its abolition. It is none the less true that the rapidity with which the development of the remote West has been pushed must be attributed, very largely, if not mainly, to the land grant policy. In justice to the Illinois Central company and its management it should be added, that its land department has from first to last been conducted honestly, and in a way calculated to increase the productive wealth of the state.

§ 14. If we were to go back a generation or so we should find society divided into two classes on the railroad question. The more conservative looked upon the locomotive as a desolating Vandal. Others, again, were completely carried away. The speed would soon be quickened to at least one hundred miles an hour, and transportation rates would be so very low that everybody would get rich. Experience has taught both extremes some wisdom. No one could have foreseen how completely the carrying trade by land would be revolutionized, nor how readily all things would adapt themselves to the change.

§ 15. The science of railroading (for a science it certainly is), no one has more than fairly begun to master, although a very large per cent. of the best talent of the country is engaged in the conduct of the business, in one form or another. Especially is this true of the legal profession. So long as the more knotty railway problems remain partially unsolved there will be more or less clashing between production and consumption, on the one hand, and transportation on the other. But, be it remembered, each is equally indispensable to the other, and a basis of good fellowship is mutually desirable. It is quite conceivable that the interests of all concerned will yet be essentially unified by the adoption of a better method of operating railroads, dictated by railway self-interest, no less than by considerations of public policy.

§ 16. Five distinct ways of operating railroads have thus far been recognized. Each deserves special mention.

§ 17. The primitive idea of railway management was borrowed from turnpikes. Examination of an English railroad charter would lead one to suppose that the British railroads were toll-roads. It was originally thought that large aggregations of capital would construct paths for the locomotive, provide station accommodations, etc., then throw the line open to the public, depending for returns on the investment solely upon the tolls received. That crude idea was early abandoned as utterly impracticable. There must be unity in the management of all the trains that run over a line. This is absolutely essential to safety. Then, too, the expense of fitting out one train, however small and poorly equipped, would be too great to admit of its being done miscellaneously. Any haphazard system would surely work disastrously, and be abandoned.

§ 18. Another method is to have the railroads form a part of the government, state or national. This plan has been tried with success in the management of canals. It proved a failure when the general government adopted it in the case of the Cumberland wagon road. The state of Pennsylvania tried it with the Pennsylvania Central railroad; but after incurring a heavy debt gave it up, either at the dictates of sound policy or at the connivance of a corrupt ring. Illinois has never taken a single step toward that method of railway management. It is being urged in Great Britain, and works well on the continent of Europe, where the governments are conducted by and for the few. Its feasibility for this country is being discussed somewhat, but the subject is now confined to the region of abstract speculation. If adopted at all it would be upon a national scale, yet through the co-ordinate action of the several states and of the United States.

§ 19. A third method is for each railroad company to own or lease all the rolling stock in use on its line. That was the system adopted when the primitive method was abandoned. If it were necessary to the *proper supply of facilities* for transportation by rail that the owners of the road should furnish all the equipments, then self-interest and duty to the public would require it; but it was early found impracticable, and was long ago abandoned. The Philadelphia and Reading railroad company alone adheres to it. That corporation, with its numerous branch roads, is complete in itself, while the other railroads of the country, whether long or short, form links in a vast continental chain. The greater part of the business of our railroads begins with one road and ends with another, often passing over many roads. To transfer the consignment from one car to another every time a change of roads was necessary, would be an intolerable delay and expense, besides greatly increasing the danger of damage from handling. This led to a system of railway comity which was some years ago recognized and made binding by legislation. That legislation has been unchallenged in its validity.

§ 20. This necessity of railway comity led, not necessarily, but still naturally, to the formation of fast freight lines and palace car lines. By means of this fourth system all unnecessary delays and transfers are avoided. The expense of palace cars are such that only one, the Pullman line, has attained any considerable proportions. The expense of freight cars is so light that there are many transportation companies, and the greater part of through freight business is carried on in the cars of such companies. There is professedly no discrimination of any kind, and the railroad companies claim to be entirely ready to haul at impartial rates all cars offered them, whether by other railroad companies, by transportation companies, or by individuals.

§ 21. The fifth and final method is in theory the same as the fourth, and rests upon precisely the same legal basis; but practically it is altogether different. The fourth has proved a monopoly system, while the fifth, when once fairly in operation, would prove a competitive system. Thus far car owners have allowed the railroad companies to dictate the terms on which consignments should be taken. This servitude has been submitted to because the evils of it fell entirely upon the producer and shipper, while its benefits were shared between servant and master. Usage has now established the right to car-service as an integral part of common law, and one person, or any number of persons, interested in cheap freight, can put into operation the competitive system. This feature of common law exists throughout the country; Illinois alone has distinctly recognized it by statutory provision. The competitive system, once generally established, would unify the railway and the popular interest. It would be alike for the interest of the owners of the highways and of the patrons thereof to have an increase of facilities. Competition would secure more cars and lower freight charges, while the railroad company would derive revenue in proportion to that increase of facilities. The work of legislation and adjudication in preventing extortion would be vastly simplified. It would be necessarily only to establish by law a fair scale of compensation for car-hauling, and competition would take care of the rest as surely as it now does of mercantile charges. Theodore Bacon justly remarks that "to give scope to competition there must not only be large and free demand, but the possibility of supplying by many persons, from many sources, the very commodity demanded." Such possibility would be rendered a certainty by this fifth system. Mr. Adams was entirely correct in his comment upon competition between railroad corporations when he said: "While the result of ordinary competition is to reduce and equalize prices, the result of railroad competition is to produce local inequalities and arbitrary raise and depress prices." Competition must be of such a nature as to reach every station on the line, else a few points of intersection will enjoy its benefits at the expense of the many.

§ 23. The fourth system is, Regulation by Combination; the true and inevitable system is, Regulation by Competition. This fifth method was first distinctly recognized and rendered attainable by the Illinois railway legislation of 1873. It would be easy to increase the profits of the railroads and lessen the cost of transportation by an equitable division, in accordance with the laws of trade, of the enormous profits now divided between transportation companies belonging to the monopoly ring.

§ 24. The entire nation is becoming profoundly agitated and perplexed over the railway question. There is imminent danger that production and transportation, interests which in their permanent thrift are mutually dependent, will be drawn into disastrous conflict. Statesmen, jurists and economists have seldom been confronted by a graver or more exacting problem. Unless it is rightly adjusted, and that with reasonable dispatch, the antagonism will be fraught with exasperation and peril. To dispel ignorance is the first step towards reconciliation. The aim of this treatise is to set forth those legal principles and rules which admit of no intelligent controversy, and which must guide and condition all successful attempts to effect an equitable and lasting adjustment.

CHAPTER II.

RAILROAD CORPORATIONS.

I. Corporate Organization.

§ 25. A railroad is defined as "a road on which iron rails are laid for wheels to run on for the conveyance of heavy loads in vehicles." This definition has reference to the practical working of railway business. The legal definition of the term, as given by the constitution of Illinois, is simply: "a railway is a highway," and, "a highway is a road open to the public." No railroad is a strictly private enterprise. The right to construct the same is not obtained in the usual methods of property transfers. The right of private way is secured only by the consent of the original owner or owners of the ground;[1] while the right of way for a railroad must be secured, to a greater or less extent, by condemnation, or the exercise of the sovereign power of eminent domain.

§ 26. The enterprise having started as a public project, and been given special privileges on that account, the contract thus entered into cannot be set aside at the option of one of the parties thereto. The perversion of a highway into a private road would justly forfeit the original franchise. We have herein the explanation of the fact that railroads which are highways are always corporate property.

§ 27. A corporation has been defined as an artificial being created by law, and composed of individuals subsisting as a body politic under a special denomination, with capacity to succeed each other in perpetual succession, and to act in many respects as a natural person. The privilege of being a corporation is conferred on individuals by grant from the sovereign power, and is a franchise. A private corporation is one founded by private individuals, the stock

[1] Nesbit *v.* Trumbo, 39 Ill. 110; Crear *v.* Crossly, 40 Ill. 175.

of which is owned, at least in part, by private persons; and is distinguished from a public corporation, which is created by the government for political purposes, or whose stock is owned exclusively by the government.[1]

§ 28. The right of a government to vest in a corporation certain functions of its own authority, for the public interest and with certain restrictions, expressed or implied, has never been in dispute. This right rests upon a foundation essential to the very existence of the state, and in its exercise dates back to the earliest conception of political economy. However it may be perverted, it is absolutely essential to the well-being of society. Under the code of Solon Athens granted corporate charters, and the Eighth of the Twelve Tables of Rome was in effect a recognition of the corporate system as an economic necessity.

§ 29. While the corporate principle is common to all civilized governments, there is wide range and great variety in the methods of its application. Until a relatively recent date, in England the granting of charters was a royal prerogative. All corporations formed in that country at the present time must organize under a general incorporation act. In this country not only has each state its own mode of procedure, but the same state often has more than one way. Such was the case in Illinois from its existence as a state until the adoption of its present constitution. Since then, all railway organizations have been formed on one general plan.

§ 30. It has always been competent for the general assembly of Illinois to require corporations to organize

[1] Chief Justice Marshall, in Dartmouth College *v.* Woodward, 4 Wheaton, 543.

under general law. The organic law has always, in theory, contemplated the issuance of special charters only in special cases. Practically, the charter system was in use to the almost entire exclusion of the general system, until absolutely forbidden.

§ 31. The present constitution provided that "all existing charters or grants of special or exclusive privileges, under which organization shall not have taken place, or which shall not have been in organization within ten days from the time this constitution takes effect, shall thereafter have no validity or effect whatever."[1] The evident intention was to forbid the entering upon new corporate enterprises on the strength of old charters; or at least to prevent "sleeping" upon vested rights.[2] Such has not been its effect. Organization deemed sufficient to comply with the constitution was easy and inexpensive. The mere election of officers, adoption of by-laws, and the like preliminary work, has been deemed compliance with the constitution. The greater part of the railway schemes put in operation in Illinois during the current decade rest upon old charters, rather than upon the general law. It would be quite impossible to estimate how long it will take to exhaust this "reserve fund" of special charters. The validity of some of these charters will doubtless be called in question, eventually, on a writ of *quo warranto*, based

[1] Illinois Constitution, art. xi, sec. 2.

[2] A great many charters were procured under the old constitution without any expectation on the part of the corporators of making any legitimate use of the same. Franchises were secured with a view to selling them. This hawking about of charters is not wholly at an end in this state even yet.

on the constitutional limitation quoted; but no such case has yet reached the docket of the Supreme Court.

§ 32. Classified from the standpoint of organization the railroads of Illinois are: First, those organized and existing under specific charters; and, second, those organized and existing under the general incorporation act.[1] It should be borne in mind that the organization of a company is a vital part of its continuous existence. It is liable at any time to be obliged to show the title to its franchises, and its right to acquire and hold property.

§ 33. The railway charters granted in Illinois differ in some of their details, but agree in their general characteristics. They quite uniformly lay special stress upon the rights of the corporation, while passing lightly over its liabilities. This is not, however, a matter of real importance, a charter being declatory of rights, rather than creative of them. Subjected to the actual test of law, railway corporations existing under the general act of the state have essentially the same rights as those existing under special charters, and, conversely, those existing under special charters are subject to the same control, judicial and legislative, as those existing under general law.[2]

§ 34. A general law for the organization of railroad companies was passed in 1849. In a subsequent railway case it was claimed that a charter granted after the passage of that act would not be valid unless it was expressly declared that special reasons existed for

[1] For a complete list of the railway companies of the state, arranged according to this classification, see Appendix.

[2] For a discussion of this subject and authorities for this statement, see chapter on the Doctrine of Uniformity.

not organizing under the general law. The court held that such declaration was not necessary.[1] As a matter of fact very few organizations were affected under the law of 1849, and it is believed that no railroad company in the state now holds its franchises under that act, or any general statute ante-dating the present constitution. Those originally organized thereunder either secured special charters afterwards, or reorganized under the statute of 1872.

§ 35. The most notable instance of beginning under the general law, and then securing a charter, occurred under the administration of Gov. Matteson, in 1854. As it was ultimately made a test case in the courts it deserves notice.[2] The Mississippi and Atlantic railroad company found it difficult to raise money and preferred a special charter. The governor called an extra session of the general assembly, specifying, among other things, this object, "to pass laws recognizing the existence of, and conferring additional powers upon, corporations formed, or which may be formed prior to the action of the legislature thereon under the act to provide for a general system of railroad incorporations." It was claimed that organization having been effected under the general law there could be no transference of the company to a charter basis. The court did not take this view of the case. It held, on the contrary, that such legislation was valid.[3]

[1] Johnson *v.* Joliet & Chicago R. R. Co. 23 Ill. 203.

[2] People *v.* Mississippi and Atlantic R. R. Co. 14 Ill. 440.

[3] There was an eminent array of counsel in the case. C. Beckwith, conspicuous in the latest test railway case, was associated with Messrs. Constable, Gillespie and Blackwell as

§ 36. The right of the legislature to cure defects of organization was the principle of chief importance set forth, in the opinion of the court, in that case. The doctrine of the validity of retroactive corporate legislation has been reaffirmed in several cases, and alluded to always as a settled point.[1] If the legislature had the right to cure organic defects by special legislation it has the right to do so by general legislation. This is a vital point in view of a law passed in 1873 for the purpose of curing defects in railway organization.[2]

§ 37. Some railroad companies organized under the general railway law of 1849, amended in 1869, have since organized under the law approved March 1, 1872. A few companies possessing special charters have seen fit to organize under that law, in accordance with a provision therein contained. The mode of procedure in such cases is the same as in effecting an entirely new organization. We need only add of the law of 1849 that it was amended in 1857, and again in 1869, and the whole repealed, except certain specified sections, by the law of 1872.[3]

§ 38. In addition to positively forbidding the creation of corporations by special enactment, except those

counsel for the people; Lyman Trumbull, B. C. Cook, J. A. Glover, V. Worthington and Gen. McClernand, appeared for the corporation.

[1] Goodrich *v.* Reynolds, Wilder & Co., 31 Ill. 490.

Laws of Illinois, Twenty-Eighth General Assembly, First Session, page 140.

[3] The sections not repealed are 34, 35, 36, 37, 38, 39, 40, 41, 42 and 45. All except the latter apply entirely to the operating of the road. That defines the companies to which the law is applicable.

for charitable, educational, penal, or reformatory purposes, and which are to be and remain under the patronage and control of the state, the constitution provides that the general assembly shall [not may] by general law make provision for the incorporations thereafter to be created.[1] It would have been competent for the legislature to have passed a statute analogous to the British law called "The Companies Act of 1872," which applies to all corporations; but as a matter of fact the general incorporation acts of Illinois do not apply to railroads.[2]

§ 39. The main statute for the formation of railway companies was approved March 1, 1872. It contained an emergency clause, and consequently became at once operative. The supplemental act was approved April 26, 1873, and went into effect July 1, 1873.[3]

§ 40. Any number of persons, not less than five, may form a railway company. In organizing an ordinary corporation the number must not be less than three, nor more than seven.

§ 41. The articles of incorporation must set forth the facts on each of the eight following points, viz.: 1. The name of the proposed corporation. 2. The

[1] Illinois Constitution, art. xi, sec. 1.

[2] There is an act authorizing the formation of union depots, the details of which will be explained hereafter. Besides railway laws there are three general incorporation acts non-applicable to railroads. The first gives the details of procedure in creating and operating stock companies; the second is purely supplemental to the first, and the third is designed to enable associations of persons to raise funds to loan only to their members. See Gross Statutes, vol. 2, pp. 124, 556 and 571.

[3] The first is given in Gross Statutes, vol. 2, p. 64; the second in the statutes of the state of Illinois, 1873, p. 117.

places from and to which it is intended to construct the proposed railroad. 3. The place at which shall be established and maintained the principal business office of such corporation. 4. The time of the commencement and the period of continuance of such corporation, the same not to exceed fifty years. 5. The amount of capital stock. 6. The names and places of residence of the several persons forming the association. 7. The names of the members of the first board of directors, and in what officers or persons the government of the proposed corporation and the management of its affairs shall be vested. 8. The number and amount of shares in the capital stock of the corporation.

§ 42. These articles of incorporation must be signed by the corporators and recorded in the office of the recorder of deeds in each county through or into which the railroad is proposed to be run, also in the office of the secretary of state.

§ 43. The filing and recording having been effected, the persons named as corporators thereupon become a body corporate, clothed with the usual powers of a corporation, and duly authorized to proceed with the business in hand. The statute defines this authority to be the power to have succession; sue and be sued; plead and be impleaded; have and use a common seal, which it may alter at pleasure; declare the interest of its stockholders transferable;[1] establish by-laws, and make all rules and regulations for the management of its affairs in accordance with law.

[1] The old idea that a corporation can only act under its corporate seal is obsolete. See New England Fire and Marine Ins. Co. v. Schatler, 38 Ill., 166.

§ 44. A copy of any articles of incorporation, filed and recorded as the law directs, certified as correct by the secretary of state or his deputy, must be accepted as *prima facie* evidence of the incorporation of the company and of the facts therein set forth.

§ 45. Under the obsolete law of railway incorporation there had to be at least twenty-five original incorporators. The life of the company was limited to fifty years, with no provision for renewal.[1] Under the present law the corporation may renew from time to time, for a period of not longer than fifty years, provided that three-fourths of the votes cast at any regular election held for that purpose shall be in favor of continuance; and provided, further, that those desiring to renew shall purchase, at its current value, the stock of those opposed to continuance, in case any of the stockholders are opposed thereto.

§ 46. The original by-laws and all subsequent amendments must be recorded in the office of the secretary of state, and of the county recorder, or recorders, the same as the articles of incorporation. The copy must be certified. This record must be made always within ninety days after the adoption of the same.

§ 47. As transfers of stock generally precede, to a greater or less extent, any actual operation, it should be mentioned in this connection that all such transfers must be made at the headquarters of the company in the state. In the case of ordinary stock companies incorporated in Illinois, all transfers of shares not fully

[1] The mode of procedure in reorganizing an old company under the existing general law is precisely the same as in organizing a company *de novo*.

paid up must be made a matter of corporate and public record; but fully paid up shares can be transferred in blank without any record whatever. Common companies may have secrets; the law attempts to make all the operations of a railway company so far a matter of record that in case of need every step and phase of the company could be brought to light.

§48. A statute amendatory to the general railway incorporation act went into force July 1, 1873. It was designed and had the effect to extend the privilege of reorganization under the general law passed by the previous general assembly to associations or corporations that had attempted to be formed, giving to such inchoate companies the same rights and privileges as were previously enjoyed by perfected organizations, "notwithstanding any defects or omissions in their articles of association." The same idea is contained in the clause, "all such corporations that have adopted or that will adopt this act are hereby declared legal and valid corporations, within the provisions of this act, from the date of the filing of their respective articles of association. And the fixing of the termini by any such corporation shall have the same effect as if fixed by the general assembly." [1] Two provisos are added to the law; but they will come under the head of construction and municipal aid bonds.

§49. The association is not binding upon the corporators until the organization has been completed. At the same time, if one actually becomes a subscriber

[1] These quotations contain the only really new and vital parts of that statute and was evidently designed to remedy a defect in a particular railway organization which had recently been pointed out by the supreme court.

he is bound by the terms of his subscription, and must bear his share of the preliminary expenses, unless the subscription provide the contrary, although several decisions favor the opinion that merely taking shares in a railroad project does not obligate the subscriber to pay any preliminary expenses, unless there is a contract to that effect. If the scheme should prove abortive, the terms of the subscription, whatever they may be, must be observed in good faith. When fully organized the company may and generally does assume the liabilities incurred by the provisional association in securing a completed organization.[1]

II. Corporate Rights and Liabilities.[2]

[1] For a full discussion of the points stated in this paragraph see Spear *v.* Crawford, 14 Wend. 20; Thrasher *v.* Pike Co. R. R. Co. 25 Ill. 393; Illinois River R. R. Co. *v.* Zimmer, 20 Ill. 654; Ill. Grant *v.* Green, 46 Ill. 469.

[2] It is proposed in this connection to consider only the rights and labilities of railway companies as corporations. Their obligations and privileges as common carriers, and their general operative relations to the public will be set forth elsewhere.

§ 50. It is the doctrine of the supreme court of the United States that if the law requires a certain amount of capital stock to be paid in before the corporation is fully formed, this condition precedent must be fairly complied with. But unless the charter or general law, as the case may be, specifically require it, such prepayment is not necessary.[1] The general law of Illinois does not make any such requirement.

§ 51. A corporate person, as well as a private individual, has a citizenship. Many cases at law have turned upon this point: what determines the local habitation of a joint stock company? It has been claimed that the residence of a majority of the stockholders is decisive of the question. But the doctrine of the courts is that the residence of the stockholders in no wise affects the citizenship of a corporation.[2] All the stock of all Illinois railroads might be owned outside of the state, and still each and every company

[1] Minor *v.* Mechanics' Bank of Alexandria, 1 Peters, 46.

[2] Louisville R. R. Co. *v.* Letson, 2 Howard, 497; Ohio R. R. Co. *v.* Wheeler, 1 Black, 286; Covington Bridge Co. *v.* Shepherd, 20 How. 227; Marshall *v.* Baltimore and Ohio R. R. Co, 16 How. 314; Regina *v.* Arnaud, 9 Q. B. 806.

would be a citizen of this commonwealth. A private person may change his citizenship at pleasure. A corporation has no such power.

§ 52. This is liable to be a matter of great practical importance. In litigation, the general policy of railway companies is to delay a final judgment. Under the constitution of the United States, the federal judiciary has appellate jurisdiction in all suits between citizens of different states; but not in cases between citizens of the same state, unless arising under the national constitution or acts of congress.[1] The right of appeal often involves immensely important practical results.[2]

§ 53. An undertaking to subscribe a certain amount of stock does not make one a stockholder. Such a promise is like the promise to purchase any other specific piece of property. If there is no delivery nor any offer to deliver, the company in a suit against such a promisor could not recover, as damages, the value of the stock, because they still hold it in their own name. The true measure of damage in such a case would be the actual damage resulting from the loss of the bargain; that is, the difference between the par and market value of such stock.[3]

§ 54. In common law, subscription may be made to a capital stock by installments. When this is done

[1] U. S. Constitution, art. iii. sec. 2,

[2] For elaborate discussion of this subject see Bank of Augusta *v.* Earl, 13 Peters, 519; Zabriskie *v.* Cleveland, Columbus and Cincinnati R. R. Co. 23 How. 381; Bank of U. S. *v.* Dandridge et al. 12 Wheaton, 64.

[3] Thrasher *v.* Pike County R. R. Co. 25 Ill. 393; Chase *v.* Sycamore and Courtland R. R. Co. 38 Ill, 215.

without condition or reservation and certificate of stock issued, the person becomes a member of the corporation and as such is liable for the calls of the company. Nothing remains to be done concerning the contract except payment of the money. This may be recovered by a suit *indebitatus assumpsit* for the money due on the installments.[1] But one corporation can not recover upon subscriptions made to another, however identical the objects sought by the organization or the parties composing them.[2] Under the statutory law of Illinois the directors of a railroad company have almost unlimited power in regard to the payment of railway stock subscriptions.[3]

§ 55. The supreme court of Illinois holds that a railroad company has the same claim upon an unpaid subscription to its stock that it has upon a promissory note. The corporation may sell the subscription, or make a contract to dispose of it, as a part of its assets. The sale must be for the purposes of the road, as must be the expenditure of all the funds of the company.[4] No stock or bonds can be issued or money disbursed for an object foreign to the designs of the company. Whatever the railway *facts* might show, railway *law* is very plain on this point.

§ 56. No stock or bonds may be issued except for money, labor or property actually received and applied to the purposes for which the company was organized. This is the constitutional law.[5] No stock dividends or

[1] Peake *v.* Wabash R. R. Co. 18 Ill. 88.
[2] Thrasher *v.* Pike R. R. Co. 25 Ill. 393.
[3] See Duties of Directors.
[4] Morris *v.* Cheney, 51 Ill. 451.
[5] Ill. Constitution, art. xi, sec. xiii.

other fictitious increase of stock or indebtedness would be legal, though every stockholder concurred therein. In the contemplation of the organic law of Illinois such "watering," as it is called, is against the public policy. The common law recognizes the right of the government to make such restrictions.

§ 57. Under certain conditions, for legitimate purposes and in a manner prescribed by law, a railway company may increase its capital stock. The condition requires that sixty days notice shall be given "in such manner as may be provided by law:" The statute provides[1] that in case the original capital shall prove insufficient for the construction and operation of the road, the same may be increased to any amount required for the purpose. This increase must be sanctioned and authorized by two-thirds in value of all the stock. The question of increase must be decided at a meeting called for that especial purpose.[2]

§ 58. Every railway company organized or doing business in Illinois, "under the laws and authority thereof," is compelled to maintain a public office in this state for the transaction of its business. It is there that its transfers of stock must be made. The company is required by the constitution to keep at that office, or place, books in which shall be recorded: 1. The amount of capital stock subscribed. 2. By whom subscribed. 3. The names of the present owners of the stock. 4. How much each shareholder holds. 5. The amount of stock paid in. 6. By whom paid in. 7. The amount of its assets. 8. The amount of its

[1] Gross, vol. ii, R. R. chap. sec. 174.

[2] For the method of its call, which is by the directors, see Duties of Directors.

liabilities. 9. The name and residence of the officers of the company. The statute reaffirms these requirements, adding one more, viz.: how the shares held by each is designated.[1] This law is only partially respected, especially by the older companies.[2]

§ 59. The corporation may not only increase its capital stock, but mortgage its property, if necessary, to complete or operate its road. In the nineteenth section of the statute of 1872, wherein numerous rights are specified, it is declared that the company shall have power[3] "from time to time to borrow such sums of money as may be necessary for completing, finishing, improving or operating any such railway, and to issue and dispose of its bonds for any amount so borrowed, and to mortgage its corporate property and franchises to secure payment of any debt so contracted." The concurrence of a two-thirds majority of the stock must be secured as first defined in the preceding section, and the increase, or mortgage, must be made a matter of public record, as provided in the case of the articles of incorporation.

§ 60. This statutory permission to borrow money on a mortgage of franchises and property formed a part of the present general railway incorporation act, and did not apply originally to railroads existing under charters. A statute was passed in 1873 extending its

[1] Gross, vol. ii, R. R. chap., sec. 166.

[2] A very large proportion of the stock is bandied about on 'Change in New York, or held by persons living remote, and the actually ownership is often unknown. See second annual report Railroad and Warehouse Commissioners, Illinois, for abundant evidence of the partial inoperativeness of this feature of organic law.

[3] Gross, vol. ii, R. R. chap. sec. 186.

provisions to all other railroad companies. It went into force July 1, 1873.[1] Besides extending this power to other or charter railroads in the state, the law contained this safeguard: "This act shall not in any manner legalize the subscription of any township, county or city to the capital stock of any railroad company, nor authorize the issuing of any bonds by any township, city or county in payment of any subscription or donation."

§ 61. The need of this special authorization to mortgage its franchise and property rests upon the fact that a corporation, whether public or private, possesses and is empowered to exercise no other functions than those specifically conferred by the act creating it, or such as are necessary to carry into effect the purposes for which it was created.[2] The courts are strict in limiting and preventing the abuse of corporate authority.

§ 62. The stock is defined by statute[3] to be personal estate, transferable in the manner prescribed by the by-laws. In the case of companies organized under the new law, "no shares shall be transferable until all previous calls thereon shall have been paid." The statute further provides that "it shall not be lawful for such corporation to use any of the funds thereof in the purchase of its own stock, or that of any other corporation, or to loan any of its funds to any director

[1] Laws of Illinois, 1873, page 141.

[2] Caldwell *v.* City of Alton, 33 Ill. 416; Newhall *v.* Galena and Chicago Union R. R. Co. 14 Ill. 273; Ohio and Mississippi R. R. Co. *v.* McClelland, 25 Ill. 140; Galena and Chicago Union R. R. Co. *v.* Crawford, Ibid, 529.

[3] Gross, vol. ii, Ibid, sec. 173.

or other officer thereof, or to permit them or any of them to use the same for other than the legitimate purposes of such corporation."

§ 63. It is worthy of note in this connection that an act of congress passed in 1848 contains a clause pertinent to such of our railroad companies as have foreign stockholders.[1] It provides that "all powers of attorney executed in a foreign land for the transfer of any stock of the United States, or for the receipt of interest thereon, shall be verified by the certificate and seal of a consul, vice-consul, or commercial agent, or vice-commercial agent, at the place of execution, if any such there be."[2]

§ 64. Some Illinois railway charters expressly permit any and all consolidation, and only a very few of them explicitly restrict it. The United States supreme court, in a recent case, held that where railroad companies are consolidated by act of legislation, the presumption of law is that each of the united lines of road will be held with the privileges and burdens originally attached thereto, unless the contrary is expressed.[3] The Illinois supreme court holds that in case of consolidation the powers vested in the companies consolidated will be conferred upon and center in the company taking the name of the consolidated company.[4] The grant of a right to a railroad com-

[1] The term foreign is often applied to a state; but in this connection it is used in its more familiar sense, as applying to persons living outside of the United States.

[2] The careless wording of this law is noticeable. As a rule state statutes are drawn with greater precision than national statutes.

[3] Tomlinson *v.* Branch, 15 Wall. 460.

[4] Robertson *v.* City of Rockford, 21 Ill. 458.

pany to extend and unite with any other railroad in the state gives a general authority to extend to any other railroad within the prescribed limits.[1]

§ 65. The present constitution declares that "no railroad corporation shall consolidate its stock, property, or franchises with another railroad corporation owning a parallel or competing line."[2] It may be questioned whether such a prohibition is valid in the case of some corporations; but no decision on that point has yet been rendered, and it is believed that no issue thereon has been joined. The same clause of the constitution adds that "in no case shall any consolidation take place, except upon public notice given sixty days to all stockholders, in such manner as may be provided by law." The statute makes the same provision for notice in this case as in the case of a proposed increase of stock.[3]

§ 66. The more frequent method of unifying two or more railway interests is by leasing, without the formal consolidation of stock. It will be observed that the constitution and the statute regards leasing and stock consolidation as so nearly the same as to place precisely the same restrictions upon both, using the term "consolidating its stock, property, or franchises." In a case which was adjudicated long prior to the present constitution the court held that, if a railroad company use the road of another company it must conform to the charter of the other corporation while doing the business.[4] A railroad company may lease

[1] Belleville R. R. Co. *v.* Gregory, 15 Ill. 20

[2] Illinois Constitution, art. xi, sec. 11.

[3] Gross, vol. ii, R. R. chap. sec. 189.

[4] City of Chicago *v.* Evans, 24 Ill. 52.

its road, but cannot thereby avoid liability. Whether the road be run by agents, servants, or lessor, they will all be considered agents of the corporation owing the road.[1] As corporations outside of the state have leased several Illinois railroads, and are likely to lease still more, this doctrine is of more than ordinary importance.

§ 67. The statute of 1872 contemplates that a railroad company may desire to offer inducements to secure donations of land or private subscriptions to the stock from persons along the proposed route. It therefore provides that if the company shall wish to fix the rates for any period of time for the transportation of passengers or freight, "such corporation may adopt a resolution fixing such rates and the time for which the same is to be fixed, and have the same recorded in the office of the recorder of deeds in the several counties through which said road is proposed to be run.[2] These rates shall be binding upon the company and its successors, forming a vested popular right. It is added, however, "Provided that said rates shall not exceed the rates provided by law."[3]

§ 68. There has been considerable controversy at different times in regard to the personal property of a railroad corporation, and the corporate liabilities thereto attached. The constitution declares, and it is the common law doctrine as held by the courts, that

[1] Ohio and Mississippi R. R. Co. *v.* Dunbar, 20 Ill. 623; Chicago and Rock Island R. R. Co. *v.* Whipple, 22 Ill. 106.

[2] Gross, vol. ii, R. R. chap. sec. 193.

[3] Diligent inquiry fails to bring to light a single instance in which this cheap transportation privilege has been exercised by any railroad corporation in Illinois.

"the rolling stock, and all other movable property belonging to any railroad company or corporation in this state, shall be considered personal property, and shall be liable to execution and sale in the same manner as the personal property of individuals, and the general assembly shall pass no law exempting any such property from execution and sale." This clause is substantially embodied in the twentieth section of the railway incorporation act.[1] The court would interfere, however to prevent the diversion of railway property from its original use to satisfy a creditor, when such satisfaction would have been a hardship upon the public. The people have a certain right in railway property, and it is conceivable that a case might arise of such a nature that the court would be compelled by regard to the general welfare and the necessities of travel to prevent the execution and sale of the personal property of a railroad company. No such case has occurred since the adoption of the existing constitution.

§ 69. "In all elections for directors or managers of a corporation of Illinois, of whatever nature, and under whatever legislation created, special or general, every stockholder has the right to vote, in person or by proxy, for the number of shares owned by him, for as many persons as there are directors or managers to be elected, or to cumulate said shares, and give one candidate as many votes as the number of directors multiplied by the number of his shares of stock shall equal; or to distribute them, on the same principle, among as many candidates as he shall think fit; and

[1] Gross, vol. ii. R. R. chap. sec. 187.

such directors or managers shall not be elected any other way."[1]

§ 70. Each stockholder is individually liable to the creditors of the company to an amount not exceeding the amount unpaid on the stock held by him, for any and all debts and liabilities of the company, until the whole amount of the capital stock so held by him shall have been paid. But if a person holds stock as an executor, administrator, guardian or trustee, or if he holds it as collateral security, he is subject to no personal liability as a stockholder. The person pledging the stock is considered as holding it, and is subject to the liability of a stockholder accordingly. This provision is statutory, rather than constitutional, and applies in some of its features only to railway companies. In corporations organized under the general incorporation act of the state, the stockholder incurs no liability except that whatever he has agreed to pay into the treasury of the company he must pay, or forfeit his stock.

§ 71. It is contemplated by common and statutory law that the main business of a corporation will be transacted at stated and regular meetings. It is further contemplated that special meetings will usually be called by the directors. But this is a rule with exceptions. The statute of 1872 provides (sec. 9), that a meeting may be called at any time by the stockholders owning not less than one-fourth of the stock, as well as by the directors. The method in both cases is the same.

[1] This bunglingly stated provision forms section 3 of article xi, of the constitution of Illinois, and is put into railway act, section 25.

§ 72. A two-thirds majority, in value, of all the stockholders, may at any special meeting remove any president, director, or other officer of the corporation, and elect others in their stead. A majority of those present may at any meeting require the officers to make a full statement of the affairs of the company. It is competent for the majority, in value, of the stockholders to fix the rate of interest to be paid by the company for the money borrowed to build or equip the road; also to fix the amount of the loan.

§ 73. Each stockholder shall at all reasonable hours have access to and may examine all the books, records, and papers of the company.[1]

§ 74. Corporations are held to a strict construction of their corporate rights. A contract is *ultra vires* when it reasonably appears that the legislature intended that such a contract should not be made.[2] "Where a corporation exceeds its powers in making a contract the contract is absolutely void."[3] Corporate limitations are well defined in the following authoritative utterances: "That contracts which do in reality contravene any principle of public policy are illegal and void, is not and cannot be denied. The doctrine is universal. There is no exception. Although the unauthorized act may be neither *malum in se* nor *malum prohibitum*, but, on the contrary, may be for some worthy or benevolent object, yet, if it is a vio-

[1] Gross, vol. ii, R. R. chap. sec. 169.

[2] S. Y. and C. Co. *v.* G. N. R. Co. 9 Exch. 55, 84; 30 Eng. Law and Eq. 120; 24 Law J. N. S. Q. B. 105

[3] Rock River Bank *v.* Sherwood, 10 Wis. 230; Beach *v.* Fulton Bank, 3 Wend. 573; N. Y. F. Ins. Co. *v.* Ely, 2 Cow., 678; Bateman *v.* Ashton—under—Ly. — 3 H. and N. 323; 4 Ellis and B. 397; 2 Exch. 711; id. 718; Angell and Ames, Corp. 9th Ed. 240.

lation of public policy for corporations to exercise powers which have never been granted to them, such contracts, notwithstanding their praiseworthy nature, are illegal and void."[1]

[1] Bissell *v.* The M. S .and N. I. R'y, 22; N. Y. Ct. Ap. Repts. 258; 13 Eng. Law and Eq. 506; 7 id. 505; 12 id. 224; 6 id. 106; 16 id. 180; 3 id. 144. The following summary of the law on this point is from the argument submitted by Hon. Robert G. Ingersoll in the case of the Peoria and Rock Island R. R. Co. *v* Coal Valley Mining Company, not yet officially reported: 1. That railroad corporations are the mere creatures of the statutes—that their powers are all derived from the legislature, and that they have no right to construct, operate and manage their property except for the accomplishment of the purposes for which they were created. 2. That they are created for the public benefit, and have no right to do any act inconsistent with their charters. 3. That a corporation itself cannot add to its powers in any manner whatever. 4. That the corporation cannot delegate some of its powers to another corporation, for the reason that corporations cannot get powers from each other, but must get them from the law making power. 5. That a corporation has no right or power to agree that it will not exercise all its powers and franchises for the purpose of carrying out the object of its creation, and that it cannot incapacitate itself. 6. That the corporation can cease to exist under certain circumstances, and render back to the state its powers and franchises; but it cannot confer *some* of its powers upon some other corporation. 7. All agreements to do certain acts unauthorized by the charter and inconsistent with it, and inconsistent with the obligations of the corporation to the public, and inconsistent with the accomplishment of the objects for which the same was created, are *ultra vires*, contrary to public policy, and void.

III. The Duties of Directors.

§ 75. We have seen that a railway corporation has a board of directors as a part of its organization; that the board must classify themselves; that the elections of directors must be upon the cumulative plan, sometimes erroneously called the "minority representation" plan. It can hardly have escaped notice that the policy of the state is not only to restrict the powers of corporations, but to vest, as far as practicable, in individual stockholders the power to prevent and arrest abuse of authority by the officers of the company. The importance of this was much greater than the public is accustomed to suppose, or rather, than it was accustomed to suppose at the time the existing constitution of Illinois was adopted.

§ 76. By virtue of a clause of the constitution of Illinois, incorporated also into the statute of 1872, a majority of the directors of a railroad company must be residents of the state. This provision is expressly extended to all railway corporations created by this state, in whatever way or at whatever time.[1] It does

[1] Illinois Constitution, art. xi, sec. 11.

not, as a matter of course, apply to companies existing by virtue of charters derived from other states and doing business in Illinois. The greater part of the constitutional provisions made in regard to railroads admit of no distinctions between those merely doing business in the state and those created by the laws of this state.

§ 77. The directors must be elected at the annual meetings of the shareholders, held at the public office of the company in Illinois. This provision in regard to the place of election not being found in the constitution, nor by its express terms made applicable to railroad companies existing under special charters, may be held obligatory only upon those corporations created under the general statute. While the law requires these elections to occur at the regular meeting, at a given time, it is provided that "in case it shall happen, at any time, that an election of directors shall not be made on the day designated by the by-laws of such corporation for that purpose, the corporation, for such cause, shall not be dissolved, if within ninety days thereafter the stockholders shall meet and hold an election for directors in such manner as shall be provided by the by-laws of the corporation."[1]

§ 78. The statute declares that all corporate powers of a railroad company shall be vested in, and be exercised by a board of directors, adding that the same shall be stockholders of the corporation, to be elected at the annual meetings of the corporation. At special meetings a two-thirds majority in value of the stock may depose an officer for cause; but the mode of filling

[1] Gross, vol. ii, R. R. chap. sec. 170.

vacancies prescribed in the by-laws shall not be changed except at a regular annual meeting.[1]

§ 79. The law, as we have seen, specifies what may be done by a two-thirds majority of the stockholders; what by a plurality; what by one-fourth; and what by a single shareholder, making, in a sense, a four-fold division. Directors must act as a whole. No provision is made for the individual or the minority action of the directors. The board is in itself a unit. There are no property rights involved; but simply official or functional authority. This does not preclude the delegation of certain powers to an executive committee, selected from and by the board. Such selection, although not specifically provided for, is not infrequent, and may be said to exist, if at all, in contemplation of law. The by-laws generally determine that matter. At common law the general duties of the board are regarded as ministerial. In case the action in a given instance is judicial in its nature, the concurrence of all the directors is required, at least the whole must assemble and take action thereon. In fine, if the matter is of public concern, the decision of the majority will bind; but in private concerns, as arbitration, all must concur.[2]

§ 80. The directors must chose, and that from their own membership, a president and "such other subordinate officers as such corporation, by its by-laws, may designate, who may be elected or appointed, and shall perform such duties and be required to give such security for the faithful performance thereof as such corporation, by its by-laws, shall require; provided

[1] For county railroad directors, see sec. 156.

[2] See Redfield on the Law of Railways, vol. 1, p. 91.

that it shall require a majority of the directors to elect or appoint any officer."[1] This clause brings up again the powers of majorities. An early Illinois decision declares that if a number of persons are entrusted with powers in matters of public or corporate concern, and all of them are regularly assembled and consulting, the majority may act and determine, provided the authority be not otherwise limited and restricted.[2]

§ 81. It is a well-established principle of law that a director is not entitled to compensation for services performed as a director.[3] The law looks with jealousy upon the delegation of special labors by the board to its own members, and the making of contracts with themselves, for constructing the road, equipping it, etc., would be regarded as a breach of fiduciary trust, unless the contract were made with the knowledge and *consent of all the stockholders. It sometimes happens* that all the shareholders are members of the board. The directors cannot indirectly pay themselves by borrowing money of the company, or using the corporate funds for any purpose, except for the legitimate objects of the corporation.[4]

§ 82. The directors may require the subscribers to the stock of the corporation to pay the amount by them respectively subscribed in such manner and in such installments as they may deem proper. If a stockholder fails to meet the assessment the directors may declare his stock, and all previous payments upon it, forfeited for the use of the corporation. Abuse of

[1] Gross, vol. ii, R. R. chap. sec. 173.
[2] Louk *v.* Woods, 15 Ill. 256.
[3] Americen Central R. R. Co. *v.* Miles, 52 Ill. 174.
[4] Gross, vol. ii, R. R. chap. sec. 173.

this power is guarded against with special care. The directors cannot declare such forfeiture without having first caused a notice in writing to be first served upon the stockholder, personally, or by mail. The letter, in the latter case, must be directed properly. At least sixty days must be given in which to make payment. If the person in whose name the stock stands be dead, then his legal representative must be notified. The notification must state the resolution or order in accordance with which payment is requested, with full particulars as to time and place. Also the penalty of non-compliance. In case of any such forfeiture to the company of stock, the same may be sold and new certificates of shares issued therefor.[1]

§ 83. A meeting of the stockholders for the purpose of increasing the capital stock of a company may be called by the directors. The meeting called, the directors as such have no authority until the question of increase has been decided.[2] If agreed upon, the resolution to that effect must be recorded by the directors, as provided in the case of the articles of incorporation. If the stockholders, by a two-thirds majority, as previously defined in this treatise, decide to mortgage the property and franchises of the company, issuing bonds to that effect, the directors shall carry out the details of the business. The company as such adopts an order or resolution authorizing the mortgaging or bonding of the road, and the same having been duly recorded, the directors may confer upon any holder of any money so borrowed the right to convert the principal into stock at any time not exceeding ten years after the date

[1] Gross, vol. ii, R. R. chap. sec. 172.
[2] Gross, vol. ii, R. R. chap. sec. 174.

of such bond, "under such regulations as may be provided in the by-laws of such corporation."[1] There has been a vast amount of litigation, especially in the New York courts, over mortgage bonds. The explicitness of our statute will be of great use in preventing misapprehension.

§ 84. The constitution makes only two distinct references to railway directors. We have given the first. The second is the requirement that they shall annually make a report, under oath, to the auditor of public accounts or "some officer to be designated by law," of all their acts and doings. The quoted words are an intimation and a foreshadowing of the Railroad and Warehouse Board. This report must include "such matters relating to railroads as may be prescribed by law." To this is added, in conclusion, the direction to the general assembly to "pass laws enforcing by suitable penalty the provisions of this section."[2]

§ 85. At the regular annual meeting of the company the president and directors are required to exhibit a full, distinct and accurate statement of the affairs of the corporation. Similar exhibits may be required at any meeting of the stockholders by a majority of those present.

§ 86. Such are the provisions in regard to directors of railroad companies, as found in the constitution, statutes and decisions of the state. This chapter cannot better be closed than by adopting the language of Mr. Perry in his recent and exhaustive work on trusts, that "the directors of a corporation are trustees and

[1] Ibid. sec. 186; also, statutes of Illinois, 1873, page 141.

[2] See chap. on Railroad and Warehouse Commissioners.

agents of the shareholders and of the corporation, and the same rules are applied to the contracts of directors with the corporation as are applied to the dealings of other parties holding a fiduciary relation to each other. The directors are intrusted with the management of the property of the corporation for the best interest of all the members, and the directors are bound to execute their trust; nor must they allow their private interests to interfere with the duties of the trust they have assumed."[1] This states the uniform doctrine of the common law on the subject.

IV. Railway Injunctions.

[1] For a discussion of this subject see Perry on Trust, chap. 16.

§ 87. This whole subject is exhaustively treated in HIGH ON INJUNCTIONS.[1] It would be irrelevant to the purpose of this treatise to do more than to give the law of injunction as it relates to railroads. The work just named has been received by the legal profession with such general and cordial endorsement for accuracy and thoroughness as to justify its use in this connection as a substitute for original investigation. It should be remarked at the outset, that while the English and American administration of the law of injunction differ somewhat, injunction law, as administered in Illinois, has no marked peculiarity, either as found in the statutes or the decisions. The only statutory provision for receivers is in connection with the transportation of grain by rail.[2]

§ 88. It is the fundamental and inalienable right of any member of a corporation to invoke the aid of equity, if his interests are in danger from a breach of trust on the part of the company or its officers. The courts would interfere, if equity demanded it, for the protection of any shareholder, however small his interest.[3] At the same time, the courts are cautious about interfering with public enterprises in the hands of corporations. It is only as a last resort and to prevent irreparable injury that the jurisdiction of equity is invoked. The granting of an injunction and appointing of a receiver is usually called into action, either to prevent fraud, save the subject from material

[1] A Treatise on the Law of Injunctions, as administered in the courts of the United States and England. By James L. High, counselor at law. Chicago: Callaghan and Company, 1873.

[2] See chapter on Railroad and Warehouse Commissioners.

[3] Kean *v.* Johnson, 1 Stocton, 403; Simpson *v.* Westminister, 8 H. L. 717; Mozely *v.* Alston, 1 Ph. 798.

injury, or to rescue it from probable destruction. This specification was given by that eminent jurist, Chief Justice BREESE, of Illinois. If a railroad company or its officers should attempt to violate the law of corporate existence and action laid down in the foregoing chapters, ground would thus be furnished for granting an injunction and appointing a receiver. But this is by no means an exhaustive statement. At common law a corporation can only do what its charter specifically contemplates. If it should attempt to go beyond its vested rights, equity would enjoin the proceeding, and, if necessary, appoint a disinterested party to take charge of the affairs of the company.[1] For example, if an attempt were being made to make the company a stockholder in any other company, or to consolidate its stock with that of another company, without express warrant from the charter or general law.[2]

§ 89. Courts of equity rarely interfere with the exercise of discretionary powers by corporate bodies or their officers, to whom such powers are confided.[3] And it is a well-established principle of equity, that where acts requiring the exercise of judgment, science and professional skill are confided to the discretion of the officers of a corporation, the exercise of that discretion will not be lightly disturbed, nor will such officers be enjoined, except when abusing their power

[1] State *v.* Newark, 3 Dutch, 197; Foster *v.* Essex Bank, 16 Mass. 245; Satterlee *v.* Matthewson, 2 Peters, 380; Watson *v.* Mercer, 8 Peters, 88; Carpenter *v.* Pennsylvania, 7 How. 456.

[2] Smith *v.* Bangs, 15 Ill. 399; Beman *v.* Rufford, 6 Eng. Law and Equity R. 106; I. Central *v.* Collins, 40 Georgia, 582; 3 Blatchford *v.* Ross, 54 Barb. 42.

[3] Walker *v.* Mad River, etc. 8 Ohio, 38; Cooper *v.* Williams, 4 Ohio, 253.

to the injury of others. The protection of the rights of shareholders in incorporated companies against the improper or illegal action of other shareholders, or of the officers of the company, is a favorite branch of the jurisdiction of equity by injunction. And it may be asserted, as a general rule, that courts of equity will enjoin, on behalf of the stockholders of an incorporated company, any improper alienation or disposition of the corporate property for other than corporate purposes, and will restrain the commission of acts which are contrary to law and tend to the destruction of the franchise, as well as the improper management of the business of the company, or a wrongful diversion of its funds.[1]

§ 90. Railroad companies are often confronted with injunction proceedings at the very outset of their enterprise. In its reluctance to interfere with public improvements, equity will refuse an injunction in favor of a person who has been guilty of great laches in the assertion of his rights, that laches being an implied assent to the construction of the work which he afterwards seeks to restrain.[2] Where, however, an action at law is pending to test the legal right of way of the company, an injunction may be allowed to restrain operations pending the trial.[3] If the exercise of the rights to enter upon land for the construction of a railroad is under color of law, but without com-

[1] Kean *v.* Johnson, 1 Stockt. 401, a leading American case; Manderson *v.* Commercial, etc. 28 Pa. St. 379; Sears *v.* Hotchkiss, 25 Conn. 171; Bagshaw *v.* Eastern, etc. 7 Hare, 114; Colman *v.* Eastern, etc. 10 Beav. 1; Attorney General *v.* Great, etc. 1 Dr. & Sm. 154; Central, etc. *v.* Collins, 40 Geo. 582.

[2] Greenhalgh *v.* Manchester, etc. 3 Myl. & C. 784.

[3] Champlin *v.* Morgan, 18 Ill. 293.

pliance with the requirements of the statute, an injunction will be granted to estop further construction.[1]

§ 91. In Illinois, the exercise of the rights of eminent domain is minutely regulated by statute, and in addition to the general rule that compensation must be made for real estate taken for railway purposes, and that the proceedings must be according to law, the rule is that where a statute provides a mode of obtaining damages for property taken for the use and construction of a railway, but the owner of the land has neglected to avail himself of the mode of relief thus pointed out, he will not be allowed to enjoin the construction of the road because of the non-payment of damages.[2] And the owner of land through which a city has laid out a street, and who is dissatisfied with the assessment of damages, but has failed to avail himself of a legal remedy provided by statute, is not entitled to an injunction against the city authorities to prevent their entering upon his land.[3] An injunction granted against a railway company to restrain it from taking possession of private property without first making payment, or tender of damages for the occupancy, will not usually be dissolved on motion, but will be retained until a hearing upon the merits.[4] And where the bill on which an injunction is granted against the prosecution of an action of ejectment, charges that the conveyances on which defendant's

[1] Commissioners *v.* Durham, 43 Ill. 86; Ledener *v.* Norristown, 23 Ind. 623.

[2] New Albany, etc. *v.* Connelly, 7 Ind. 32.

[3] Nichols *v.* Salem, 14 Gray, 490.

[4] Ross *v.* Elizabeth, etc. 1 Green Ch. 422.

title rests are fraudulent, the injunction will not necessarily be dissolved on the coming in of the answer, unless it fully and satisfactorily negatives the fraud, and a mere general denial is not sufficient for this purpose.[1]

§ 92. But where the owner of real estate has invited a railway company to enter upon his land and has promised a right of way, though his promise, being verbal, is not binding, yet if he allows the company to go on with the construction of its road, he cannot afterward restrain the use of the track over his land until compensation is made.[2] And where a company has been permitted under claim of right for twenty years to occupy the street of a city fronting complainant's premises, without objection or remonstrance, and by such long acquiescence has been induced to enter into a contract with the city binding itself to build a depot and platform in such manner as will cause but little inconvenience to complainant in addition to that arising from defendant's track, an injunction will not be granted to restrain the erection.[3]

§ 93. Where adjoining proprietors of real estate are entitled to compensation for their interest or property in a street appropriated by a railway company, an injunction will be granted to prevent such appropriation until due compensation is made.[4] But the people, being the aggregate body politic, and having no property traversed by the line of the proposed road, and therefore no property rights to be protected, are not

[1] Roberts *v.* Anderson, 2 Johns. Ch. 202.
[2] Pettibone *v.* LaCrosse, etc., 14 Wis. 443.
[3] Higbee *v.* Camden, etc., 5 C. E. Green, 435.
[4] People *v.* Law, 34 Barb. 494.

entitled to such relief.[1] And where a municipal corporation, under claim and color of right, enters upon and takes private property for public uses, giving the owner a grossly inadequate compensation for the damages incurred, if the steps taken are regular in form so that the illegality does not appear on the face of the proceedings themselves, an injunction will be granted, the common law remedy by *certiorari* being insufficient.[2]

§ 94. Courts of equity are inclined to hold railway companies to a strict compliance with the terms and conditions upon which they have been permitted to enter upon land necessary for the construction of their lines, and in default of compliance with such conditions they are not entitled to the protection of equity. Thus, where a railway company is forbidden by statute from constructing its road upon the streets of an incorporated city without the assent of the corporate authorities, and where the city has granted a right of way to the company upon certain express conditions, which have not been fulfilled, the authorities will not be enjoined from re-entering and taking possession of the grounds granted the railway company, the privilege of re-entering in case of default on the part of the company having been reserved in the contract.[3]

§ 95. The sole object of a preliminary injunction being to protect the property or rights in controversy until a final hearing upon the merits, a court of equity will not interfere to take property out of the possession of one party and put it into the possession of another.

[1] Id.

[2] Baldwin *v.* Buffalo, 29 Barb. 396.

[3] Pacific, etc. *v.* Leavenworth, 1 Dillon's C. C. 393.

And where complainants allege that they are entitled to the possession of a railway, but that defendants are in actual possession under claim of right, it is improper to restrain defendants from using the road until the right can be determined.[1]

§ 96. Any use of public streets for purposes unauthorized by the dedication of the land to the public, or by the law under which the dedication was made, may be enjoined where special injury is shown to result to the party complaining. Thus, the laying of the track of a railway company over land which has been dedicated to the public use for streets, being unauthorized by the dedication to the public use, will be enjoined.[2] And in such case the injunction will be granted at the suit of the owner of the fee on the ground that the use of the streets for such unauthorized purpose is a special injury to him.[3]

§ 97. The unauthorized extension by a railway company of its track is the attempted exercise of a valuable franchise, and is of itself sufficient ground for a perpetual injunction.[4] But where a road has been properly discontinued, the forcible reopening thereof and removal of fences necessary in reopening it will not authorize a court of equity in interfering. Such acts are regarded as mere trespasses for which the law affords ample relief and they will not be enjoined in equity.[5]

§ 98. Equity will sometimes interfere with the construction of public works for the purpose of protect-

[1] Farmers, etc. *v.* Reno, etc. 53 Pa. St. 224.

[2] Schurmeier *v.* St. Paul, etc. 10 Minn. 82.

[3] Id.

[4] People *v.* Third Avenue, etc. 45 Barb. 63.

[5] Nichols *v.* Sutton, 22 Geo. 369.

ing parties in the enjoyment of their premises for the particular purposes for which they were acquired. Thus, commissioners of highways will be enjoined from laying out a road across complainant's railway track and grounds acquired for engine houses and other like uses of the railway. The land having been acquired for specific purposes, an injunction is regarded as the proper remedy to secure its quiet enjoyment.[1]

§ 99. Under the authority of equity to interfere for the prevention of irreparable mischief, a railway company may be enjoined from planting trees so close to one's land as to overshadow it and to cause the roots to spring up to the damage of the soil.[2] And where a statute provides that in the construction of levees over private property a just compensation shall be paid to the owners for damages thereby incurred, an injunction may properly issue to stay proceedings until the damages have been ascertained and paid according to law.[3]

§ 100. Where a railway company in its capacity as a common carrier refuses to make a personal delivery of goods to a consignee, the fact that a statutory remedy has been provided will not prevent a court of equity from entertaining jurisdiction of the matter if the statutory remedy is inadequate.[4] And where the course pursued by the carrier is such as to greatly injure if not destroy the business of complainants, and damages at law would afford no just compensation for

[1] Albany, etc. *v.* Brownell, 24 N. Y. 345; Mohawk, etc. *v.* Artcher, 6 Paige, 87.

[2] Brock *v.* Connecticut, etc. 35 Vt. 373.

[3] Horton *v.* Hoyt, 11 Iowa, 496.

[4] Vincent *v.* Chicago, etc. 49 Ill. 33.

the injury, an injunction is the proper remedy.[1] Nor will such carrier be allowed to impose upon certain warehousemen additional charges beyond what are imposed upon others, and it may be enjoined from attempting to levy such charges.[2]

§ 101. With regard to the interference of equity in restraint of public nuisances, resulting from railroads, it is to be noticed in the first place that the erection of a railway and the running of cars through the streets of a city or village do not, *per se*, constitute such a nuisance as will be enjoined in the absence of proof that the railroad is a nuisance in fact.[3] Nor will a general averment that the road is a flagrant nuisance suffice in the absence of facts proving it to be such.[4] And the fact that the change in the mode of travel thus induced in the street or thoroughfare may have had an injurious effect upon business or rents in such thoroughfare, affords no ground for relief.[5] And where a railroad is authorized by the terms of its charter to construct its road in a particular manner, or through a particular street, such construction, being authorized by law, is not a nuisance and will not be enjoined.[6] Even where the road is being built without authority of law, it will not be enjoined at the suit of one who owns no real estate over or adjoining which

[1] Id.

[2] Id.

[3] Lexington, etc. *v.* Applegate, 8 Dana, 289; Hentz *v.* Long Island, etc. 13 Barb. 646; Bell *v.* Ohio, etc. 25 Pa. St. 161.

[4] Hentz *v.* Long Island, etc. 13 Barb. 646.

[5] Lexington, etc. *v.* Applegate, 8 Dana, 289.

[6] Currier *v.* West, etc. 6 Blatch. 487; McFarland *v.* Orange, etc. 2 Beas. 17.

it is to pass, and who will not be specially injured by its construction.[1]

§ 102. Where the corporate authorities of a city are proceeding to open a street through the embankment of a railway, upon the ground that it constitutes a nuisance by obstructing the street, and the railway company, relying upon twenty years possession, enjoins the municipal authorities from proceeding, the right of the city being doubtful, it is not error to continue the injunction until a hearing upon the merits. The question being properly triable by a jury, a court of equity will not assume its functions and decide the issue in advance of a trial at law.[2]

§ 103. The interest in and use of public streets being *publici juris*, their appropriation to private or corporate use in the construction of a railway, without authority of law, and the obstruction thus caused to travel, constitute a public nuisance which may be enjoined on behalf of the people.[3] A city, however, in its corporate capacity, has not such an interest or property in the streets and public squares over which a railway is built as to entitle it to an injunction restraining the erection of a road.[4] And the construction of a railroad through a city, by authority of the common council, will not be enjoined as a nuisance to adjacent property owners, the right of passage not being obstructed to the public for other purposes.[5]

[1] Currier *v.* West, etc. 6 Blatch. 487; Davis *v.* Mayor, etc. 4 Kern. 506.

[2] Mayor, etc. *v.* Georgia, etc. 40 Geo. 471.

[3] The People *v.* New York, etc. 45 Barb. 73.

[4] Milwaukee *v.* Milwaukee, etc. 7 Wis. 85.

[5] Drake *v.* Hudson, etc. 7 Barb. 508.

§ 104. Where one under contract with a railroad company which has failed to construct its road, has gone on with the construction of a portion of the route for his own benefit, he may be restrained on the application of owners of land through which the road passes.[1] And the fact that complainants in the bill in equity are plaintiffs in an action at law then pending against other parties, to recover damages for past trespasses thus incurred, affords no defense to the bill.[2]

§ 105. Frequent instances of the interference of equity to prevent the violation of a franchise occur in the case of roads, turnpikes and railways. Actual injury to the franchise must exist before an injunction will be awarded. In Illinois no franchise of an exclusive nature exists, such as the exclusive right to transport passengers and freight between two cities. In some states such charters have been granted, and protected by proceedings in equity, and the granting of injunctions.[3]

§ 106. Where town officers are about to deliver to a railway company the bonds of the town, issued in aid of the railway, and are proceeding in violation of the conditions of subscription, they may be perpetually enjoined, on the ground that if the bonds should be negotiated the town might be embarrassed in defending against them at law.[4] But a tax-payer of a town which has issued bonds in aid of a railway, can not

[1] Stewart and Foltz's Appeal, 56 Pa. St. 413.

[2] Id.

[3] Delaware, etc. *v.* Camden, etc. 2 McCart. 1; Ibid. 1, C. E. Green, 321; South Carolina, etc. *v.* Columbia, etc. 13 Rich. Eq. 339; Boston, etc. *v.* Salem, etc. 29 Gray 1; Boston, etc. *v.* Boston, etc. 16 Pick, 512.

[4] Danville *v.* Montpelier, etc. 43 Vt. 144.

enjoin the transfer or delivery of the bonds to the officers of the company on the ground that they were not legally elected, they being officers *de facto* of the company.[1]

§ 107. Where, as is frequently if not generally the case with interlocutory injunctions, the injunction is merely auxiliary to the principal relief sought by the bill, the dismissal of the bill of necessity works a dissolution of the injunction, *ipso facto.*[2] Upon the bill being dismissed, therefore, the injunction falls as of course, and without further proceedings.[3] So where the bill for injunction is auxiliary to an action at law, on the dismissal of the proceedings at law, the injunction usually shares the same fate.[4] But where a railway company is enjoined from using complainant's land until satisfaction of a judgment obtained against the company for the appropriation of his land, the order for the injunction will not be reversed because of the reversal of the judgment for want of jurisdiction.[5]

[1] Sauerhering *v.* Iron Ridge, etc. 25 Wis. 447.

[2] Green *v.* Pulsford, 2 Beav. 72; Coleman *v.* Hudson, etc. 5 Blatch. 56.

[3] Green *v.* Pulsford, 2 Beav. 72.

[4] Phelps *v.* Foster, 18 Ill. 309.

[5] Sturtevant *v.* Milwaukee, etc. 11 Wis. 63.

V. Transportation Companies.

§ 108. The first statute of Illinois designed to prevent railway extortion and discrimination defined the term "railroad corporation," as contained in that act, to mean "all corporations, companies or individuals now owning or operating, or which may hereafter own or operate any railroad, in whole or in part, in this state."[1] That definition left out of consideration express companies, the Pullman Palace Car company, and the many fast freight lines through which, as a matter of fact, the major part of railway business is conducted.

§ 109. The statute of 1873 remedies this defect. It incorporates in its definition of the term, "railroad corporation," the foregoing, without a change, and in addition thereto declares, "and the provisions of this act shall apply to all persons, firms and companies, and to all associations of persons, whether incorporated or otherwise, that shall do business as common carriers upon any of the lines of railways in this state (street railways excepted), the same as to railroad corporations hereinbefore mentioned."[2]

[1] Gross, vol. ii, R. R. chap. sec. 147.

[2] For full text of this statute see chapter vii.

§ 110. The policy of holding all companies and individuals engaged in the business of transportation by rail to the same restrictions is founded on clearly established principles of common law. To forbid unjust discrimination and charges on the part of the owners of road beds and locomotives, which may or may not have cars of their own, and exempt the very persons, individual or corporate, with whom the public has most to do, would be subversive of the end sought. There has grown up a system intermediate between the companies owning the railroads and the shippers patronizing them, and of the two, it is more important to regulate this intermediate system than to control the owners of the roads and engines.

§ 111. While no suit at law has arisen under the foregoing statutory definitions of a railroad corporation, the principle on which it rests has been established by frequent precedents. The supreme court of Illinois has pronounced that "companies who receive goods for transportation to remote points, without any special undertaking, except what is implied from the manner of accepting the charge, are responsible as common carriers."[1] That eminent jurist and legist, Chief Justice REDFIELD, states that "it was decided at an early day that persons assuming to carry goods upon railways for all who applied, were responsible as common carriers, and indeed it is now regarded as an elementary principle in the law that all who carry goods, in any mode, for all who apply, are common carriers." It is entirely safe to conclude that if the propriety and justice of classing transportation companies and individuals as railroad corporations, in the

[1] Baldwin v. Am. Express Co. 23 Ill. 197; S. C. 26, ibid. 504.

sense of being amenable to the statutes designed to declare and enforce the common law liabilities of common carriers by rail, should be called in question. the courts would sustain the classification.[1]

§ 112. Careful research has failed to disclose that any charter was ever granted to a railway transportation company by the general assembly of Illinois Two public statutes are to be found in which transportation companies are mentioned; but neither is really applicable to such companies as those now under consideration. One refers to companies organized to do business by water, in part or in whole; the other is a general incorporation act for such companies only as are engaged in coal mining. Those statutes have in effect, if not in terms, been repealed.

§ 113. All the express companies and fast freight lines doing business in Illinois at the present time, or that have ever done business here, were created by other states. They are, however, as much subject to the laws of Illinois in their operations within the limits of this state as if they were domestic companies. This proposition is so far axiomatic that no authorities to the contrary could be given, and none in its support are necessary.

§ 114. While no domestic transportation company is doing business in the state at this date, one has

[1] Aurora R. R. Co. *v.* Thompson, 19 Ill. 578; Ponnelee *v.* Mc-Nulty, 19 Ill. 556; Mercantile Mut. Ins. Co. *v.* Chase, 1 E. D. Smith, 115; Sherman *v.* Welles, 28 Barber, 403; Lowell Wire Fence Co. *v.* Sargent, 8 Allen, 189; Langworthy *v.* N. Y. & Harlem Ry. Co. 2 E. D. Smith, 195; Farmers' & Mechanics' Bank *v.* Champlain Transportation Co. 23 Vermont, 186; N. Y. Steam Nav. Co. *v.* Merchants' Bank, 6 Howard, 344.

been authorized aud others may follow.[1] Such companies must organize under "an act concerning corporations," and in their management be consistent with the rules laid down in that law, and the supplemental act, in os far as those statutes apply to companies formed for profit.[2]

§ 115. The organization of a transportation company must be effected under, and conducted in accordance with, the general corporation law of the state, which for simplicity and thoroughness of safeguard against corporate dishonesty is a model.

[1] Reference is had to the Mutual Transportaiton Company, Hon W. C. Flagg, President of the Illinois State Farmers' Association and Ex-Gov. John M. Palmer are among the prime movers. The success of one corporation of this kind will inevitably result in the formation of other companies of a similar nature, and be of incalculable benefit in bringing about the system of railway control discussed in the first chapter, and designated "Management by Competition."

[2] Gross, vol ii, page 102.

CHAPTER III.

MUNICIPAL AID TO RAILROADS.[1]

I. Issue of Bonds.

§ 116. The term "municipal" in its more frequent use applies only to cities. When used in connection with subscriptions to the stock of a railroad company, or donations made to stimulate the enterprise, it has come to include also counties, towns and townships.

[1] The latest U. S. Supreme Court decision on this subject, agreeing with all kindred decisions of that tribunal previously rendered, is Cheete *v.* Winnegar, 15 Wallace.

In that wider significance it will be employed in this chapter

§ 117. It has ever been unconstitutional in Illinois for the state as such to aid private enterprises of any kind, however needful they might be to the public.[1] The constitution of 1848 provides that "the credit of the state shall not in any manner be given to or in aid of any individual, association or corporation." The same organic law forbid the aiding of private persons or enterprises by exemption from taxation. Many questions, then, which arise in some states touching railway aid have no place in a treatise on railway law in Illinois. The only aid the general assembly could extend to such enterprises, in obedience to the constitution of the state, was to encourage internal improvements by passing liberal general laws of incorporation for that purpose.[2] Even special liberality in charters has no warrant in the constitution under which every railway charter in Illinois was granted.

§ 118. The constitution of 1870 went still further,

[1] In the period just prior to railroads, when canals were the hope of the people for cheap and rapid transit, all sorts of wild and disastrous schemes were devised in aid of "internal improvements," resulting finally in failure and disaster, with few exceptions. The Michigan & Illinois Canal, a wholly public enterprise, yet not wholly so in fact, has alone justified the hopes of its projectors. See Ford's Illinois and Lamon's Lincoln.

[2] Constitution of Illinois, 1848, art. x, sec. 6. A case was quite recently decided in the Supreme Court of the United States, wherein the Commonwealth of North Carolina was the defendant. The State government had promised a railroad company perpetual exemption from all taxation. It was on the strength of that promise that the road was built. The court held that the State could not repudiate the contract, or in any way evade its provisions.

and absolutely forbid the further issuance of municipal aid bonds, except that the city of Quincy might complete a contract then partially made with a railroad company in Missouri.[1] The municipal subscription section was submitted to the people separately, and was ratified by a majority of nearly four to one. It reads as follows: "No county, city, town, township, or other municipality shall ever become subscriber to the capital stock of any railroad or private corporation, or make donation to, or loan its credit in aid of such corporation: *provided, however*, that the adoption of this article shall not be construed as affecting the right of any such municipality to make such subscriptions where the same have been authorized, under existing laws, by a vote of the people of such municipalities prior to such adoption."

§ 119. The supreme court held in the case of *Schall v. Bowmar*, not yet officially reported, that this section went into effect July 2, 1870. Although no more railroad aid can be afforded by municipal gifts, or subscriptions to, or purchases of railway bonds, the legal basis on which such aid rests is of vital concern. That ground has been critically surveyed by the courts since the prohibition, and it had been frequently surveyed before, and is liable at any time to be the main issue in important litigation.

§ 120. It is worthy of remark in this connection that while no new railway aid bonds have been issued since July, 1870, it is quite possible at this time to determine the amount of the municipal indebtedness

[1] See sec. 24 schedule of the constitution for the Quincy provision. The corporation benefited by that exception was the Quincy, Missouri and Pacific R. R. Co.

of the state in furtherance of railroad projects. In some cases the conditions precedent, on which the final issue will be legal, may or may not hereafter be complied with. The aggregate will probably foot up not far from $15,000,000.

§ 121. The main statute authorizing municipalities to take stock by subscription or purchase in a railroad company, dates back to 1849. Subsequent legislation modified some of its details, but in its general features that law stood intact until repealed by organic law. The changes made were at the instigation and in the interest of the railroad companies being benefited.[1]

§ 122. No city or county could invest more than $100,000 in any one railway project. This maximum was not often reached. The rate of interest that could be paid on bonds so subscribed or purchased, or on money borrowed to make such investments, was limited to ten per cent. per year. The second annual report of the railroad and warehouse commissioners shows that this maximum of interest has been the rule, but has had many exceptions.

§ 123. The question of aiding a railroad project by subscribing to its stock, or by purchase of the same, could only be decided by a direct vote of the people of the municipality. The submission of the proposition could occur in connection with a general election, or a special election for that purpose could be called. In either case notice of the proposed submission had to be given at least thirty days in advance. In the case of counties, the county judiciary issued the notice; in the case of cities that duty devolved upon the com-

[1] All the legislation of Illinois on this subject may be found in Gross Statutes, vol. i, chap. lxxxvi, div. xiii, first part.

mon council. This notice had to be given in the same manner as notices for elections of state or county officers.

§ 124. This notice was not legal unless it contained the following specifications: 1. The company in which it was proposed to take stock. 2. The amount proposed to be taken. 3. The length of time the proposed bonds would run. 4. The interest they were to bear. In case it was proposed to borrow the money to pay the subscription, then the notice had to state: 5. The terms on which the loan could be negotiated. The ballots were: "For Subscription;" "Against Subscription." The counting and returning had to be the same as in ordinary elections.

§ 125. It was not enough that a majority of the votes cast should be in favor of the proposition. The law required a majority of all the voters. If the submission was at a regular election, then the number of votes cast for county officers should be taken as decisive of the number of qualified voters in the municipality. If the submission were at a special election, then the standard should be the vote at the general election immediately preceding. It has never been claimed that in any event bonds would be good, or could be made good, if a majority of the votes cast were against the issuance, however "innocent" the party holding them at some subsequent period might be.

§ 126. It will be seen that it was contemplated that the county or city should, in effect, go into partnership with the railroad company. At that early day the subscription was not probably looked upon as a gratuity. The stock subscribed was placed under the control of the county court or common council, as the case might be, "in all respects as stock owned by individuals." It was not necessary that the municipality should take the stock as an original shareholder, or by subscription, strictly speaking, but it might be taken by purchase as well.

§ 127. In order to raise the money to subscribe for or purchase the stock, the custodian thereof, as just defined, was authorized to borrow money at a rate not exceeding ten per cent. per annum, and to "pledge the faith of the county or city for the annual payment of the interest and the ultimate redemption of the principal, or if the said judges or common council should deem it most advisable, they are hereby authorized to pay for such subscriptions or purchase in bonds of the city or county, making such subscription to be drawn for that purchase, in sums not less than $50, bearing interest not exceeding ten per cent. per annum."

§ 128. There seemed to be considerable solicitude about the par value of the bonds. A proviso to the clause quoted in the foregoing section forbid the paying out of any bond at a rate less than par, and in authorizing the railroad company to accept the bonds, it is specified that it shall be at par "and in lieu of cash." To still further guard against discount it is declared that "no bonds shall be issued under the provisions of this act by any county or city except for the amounts required to be paid at the time of subscription." Lest other subscribers or purchasers should evade payment, while the municipality was held to its agreement, it is in the same connection asserted that the bonds shall be issued only "for the amounts of and at the time when assessments upon all the stockholders of said company shall be regularly assessed and made payable." Having accepted the bonds at par the company was authorized to dispose of them the same as of other assets, except that the money realized had to be used in defraying construction expenses, or for the purchase of engines or cars. The exact language of this feature of the statute is, "the company is hereby authorized to issue their bonds, bearing interest not exceeding ten per cent. per annum for any money by them borrowed for the construction of their railroad and fixtures, or for the purchase of engines and cars, and for such purpose may dispose of any bonds by them received as aforesaid."

§ 129. No change in the statutes occurred until 1854, when a supplemental law was passed. That statute removed one of the restrictions of the original act. It authorized and empowered the custodian of the bonds (the court or common council, as the case might be,) to issue and deliver to the railroad company "the whole or any portion of the bonds of such city or county, payable on such subscription at any time hereafter, when in their opinion the interest of the city or county will be promoted thereby, whether the asessments upon the stockholders of said company have been regularly assessed and made payable or not." This law dates from March 1, 1854.

§ 130. In a case recently decided by the United States district court of Northern Illinois, the court, Mr. Justice Blodgett, held that where a county had voted to subscribe to the stock of a railroad company, and after such vote, and before the issuing of the bonds, such company consolidated with another with a different capital stock, termini, and board of directors, and changed its name, and the bonds were issued to such consolidated company, that they were illegal and void.[1] The court largely relied for authority upon *Marsh v. Fulton County.*[2]

§ 131. Such is constitutional law and such is, or was, statutory law on the subject of municipal aid bonds. It should be remarked that the especial agitation of this subject in its constitutional aspects has arisen in other states, notably in Michigan, Iowa and Wisconsin. Such eminent jurists as COOLEY, DILLON, and DIXON, have denied the legality of municipal sub-

[1] For the full text of the decision see Chicago *Legal News*, vol. v, no. 48. The facts in the case are stated as follows by the same journal: A vote of the people of the county was had on the 10th of July, 1869, and on the 8th of February, 1870, upon the proposition to subscribe to the capital stock of the Kankakee and Illinois River Railroad company, a corporation possessing the power to construct and maintain a line of road between certain termini in the state of Illinois, with a capital limited to the cost of construction. The bonds in question were issued after the Kankakee and Ill. River R. R. Co. had merged itself by articles of consolidation into another corporation, now known as the Plymouth, Kankakee and Pacific R. R. Co., a road having control of a different enterprise from that of the original corporation, possessing a different capital stock, and governed by a different board of directors, elected upon a different basis, with different termini of the road: *held*, that these bonds were illegal and void; that they were issued by the board of supervisors without the power being granted to them for that purpose; that the vote of the people authorized the county authorities to issue its bonds to the Kankakee and Illinois River Railroad company, and they were in fact issued to another company without a vote. The fact that the bonds bear upon their face the statement that they were issued in pursuance of law and for the stock of the Kankakee and Illinois River Railroad company, can not be held to clothe the county authorities with power to make the issue, as the assertion is untrue.

[2] 10 Wallace, 676; also Clearwater *v.* Meredith, 1 Wall. 25

scriptions, giving cogent reasons therefor; but they have been overruled by the supreme court of the United States, the tribunal before which every court in the nation must bow in obedience, however reluctantly. The authorities in support of the position taken by the court of last resort are stated quite fully in the decision herewith given in full.

II. Latest Decisions in Illinois.

§ 132. This whole subject was thoroughly discussed by the supreme court of Illinois in an opinion filed January 22, 1872. It was rendered by Mr. Justice Thornton, the entire bench concurring. As the decision is of great importance, and will not be officially reported for some time, we give it entire, only premising that several of the positions therein taken are peculiarly significant in their support of the constitutionality of the statute to regulate railway charges and prevent extortion. Their application will be specifically noted in the discussion of that subject. The title of the case is, *Chicago, Danville and Vincennes R. R. Co. v. Frederick Smith.* The original trial was in the circuit court of Will county, before Judge TIPTON. The decision of the inferior court was adverse to the constitutionality of the bonds. The full basis of the decision is as follows:

§ 133. Defendant in error filed his bill in the circuit court to enjoin the collection of taxes levied under an act of the legislature, and in pursuance of a vote of the people, to aid in the construction of a railroad. The act authorized all towns, acting under the township organization law, to appropriate such sums of money as they should deem proper to aid in the construction of the road, to be paid as soon as the track should have been located and constructed through the towns. The road was completed before the appropriation was made; and it was a donation to the company, and not a subscription to its capital stock. Upon the hearing, the circuit court made the injunction perpetual, and pronounced the act unconstitutional. The officers of the town, who made the appropriation, and levied the tax, were the "corporate authorities" of a municipal corporation; and they acted in the premises after a majority of the legal voters of the municipality had authorized the appropriation upon the condition of the construction of the road.

§ 134. The only question is as to the power of the legislature to authorize municipalities to subscribe to the capital stock of railroad companies, and to appropriate money as a donation, to aid in the construction of the roads. The only difference between this case and numerous cases decided by this court, is that the money appropriated by virtue of the statute in question is a donation instead of a subscription. But for this difference we might stand securely upon the maxim, *Stere decisis et non quieta movere.* Frequent fluctuations in the opinions of courts of last resort involve the court in absurdities; render the law uncertain; destroy that feeling of reliance so essential to the strength and stability of all authority; and produce mischiefs innumerable. The decision of the courts had better be involved in some error, than subject to change upon every change of the judiciary.

§ 135. In the discussion of legislative power, we have nothing to do with questions of policy or expediency. The constitution has created the legislative and judicial departments; the one to make the law, the other to construe and administer it. It may be mischievous in its effects; burdensome upon the people; conflict with our conceptions of natural right, abstract justice, or pure morality, and of doubtful propriety in numerous respects; and yet we would not be justified to hold that it was not within the scope of legislative authority for such reason. The question, as to the repugnancy of a law to the constitution, is always one of much delicacy; and courts will never indulge the supposition unless the repugnancy is manifest to the understanding.

§ 136. In *Lane v. Donovan*, 3 Scam. p. 238, this court said: "The determining of a question involving the inquiry whether an exercise of power, by the legislative department of the state, is constitutional, is readily conceded to be not only a matter of delicacy, but of grave import, and demands the most deliberate and mature consideration. It should not, moreover, be decided but in cases of clear necessity, and where the character of the act done is in plain and obvious conflict with the constitution." The law should not be pronounced void in a doubtful case or upon slight implication. "The opposition between it and the constitution must be clear and strong." *People v. Marshall*, 1 Gil. 672. The infringement of the constitution must be evident before the courts will interfere and hold the act nugatory. *People v. Hatch*, 3 Ill. 130. In *ex parte McCollum*, 1 Conn. 504, SAVAGE, C. J., said that a court ought not to declare a law unconstitutional without a case is presented in which there can be no rational doubt.

§ 137. In delivering the opinion in the case of *Fletcher v. Peck*, 6 Cranch, 87, Chief Justice MARSHALL said: "The question whether a law be void for its repugnancy to the constitution is at all times a question of much delicacy, which ought seldom or ever be decided in the affirmative in a doubtful case. The court, when impelled by duty to render such a judgment, would be unworthy of its station could it be unmindful of the solemn obligation which that station imposes. But it is not on slight implication and vague conjecture that the legislature is to be pronounced to have transcended its powers, and its acts to be considered as void. The opposition between the constitution and the law should be such that the judge feels a clear and strong conviction of their incompatibility with each other." In the same court, whose decision is chiefly relied on to induce a reversal of the former opinions of this court, equally explicit language in regard to the duty of courts has been used. In *Twitchell v. Bloodgett*, 13 Mich. 152, COOLEY, C. J., said: "It is conceded to be the settled doctrine of this state that every enactment of the state legislature is presumed to be constitutional and valid; that before we can pronounce it otherwise, we must be able to point out the precise clause in the constitution which it violates, and that the conflict between the two must be clear, or free from reasonable doubt, since it is only from constitutional provisions, limiting the legislative power and controlling the legislative will, that we derive authority to declare void any legislative enactment."

§ 138. We might multiply extracts from the opinions of the ablest courts to the same effect. Enough has been cited to show the firm position of the judiciary, that the courts ought not, and in justice to the rights of a co-ordinate department of the state government, cannot declare a law to be void without a strong and earnest conviction, divested of all reasonable doubt, of its invalidity.

§ 139. An objection to this law is urged, which has been made since the origin of the character of legislation now under consideration. It is assumed that the taxes levied are to be appropriated to a private, and not a public, purpose; that the benefits resulting to the public, — the people at large, — from the construction of railroads, are merely incidental; that the profits arising from their operation enrich the individuals who form the private corporation; and, therefore, all laws imposing taxes to aid in the building of railroads, to be owned and operated by private corporations, are unconstitutional. If the premises are correct that the corporations are strictly private, and the benefits to the public purely incidental, the conclusion might logically follow. The argument assumes as unquestionable the point to be determined, as true the fact to be ascertained. In the enactment of laws the legislature must exercise its judgment and discretion. As to questions of pure policy and expediency, no express or necessarily implied constitutional provisions intervening, it is the sole judge. It has also the undoubted right to take a comprehensive view in determining the necessity of a law, and the character of the purpose to be accomplished by it. A court, with any propriety, cannot arrogate to itself all power and wisdom in such matters; and if there be grave doubt as to the nature of the purpose, the doubt must always be solved in favor of the action of the legislature. Concede that taxation for a mere private enterprise is wrong and invalid, is the construction of the road, to which the aid is proposed to be given, of that character? It is a road from Lake Michigan to a point opposite Vincennes, in the state of Indiana, traversing nearly the entire length of the state. The road was completed before the payment of any money was asked, though it was built upon the faith of it.

§ 140. Are the advantages which accrue to the public from the construction and operation of railroads merely incidental, in the sense of the term as commonly used? We are inclined to think that they rather resemble the incident in law, and appertain to and follow the principal thing. The benefits resulting to the people of the state from our system of railroads are untold and incalculable. The mind can scarcely grasp them. Railroads have almost superseded all other modes of intercommunication between the several parts of our extensive and growing states. They have become an absolute necessity, — indispensable to our increased growth and to the removal of our immense surplus. They have added millions to our taxable property; given augmented facilities to every department of trade; enriched the mass of the people; largely enhanced the value of our lands; built up manufactories, and brought us into close proximity with the best markets of the country. All share in the blessings flowing from them.

§ 141. Railroads are, in truth, the people's highways for pleasure, and business, and commerce. Without them our internal trade would languish and die, and our corn and wheat rot in our granaries. For more than a quarter of a century the courts have recognized and referred to them as public improvements, made for the public good, and to subserve the public interests. *Johnson v. The County of Stark*, 24 Ill. 75; *Cin., Wil. and Janesville R. R. Co. v. The Commissioners*, 21 Ohio (1 McCook), 77; *Sharpless v. The Mayor, etc.*, 21 Penn. (9 Harris), 149; *Nichol v. Mayor and Aldermen*, 9 Humph. 252; *Gaddin v. Crump*, 8 Leigh, 120; *Enfield Toll Bridge Co. v. Hart. and N. H. R. R. Co.*, 17 Conn. 40; *Beekman v. Saratoga and Schenectady R. R. Co.*, 3 Paige, 45; *Bloodgood v. Mohawk and H. R. R. Co.*, 10 Wend. 9; *Newbury Turnpike Co. v. Eastern R. R. Co.*, 23 Peck, 326.

§ 142. The courts, while ready and willing to protect these corporations in all their rights, have uniformly asserted, and seem determined to maintain, their obligations to the public. The principles of common law and their charters, accepted by them, and which clothe them with a portion of the sovereignty of the state, impose duties on them to the public which they must discharge. They can be compelled, by the mandates of the courts, to a full performance of them, and parties seeking redress need not resort to the imperfect action at common law, but may apply for the more effectual remedy by *mandamus*. Railways are improved public highways, and the courts have uniformly held that they are of such public use as to justify the exercise of the right of eminent domain, in taking all real estate that may be necessary for the construction and maintenance of the road, its depots, side tracks, stations, machine shops, and other necessary appendages; disfiguring and rendering unfit for cultivation farms, and even in destroying dwellings. The necessity and expediency for the exercise of this right, in making public improvements, either for the benefit of all the people of the state, or of a particular municipality, must be determined by the legislature. Mere convenience is not sufficient to justify the exercise of the right. The public use must be necessary and pressing. In referring to the urgency of the public use, WOODBURY, J., in the case of *West River Bridge Co. v. Dix*, 6 How. 546, said: "So, as to a road, if really demanded in particular forms and places, to accommodate a growing and changing community, and to keep up with the wants and improvements of the age, — such as its pressing demands for easier and social intercourse, quicker political communication, or better internal trade, and advancing with the public necessities from blazed trees to bridle paths, and thence to wheel roads, turnpikes, and railroads."

§ 143. Though the distinction between the right of eminent domain and the power of taxation may be manifest, yet when the public use, necessary for the exercise of the former, has been settled by both the legislative and judicial departments, and a particular enterprise has thus been fixed as of public importance, the position is very much strenghtened that taxation for such an enterprise is for a public purpose. This court has decided that such corporations are created for the public good; to increase the facilities and conveniences, and promote the great ends of commerce; and that they cannot organize monopolies and make contracts injurious to the public interests. *Vincent v. C. and A. R. R. Co.*, 49 Ill. 33; *C. and N. W. R. R. Co. v. The People, ex rel. Hempsted.* In view of the past history of railroads; the impossibility of dispensing with them; the necessity of an increase of the number, to open more outlets for the products of our fertile and inexhaustible soil, — all of which were well-known to the legislature, and sustained by numerous authorities, — we must hold that, even if the appropriation in this case was not for a public purpose, in the broadest sense, the character of the purpose is involved in such doubt that we cannot declare void the action of the legislature.

§ 144. Is the law, under consideration, in violation of the fifth section of the ninth article of the constitution of 1848? That section provides that "the corporate authorities of counties, townships, school districts, cities, towns and villages, may be vested with power to assess and collect taxes for corporate purposes; such taxes to be uniform in respect to person and property within the jurisdiction of the body imposing the same." It is contended that the appropriation was not for a "corporate purpose." If it was for a public purpose—for the benefit of the inhabitants of the municipality—then it would be for a corporate purpose. The latter cannot be distinguished from the former; and all that we have said in relation to the public purpose of the tax will apply with equal force to a corporate purpose. We refer to the following cases in which the questions discussed have been settled by this court: *Prettyman v. The Supervisors of Tazewell County*, 19 Ill. 406; *Johnson v. The County of Stark*, supra; *Perkins v. Lewis*, 24 Ill. 208; *Butler v. Dunham*, 27 Ill. 474; *The President and Trustees v. Frick*, 34 Ill. 405. In the case of *Nichol v. The Mayor and Aldermen*, supra, a subscription by the city of Nashville to a railroad was held to be for a corporate purpose. The constitution of Tennessee provides that "the general assembly shall have power to authorize the several counties and incorporated towns in this state to impose taxes for county and corporation purposes respectively." The language is substantially the same as in our own constitution. The city of Nashville having subscribed, a bill was filed to restrain the issue of bonds; and the court decided that the legislature had power to authorize the subscription; that the construction of the road was a corporate purpose, and that the city might either levy the tax or issue bonds to obtain the money.

§ 145. In *Taylor v. Thompson*, 42 Ill. 9, this court defined a corporate purpose to mean "a tax to be expended in a manner which shall promote the general prosperity and welfare of the municipality which levies it." We adopt this definition; and are of the opinion that no person can doubt but that taxes expended to aid in the construction of a railroad must promote the general prosperity.

§ 146. The remaining question is whether a distinction exists between a donation in aid of the road and a subscription to the capital stock of the corporation. The distinction is more apparent than real; indeed, to our view, is entirely shadowy. No principle would justify the authority to a municipal corporation to become a stockholder in a railroad company, merely to acquire equitable rights and to prevent the misapplication of the funds. The power is granted in consideration of the public benefits; and these are as great in the one case as in the other. The decree of the court below is reversed and the cause remanded. Decree reversed.

III. Funding and Relief.

147. The statute of 1865.
148. The statute of 1869.
149. Refunding State taxes: Ten years.
150. Registration of municipal aid bonds.
151. Certificate of the County Clerk.
152. Payment of interest on the bonds.
153. The State the custodian of the bonds.
154. Surplus taxes: Eight years.
155. Conditions of registration.
156. County railway directors.
157. Auditor of Public Accounts.
158. Entry of payment ordered.
159. When the statute will expire by its own limitation.
160. Bonds of collectors: Fees.
161. Act of 1871.
162. Allotment of surplus taxes.
163. Railway taxation and surplus.
164. Act of 1872.

§ 147. In 1865 the general assembly passed a statute to allow counties and cities to fund their railway aid bonds, with a view to their general extinction. The state was made custodian of the tax necessary to meet the annual liabilities incident to those bonds, and the auditor of public accounts was required to do a portion of the work of making out the assessment rolls of the several counties or cities, as the case might be. It was expressly declared that the state assumed no obligations thereby. The entire scope and effect of that statute was to make the state, through its auditor of public accounts, fiscal agent for the several municipalities.

§ 148. In 1869 a seemingly similar but radically different law was passed. By the provisions of the latter statute the whole state was made to bear some portion of the burden of the municipal aid bonds, although less than half the counties had incurred any such obligations. The constitutionality of the measure was called in question when the bill was pending before the general assembly. The supreme court has not had occasion to pass upon it. The law was so difficult of construction in some of its details that two supplemental acts have been passed. All are herewith given just as found on the statute books of the state.

§ 149. Whenever any county, township, incorporated city or town, shall have created a debt which still remains unpaid, or shall create a debt under the provisions of any law of this state, to aid in the construction of any railway or railways, that shall be completed within ten years after the passage of this act, whose line shall run near to, into or through said county, township, city or town, it shall be lawful for the state treasurer, and he is hereby required, immediately upon receiving the revenue for each year, to place to the credit of such county, township, city or town so having incurred such indebtedness, in the state treasury, annually, for and during the term of ten years, all the state taxes collected and paid into the state treasury on the increased valuation of the taxable property of said county, township, city or town, as shown by the annual assessment rolls over and above the amount of the assessment roll of the year 1868, excepting the state school tax and the two mill tax provided for by the constitution of this state for the payment of the state debt. And whenever any county, township, city or town shall have created a debt as aforesaid, it shall also be lawful for the collector of taxes, and he is hereby required, annually, for and during a term of ten years, to pay into the state treasury all the taxes collected for any purpose whatever, on the assessment of the railroad or railroads for whose aid the said debt was incurred, including the road-bed and superstructure, and all fixtures and appurtenances thereof, the locomotives, cars, machinery and machine shops, depots and all other property, real and personal, of said railway company within such county, township, city or town; and immediately upon receiving the same the state treasurer shall place to the credit of such county, township, city or town in the state treasury the whole amount so received, except the state school tax and the two mill tax provided by the constitution of this state for the payment of the state debt; and it shall be the duty of the said collector of taxes to furnish the state auditor a separate and detailed account of the amount of taxes collected from said railway or railways, at the time of his annual settlement with the state auditor. And the state treasurer shall give to said collector separate receipts for the respective amounts paid into the state treasury to the credit of said county, and said receipts shall be taken and received by the county court, or other legal authorities, as vouchers for the amount collected on account of the county and local assessments on said railroad property in the annual settlement with such collector, and the several amounts of money in this section provided and ordered to be placed to the credit of such county, township, city or town, shall be applied by the state treasurer to the payment of the bonded railroad debt of such county, township, city or town, as hereinafter provided.

§ 150. And the county clerk or other proper officer, upon the issuing of the bonds in payment of said railroad debt, shall make a registration thereof in a book to be kept for that purpose in his office, showing the date, amount, number, maturity, and rate of interest of such bonds, and upon the subscription or donation to what railroad the same was given. And the said bonds, and bonds heretofore issued and still unpaid, in order to receive the benefits of this act shall be registered by the holder thereof at the office of the auditor of public accounts, who shall cause the same to be registered in a book kept for that purpose. Such registration shall show the date, amount, number, maturity and rate of interest of such bond, under what act and by what county, township, city or town issued; and the auditor shall, under his seal of office, certify upon such bond the fact of such registration, for which registration and certificate the auditor shall be entitled to a fee of $1 from the holder of each bond.

§ 151. In all cases when any county, township, incorporated city or town shall issue bonds under the provisions of law, and be entitled to the benefits of this act, it shall be the duty of the county clerk of such county or of the officer to whom or to whose office the assessment rolls for state taxation are or shall be returnable, within five days after such return, to make out and transmit to the state auditor, to be filed in his office, a certificate stating the total value of all property, real and personal, within such county, township, city or town, as exhibited by such assessment.

§ 152. When the bonds of any county, township, city or town shall be so registered, the state auditor shall annually ascertain the amount of interest for the current year due, and accrued, and to accrue upon such bonds, and from the amount so ascertained he shall deduct the amount in the state treasury placed to the credit of such county, township, city or town, as herein provided and directed, and from the basis of the certificate of valuation of property heretofore provided to be transmitted to him, or in case no such certificate shall be filed in his office, then upon the basis of the total assessment of such county, township, city or town, for the year next preceding, he shall estimate and determine the rate per centum on the valuation of property within such county, township, city or town, requisite to meet and satisfy the amount of interest unprovided for, together with the ordinary cost to the state of collection and disbursement of the same, to be estimated by the auditor and treasurer, and shall make and transmit to the county clerk of such county, or the proper officer or authority whose duty it is or shall be to prepare the estimates and books for the collection of state taxes in such county, township, city or town, a certificate stating such estimated requisite per centum for such purpose, to be filed in his office, and the same per centum shall thereupon be deemed added to and a part of the per centum which is or may be levied or provided by law for purposes of state revenue, and shall be so treated by such clerk, officer or authority in making such estimates and books for the collection of taxes, and the said tax shall be collected with the state revenue, and all laws relating to the state revenue shall apply thereto, except as herein otherwise provided.

§ 153. The state shall be deemed the custodian only of the several taxes so collected and credited to such county, township, city or town, and shall not be deemed in any manner liable on account of any such bonds, but the tax and funds so collected shall be deemed pledged and appropriated to the payment of the interest and principal of the registered bonds herein provided for until fully satisfied. The state shall annually collect and apply all the said taxes and funds placed to the credit of such county, township, city or town for and during the term of eight years, to the payment of the annual interest on such registered bonds of such county, township, city or town, in the same manner as interest on the bonds of the state is or may be collected and paid, but in like moneys as shall be receivable in payment of state taxes; and for and during the remainder of the term of years during which said registered bonds shall remain unpaid, the funds provided in § 1 of this act accruing from taxes collected on the property of said railroad and railroads, and the surplus, if any, of the other funds in this act provided, remaining after the payment of the interest on the bonds, shall be applied to the payment of the principal of said registered bonds on presentation at the state treasury; or the treasurer shall purchase the same in open market at not more than par; and upon such payment or purchase of the said bonds, the amount paid upon the principal of said bonds shall be indorsed thereon and receipts therefor shall be taken and filed in the office of the state treasurer; and the interest-coupons or bonds, when fully paid, shall be returned to the office of the state treasurer, and shall be canceled and destroyed in the same manner as those appertaining to the state debt; and the fund derived from the taxes collected on the increased assessment over the year 1868, and the tax levied to meet the interest on said registered bonds, shall continue to be annually applied to the interest of said bonds; and the said taxes and funds required in this act to be placed to the credit of counties, townships, cities and towns, shall be applied by the state treasurer to the payment of the registered railroad bonds of such county, township, cities or towns, equally and without discrimination.

§ 154. The state may, out of such funds, first retain or satisfy the ordinary costs of the state of the collection and disbursement thereof; and in case of non-presentment of any such bonds or interest-coupons for payment at the time and place, when and where the interest on the state debt is or may be paid, then, on the beginning of the next year, the money by reason thereof undisbursed, together with any surplus for any cause remaining, shall be carried to the fund of such county, township, city or town of the current or ensuing year, and be considered by the auditor in making his next estimate for taxation therein for such year under this act, and shall be applied accordingly during the first eight years of the operation of this act. All laws relating to the payment of interest on the state debt, or the cancellation of evidences thereof, not inconsistent with this act, shall apply to the receipt, custody, and disbursement of the taxes and funds provided by this act.

§ 155. And it shall not be lawful to register any bonds under the provisions of this act, or to receive any of the benefits or advantages to be derived from this act, until after the railroad in aid of the construction of which the debt was incurred, shall have been completed near to, or in such county, township, city or town, and cars shall have run thereon; and none of the benefits, advantages, or provisions of this act shall apply to any debt unless the subscription or donation creating such debt was first submitted to an election of the legal voters of said county, township, city or town, under the provisions of the laws of this state, and a majority of the legal voters living in said county, township, city or town, were in favor of such aid, subscription or donation, and any county, township, city or town, shall have the right upon making any subscription or donation to any railroad company to prescribe the conditions upon which such bonds, subscriptions, or donations shall be made, and such bonds, subscriptions, or donations, shall not be valid and binding, until such conditions precedent shall have been complied with, and the presiding judge of the county court, or the supervisor of the township, or the chief executive officer of the city or town that shall have issued bonds to any railway or railways, immediately upon the completion of the same near to, into, or through such county, township, city or town, as may have been agreed upon, and the running of the cars thereon, shall certify, under oath, that all the preliminary conditions in this act required to be done to authorize the registration of such bonds, and to entitle them to the benefits of this act, have been complied with, and shall transmit the same to the state auditor with a statement of the date, amount, number, maturity and rate of interest of such bonds, and to what company, and under what law issued, and thereupon the said bonds shall be subject to registration by the state auditor, as hereinbefore provided.

§ 156. And each railway company in aid of which any bonds shall hereafter be issued by any county, township, incorporated city or town, to pay for any subscription to the capital stock of such company or for any donation made to such company, shall give to such counties, townships, cities and towns, collectively, a representation in the board of directors of such company of one-fourth of the number of such board of directors, until after the said railway shall have been completed, and the cars shall have run thereon, and until all the conditions of the subscriptions and donations to such railway company by such counties, townships, cities and towns, shall have been fully settled and complied with by said railway company; and thereafter the said counties, townships, cities and towns, shall be represented in said boards of directors only in the manner and proportion that other stockholders are represented; and the governor of the state is hereby authorized and empowered to appoint the directors herein provided to represent the interests of said counties, townships, cities and towns, in the boards of directors of such railways as shall receive bonds to be entitled to the benefits of this act.

§ 157. And the state auditor from the total value of all the property in the state, after the same shall have been equalized in accordance with the provisions of "An act to amend the revenue laws, and to establish a state board of equalization of assessments," approved March 8, 1867, shall deduct the amount of the said increased valuation of the taxable property above the valuation of the year 1868, in such counties, townships, incorporated cities and towns as may be entitled to the benefits of this act, and the taxes upon which are herein directed to be credited to counties, townships, cities and towns, and upon the amount remaining, he shall cause to be collected such a per cent. as shall be sufficient to pay the appropriations and other demands upon the treasury due to the end of each fiscal year, and the same per cent. shall also be collected on the said increased valuation above the valuation of the year 1868, and applied as herein provided.

§ 158. Upon the payment of any such registered bond or interest-coupons by the county, township, city or town issuing the same, and presentation thereof to the state auditor, he shall cause due entry thereof to be made in his office.

§ 159. And if the principal and interest of the bonds registered under the provisions of this act shall be fully paid and canceled at any time before the expiration of the full term of 10 years, during which the funds provided in § 1 of this act, are to be applied to the credit of such county, township, city or town, then the provisions of this act in respect thereto, shall cease and determine, and no further money derived from said taxes shall be so applied.

§ 160. The collector's bonds in counties, townships, cities and towns where collections shall be made under the provisions of this act, shall be increased 50 per centum, and collectors in counties not under township organization, shall pay into the state treasury a sufficient amount of the taxes collected in such county to meet the interest to be annually paid on such registered bonds, on or before the 20th day of June in each year; and there shall be allowed and paid to county, township, city and town collectors, for collecting and paying over the taxes levied by virtue of this act, the following rates of commissions, to be ascertained and computed in the same manner that commissions for collecting and paying over the state taxes are ascertained and computed, and paid from the taxes so collected, to-wit: To township, city or town collectors, at the rate of two per centum on all sums collected, and to county collectors at the rate of one per cent. on all sums received by them from township, city and town collectors, which shall be in full for reciving the same and paying it into the state treasury, and for adjusting the accounts of and settling with the township, city and town collectors for their collections of said tax, and a commission of three per cent. on all sums by themselves collected and paid over into the state treasury.

§ 161. In 1871, the general assembly, at the solicitation of the auditor of public accounts, passed an act defining the foregoing, and virtually superseding the first section of that circuitous statute.[1] This supplemental act became a law April 28, 1871, going into effect July 1 of the same year. It is as follows:

§ 162. Whenever the valuations of property, as shown by the assessment returns of two or more corporations, embrace the same surplus valuation, the auditor of public accounts, in determining the amount due by virtue of said act of 16th April, 1869, to the county, the township, the city or town, shall distribute the tax on such surplus valuation in equal proportions, between such corporations; that is to say, should the valuation of the county show a surplus of $3,000, the township a surplus of $3,000, the town or city a surplus of $3,000, each shall be entitled to the proportion of $1,000. Any excess of such surplus valuation, in either of said corporations, and not embraced in the surplus valuation of either of the other, shall be apportioned to such corporation; or if in either two of such corporations, and none in the third, such amount shall be equally divided betwen such two corporations.

§ 163. The tax on the property of railroads aided, appropriated in section 1 of said act of 16th April, 1869, shall be apportioned by the auditor, between counties, townships, cities and towns, in similar cases, in the same manner as the surplus tax is required to be apportioned by section 1 of this act: *Provided*, that the amount of surplus tax shall be deducted from the amount of state tax on the railroads aided,

[1] See section 149.

in each corporation, so that no county, township, city or town, shall receive both the surplus and railroad tax; or when the amount of surplus tax exceeds the amount of state tax on railroads aided, in any corporation, then, in such case, no state tax on railroads aided, shall be placed to the credit of such county, township, city or town.

§ 164. The latest legislation on this subject dates from March 7, 1872, going into force July 1 of the same year. It reads as follows:

§ 165. The treasurer of state, and all county treasurers in the state, at whose office any county, town or city bonds or coupons are made payable by law, which have been issued in aid of any railroad or other corporation or in payment of the stock of any such railroad or other corporation in this state, shall, at least once in each year, after this act shall be in force, if so requested by the proper authorities of any such county, town or city, account to and with any person designated by any such county, town or city, for any and all money that may have come to his or their hands for the payment of any bonds or coupons, so issued as aforesaid, and shall, upon such accounting, deliver up to such person so designated by any of the counties, towns or cities aforesaid, any and all bonds or coupons that he or they may have fully paid off and discharged out of the money coming into their hands for such purpose, and to take a voucher for all such bonds or coupons so delivered.

§ 166. There shall be allowed and paid out to the county treasurers, and to the county, town and city collectors for collecting, receiving and paying out any and all taxes levied for the payment of any such bonds or coupons or interest on the same, the amount of one-half per centum, as fees for such service, and no more for such amount so paid out: *Provided*, if any of the above officers are now or may be hereafter paid a salary for the performance of these duties, then they shall not be paid any other compensation whatsoever.

§ 167. All laws in conflict with this act are hereby repealed.

NOTE.—The full text of this legislation is given without note or comment, on account of the danger of misstatement, and there has been no authoritative interpretations of the same.

CHAPTER IV.

EMINENT DOMAIN.

§ 168. "Eminent domain is the power to take private property for public use."[1] In this perfectly plain statement Chief Justice MARSHALL condensed one of the most intricate and important features of law. By whatever name called, the subject has challenged discussion by all the great legists, from Bracton down. Indeed, the subject was old when introduced into English law. The Roman jurisprudence had nearly mastered its every detail of principle. The term *dominsium eminens*, betrays its Latin origin. Blackstone's Commentaries, Napoleon's Code, Vattel, Kent, and all the great embodiments of law, are largely taken up with it, under various heads and designations. The judicial reports show that a vast amount of litigation grows out of some phase of this subject.

§ 169. It would be quite foreign to the object of this treatise to enter upon any extended discussion of this subject. It would be presumption, or a sheer waste of time, for any one to do so at this late day. Every point has been fully considered and clearly stated by jurists and authors of the highest eminence. Abstract philosophy may never determine precisely how this right of eminent domain was included in the original contract between the people and the government (a mystic if not a mythical contract); but no

[1] 6 Howard, 536.

practical doubt of its existence and validity can be entertained. Without such an attribute of sovereignty no government could accomplish the object of its existence, or deserve the loyalty of its citizens. Civilization itself would be at an absolute stand-still. It would be impossible to overestimate the importance and necessity of this right to take private property for public uses.

§ 170. The uses and occasions for this law of eminent domain are almost infinite, and apply to personal property no less than to real estate, and may apply to a temporary use of the same.[1] The term generally suggests to the mind the appropriation of land belonging to a private person for some public use. During the present generation it has come to mean, chiefly, the acquirement of the right of way to construct a railroad. It is to this phase of the subject that our attention will naturally be restricted.

§ 171. It has been remarked that in the organization of a railway company there is no need, intrinsically, of a different method from that pursued in forming an ordinary corporation. As soon, however, as actual operations begin a fundamental difference is developed. A corporation created to carry on any private business may have a vast capital, and be in every way a most important concern, and still have no need of invoking the government to exercise its sovereignty over private property. The corporation can acquire by ordinary purchase the necessary ground and material. The state will not concern itself with the matter, any more than with the sale of a farm or building lot. The railway company, on the contrary,

[1] See chapter on railway construction.

can do nothing without the intervention of the state. However short its proposed line it is sure to need a little real estate belonging to a great many owners. It is certain that the necessary right of way could not all be secured except at a ruinous price. Practically, then, the right to take private property for public uses must be exercised, or the enterprise die before it be born. The government must in some way help the company to get the necessary right of way for a fair price.[1]

§ 172. On some accounts the company would prefer to acquire the right by ordinary purchase, if it could. It would thus escape a degree of dependence upon the government which results from an appeal to the state for aid in securing its real estate. By every principle of justice the state is entitled to a consideration of one kind or another for the exercise of this right in behalf of the company, and clearly has certain claims upon the company which it would not have had otherwise. But necessity knows no option, and eminent domain is by an inevitable law the corner-stone of railway construction.

§ 173. In the absence of statutory provision it would be relatively easy to point out every step necessary to the acquisition of the right of way.

[1] The only exception would be in the case of a road extending over the public domain. An act of congress passed in 1852 threw the government lands open to railway construction, under certain restrictions. That was not the exercise of the right of eminent domain, for a fee simple of the land vested in the government. That exception in no way impairs the force of the rule. The law itself has never been of any utility. All rail roads since built through the public domain have had special charters and special privileges.

The provisions of the common law are copious and minute. But the written law, unless unconstitutional, is absolute in its authority, and the validity of the Illinois statute on eminent domain has never been called in question.[1]

§ 174. Prior to the present constitution the term eminent domain was not in use, but elaborate details had been laid down by statute for its exercise in the case of railroads[2]. All that was swept away by a law passed April, 1872. The latter was distinctly based on this constitutional provision: "The right of trial by jury shall be held inviolate in all trials of claims for compensation, when in the exercise of the said right of eminent domain, any incorporated company shall be interested either for or against the exercise of the said right."[3]

§ 175. This provision is recognized and acted upon in the bungling road and bridge statute passed at the second session of the twenty-seventh general assembly,[4] which was repealed by an act approved April 11, 1873, containing an emergency clause.[5] That application was only to ordinary roads. Several other laws are in part based on the provision, notably the act for the formation of bridge companies, and the statute allowing the United States to acquire real estate property by purchase or condemnation.[6] The right of trial

A statute expressly declares that the common law is in force in Illinois. See Gross' Statutes, vol. i, chap. 62, sec. 1.

[2] Gross Statutes, vol. i, chap. 92.

[3] Constitution of Illinois, art. xi, sec. 14, last clause.

[4] Gross' Statutes, vol. ii, chap. 93.

[5] Gross' Statutes, vol. ii, chap. 25, div. 19, sec. 5.

[6] Gross' Statutes, vol. ii, chap. 105, div. ii, sec. 1.

by jury enjoined in the clause of the constitution quoted, is specifically recognized in the legislation on special assessments, a kindred subject, although foreign to our consideration.[1]

§ 176. A statute entitled "An act to provide for the exercise of the right of eminent domain" was approved April 10, 1872, and went into effect the July following.[2] By its provisions all laws and parts of laws in conflict with it were repealed, but it was expressly provided in that connection that the same should not be construed to repeal any law, or part of law, upon the subject, passed by that general assembly, but rather be construed to provide cumulative remedy. So far as such laws are concerned the eminent domain act simply furnishes further details, some of which are applicable, for whatever purpose the private property is appropriated to public uses. Whatever legislation under the previous constitution of the state was pertinent to this subject was repealed, leaving only so much of the legislation under the old constitution on the right of way as refers to public lands, school sections, and state land, which, although not strictly a part of eminent domain, will be disposed of in this chapter.

§ 177. Private property cannot be taken or damaged for public use without just compensatiôn.[3] This common law doctrine has been held immemorially. A private right over property belonging to another can in no case be acquired except by gift, purchase, or

[1] Gross' Statutes, vol. ii, chap. 5, art. ix.

[2] Gross' Statutes, vol. ii, chap. 38.

[3] The details and principles of law laid down in this chapter for which no authority is given, are based on the eminent domain statute, Gross, vol. ii, chap. 38.

exchange. This doctrine and its correlative one that private property may be taken for public uses on making just compensation of necessity, take railways out of the list of private property and justifies the constitutional classification of them as public highways.[1]

§ 178. The state, in its own corporate capacity, may make the compensation. In the state is the right of eminent domain vested originally, and the statute does not attempt to prescribe the method of its direct exercise. Should the commonwealth, in its sovereignty, attempt its exercise in a manner and to an extent clearly unjust, the courts would interpose, the judiciary being charged with the authority to set aside unconstitutional laws. It will be observed that the right of trial by jury in determining the measure of damages prescribed by the constitution does not require that mode of procedure when the state acts directly in the matter. The usual, if not the uniform, mode of procedure for the state is to acquire possession by purchase or donation, except in extreme emergencies. The government is always, and justly, cautious about an assertion of its sovereignty over private property.

§ 179. The first section of the statute closes with the general assertion of the right of trial by jury, leaving the manner thereof to subsequent sections. The old method was to leave the appraisement to a commission appointed by the circuit judge, and in some cases to a justice of the peace.[2] This commis-

[1] Constitution of Illinois, art. xi, sec. 12. For a discussion of private rights in this connection, see Nesbitt *v.* Trumbo, 39 Ill. 110; Crear *v.* Crosby, 40 Ill. 175.

[2] Gross' Statutes, vol. i, chap. 92.

sion consisted of three householders. Although the act of 1852 provided for a somewhat different mode, the supreme court held that this way was not repealed and was, consequently, in force until the adoption of the present constitution.

§ 180. By the first section, the statute is extended to "all cases in which compensation is not made by the state in its corporate capacity." The last sentence of the second section (in which the foregoing provisions for jury trial are found) reads: "In cases where the property is sought to be taken or damaged by the state for the purpose of establishing, operating, or maintaining any state house, or state charitable or other institution or improvements, the petition shall be signed by the governor, or such other person as he shall direct, or as shall be provided by law.[1]

§ 181. An inability to agree on the terms may not be the only obstacle to securing the right of way by purchase. The owner may be incapable of consenting; his name and residence may be unknown; he may reside in another state. In either of these three cases resort may be had to condemnation, as well as in case of non-agreement of the parties in regard to the amount of compensation. It is not to be inferred that a non-resident could not convey the desired property in the ordinary way, that being an inherent right of property; but simply that both parties may be spared the trouble and expense of foreign negotiation.[2]

[1] This inconsistency, or at least appearance of inconsistency, has not been passed upon by the supreme court, nor is there any immediate prospect of an issue being joined thereupon.

[2] In a certain sense the several states are "foreign" to each other. See Bank of Washtenaw *v.* Montgomery, 3 Ill. 422; Bank of Augusta *v.* Earle, 13 Peters, 519.

§ 182. The first step is taken by the party desiring to acquire the property for public use. This step consists of an application to the judge of the circuit or county court. The application or petition may be presented either in vacation or term time. It must be made in the county where the property, or any part of it, may be situate. This is done by filing a document with the clerk, wherein is set forth, in detail: 1. His or their authority in the premises. 2. The purpose for which the property is sought to be taken or damaged. 3. A description of the property. 4. The names of all the persons interested therein as owners, or in any other way, as appearing of record, if known. 5. If the ownership of and interest in the property is not known, that fact must appear. 6. To this statement is appended as a part of the application a petition to the judge to cause the compensation to be paid to the owner to be assessed.

§ 183. If the proceedings seek to affect the property of persons under guardianship, the guardians of or conservators of persons having conservators shall be made parties defendant.[1] If the owner is a married woman her husband shall be made a party defendant also. The common law doctrine of the limited powers of a wife has been modified in this state very materially; but this provision, although evidently based on the old *femme covert* idea, is none the less vital.

§ 184. If the persons interested are unknown by name, they may be made parties defendant by a description setting forth all that is known of them. This

[1] In the statute the custodian of a person under age is usually designated a guardian, and of a lunatic, an imbecile, or a confirmed drunkard, a conservator.

description must be accompanied by an affidavit by or on behalf of the petitioner, setting forth the fact that the names of such persons are unknown. This affidavit must be filed. The doctrine of "due diligence" would here be recognized. The court would hold such an affidavit perjury if the person making it either knew or might have known the name by proper investigation.

§ 185. In case the petition be presented to the judge in vacation, he shall note thereon the day of presentation; also the day when he will hear the same. He shall order an issuance of summons to each resident defendant, and the publication of notice as to each non-resident defendant. This summons must be immediately issued by the clerk and the notices given accordingly. The manner of serving such summons and publishing such notice shall be the same as prescribed in chancery.[1]

§ 186. The judge may hear such causes in vacation as well as in term time. The period of ten days must elapse in the case of personal service between the service and the hearing. In the case of non-residents the time is not specified, the law simply requiring "due publication." What would be reasonable and just might not be the same in any two cases. This discretion must be exercised in the spirit and on the principles of justice.

§ 187. As a matter of convenience, and without injustice to any person, it is provided that any number of separate parcels of property, if only they are situate in the same county, may be included in one

[1] On this point see Gross' Statutes, vol. ii, chap. 21; also ibid., vol. i, same chapter.

petition. The compensation, however, for each must be assessed separately. The assessment may be by one jury or by different juries. This is left to the discretion and direction of the court or judge.

§ 188. Another provision to simplify proceedings and insure equity is that amendments to the petition, or to any paper or record in the cause, may be permitted, whenever necessary, to a fair trial and final determination of the questions involved. That no just restriction should be put upon this provision, or any opportunity for unreasonable delay be afforded, it is added: "Should it become necessary at any stage of the proceedings to bring a new party before the court or judge, the court or judge shall have the power to make such rule or order in relation thereto as may be deemed reasonable and proper; and shall also have power to make all necessary rules and orders for notice to parties of the pendency of the proceedings, and to issue all process necessary to the execution of orders and judgments as they may be entered." Although the courts are held to a specially strict construction of law in cases of eminent domain,[1] the proceedings are largely in the nature of equity. The right to bring a new party into the case is provided for specifically. "Any person," says the eleventh section of the statute, "not made a party may become such by filing his cross petition, setting forth that he is the owner or has an interest in property, and which will be taken or damaged by the proposed work,

[1] Williams *v.* Powell, 6 Wheat. 119; Beaty *v.* Knowler, 4 Peters, 168; Early *v.* Doe, 16 How. 610; Rule *v.* Parker, 1 Cooke, 365; Parker *v.* Overmann, 18 How. 137.

and the rights of such last named petitioner shall thereupon be fully considered and determined."

§ 189. No specific jury provision is made for cases in which the hearing of petition occurs in term time; but if fixed for hearing in vacation it is the duty of the clerk of the court in whose office the petition is filed, to write the names of each of sixty-four disinterested freeholders of the county on as many distinct slips of paper, and, in the presence of two disinterested freeholders, cause to be selected from the same the names of twelve persons to serve as jurors. This selection must be made by lot, "without choice or discrimination." The preparation of the list and the drawing of the lot must occur at the time of issuing summons, or making publication. The selection made, the clerk shall issue *venire*, directed to the sheriff of his county, commanding him to summon the twelve persons so selected as jurors to appear at the court house, in the county, at a time to be named in the *venire*.

§ 190. The petitioner and every party interested in the ascertainment of compensation have the same right of challenge of jurors as in other civil cases in the circuit court.[3] If the panel be not full by reason of non-attendance, or be exhausted by challenge, the judge hearing the petition shall designate by name the necessary number of persons of proper qualification, and the clerk or justice shall issue another *venire*, returnable instanter and until the jury be full.

§ 191. The jury selected, the following oath must be administered to them: "You, and each of you, do

[3] For the right of challenge as defined by statute, see Gross, vol. ii, chap. 58.

solemnly swear that you will well and truly ascertain and report just compensation to the owner (and each owner) of the property which is sought to take or damage in this case, and to each person therein interested, according to the facts in the case, as the same may be made to appear by the evidence, and that you will truly report such compensation so ascertained. So help you God."

§ 192. In ascertaining the real facts in the case the jury shall, at the request of either party, go upon the land sought to be taken or damaged, in person, and examine the same. After hearing and seeing all the evidence in the case the jury must make report in writing so as to clearly set forth and show the compensation ascertained, to each person thereto entitled. If the report is not sufficiently explicit the jury shall amend it under the direction of the court or the judge. The verdict shall thereupon be recorded. It is expressly provided, in this connection, that no benefits or advantages which may accrue to lands or property affected shall be set off against, or deducted from, such compensation in any case.[1]

§ 193. The next step is for the judge, or court, to "adjust and make such order as to right and justice shall pertain." This order shall issue to the petitioner, directing entry upon such property and the use of the same, upon payment of full compensation, as ascertained. This order, if coupled with evidence of such payment, shall constitute complete justification of the taking of such property. Payment of

[1] The original doctrine of set-off in Illinois was just the reverse of this, and gave rise to much litigation, ill feeling and injustice.

compensation adjudged may, in all cases, be made to the county treasurer, who shall, on demand, pay the same to the party thereto entitled, taking receipt for the payment. Or, if preferred, payment may be made to the party entitled, his or her or their conservator or guardian. The court or judge must cause the verdict of the jury and the judgment of the court to be entered upon the court records.

§ 194. In the event that both parties are satisfied with the verdict of the jury, the transaction is complete, and the right sought has been fully secured. But the right of appeal to the supreme court is guaranteed in all cases. If the party whose property is to be taken or damaged appeals, the petitioner shall, notwithstanding, have the right to enter upon the use of the property upon entering into bond, with sufficient surety, payable to the party interested in such compensation, conditioned for the payment of such compensation as may be finally adjudged in the case. If the appeal is taken by the petitioner the same bond shall be exacted. The bond shall be submitted to the judge or justice before whom such proceeding shall be had and be approved by him. The execution and filing shall be within such time as the judge may designate.

§ 195. The right to acquire a roadway includes the right to acquire as much land as may be needed for the work-shops and other appendages. This right may lay dormant for an indefinite length of time, provided its final exercise is in itself legitimate.[1] In case the regularity of the proceedings under which the

[1] Chicago, Burlington and Quincy R. R. *v.* Wilson, 17 Ill. 123.

right of way was acquired should be called in question, the presumption of the law would be in favor of its regularity,[1] although the requirement of regularity is strict,[2] as previously stated.

§ 196. There are a few additional points established by the decisions that remain to be noted before calling attention to the method of acquiring the right of way to enter a city or pass over school and state lands. Authorities could be given for the doctrine that the title to land acquired by a railroad company is absolute.[3] An early case held that the land taken from private persons and vested in a corporation, under the exercise of this right of eminent domain becomes really vested in the state.[4]

§ 197. The constitution is explicit on this point (article xi, section 14): "The exercise of the power and the right of eminent domain shall never be so construed or abridged as to prevent the taking by the general assembly of the property and franchises of incorporated companies already organized, and subjecting them to the public necessity, the same as of individuals." The bill of rights is more sweeping. Besides forbidding the making of any irrevocable grant of special privileges or immunities, it declares (section 13): "Private property shall not be taken or damaged for public use without just compensation. Such compensation, when not made by the state, shall be ascertained by a jury as shall be prescribed by law. The fee of land taken for railroad tracks, without con-

[1] Galena and Chicago Union R. R. Co. *v.* Pound, 22 Ill. 399.

[2] Harper *v.* Lexington and Ohio R. R. Co. 2 Dana, 227.

[3] Chicago and Mississippi R. R. Co. *v.* Patchin, 16 Ill. 198.

[4] The State *v.* Evans, 2 Scam. 208.

sent of the owners thereof, shall remain in such owners, subject to the use for which it is taken."

§ 198. When the route of a railroad lies partly in an unorganized township the notice for application to acquire the right of way through the school section (section 16) must be served upon the school commissioners of the county. The damage assessed shall be paid into the school fund of the county for the use of the inhabitants of the township in which the section may be situate. As soon as the township has been organized the money shall be paid over to the treasurer thereof.[1] The special consent of the general assembly must be secured in order to acquire the right of way through land belonging to the state for the use of any benevolent institution of the state. The courts have no jurisdiction over such cases.[2] The twenty-eighth general assembly exercised this function of legislation in granting to the Chicago and Pacific railroad company a conditional right of way over lands of the Northern Illinois Hospital and Asylum for the Insane. In a case involving the construction of a charter embodying the right of way through state lands the court held[3] that the language of a statute incorporating a railroad company might be sufficiently comprehensive to embrace any property owned by the state, still it will not be construed to include property used by the state for a specific purpose. This could not be the intention of the legislature, and all statutes are to be construed according to it.

[1] Gross' Statutes, vol. i, chap. 92, sec. 27.

[2] Ibid. sec. 28.

[3] St. Louis, Jacksonville and Chicago R. R. Co. *v.* Trustees, 43 Ill. 303.

§ 199. The fee simple to the streets of a city is generally vested in the municipal corporation.[1] The right of way to enter a city must be secured from the municipal government. This sometimes occasions vexatious delay, but has proved no serious obstacle to railway enterprise.

§ 200. Such is the present mode of procedure in acquiring the right of way in Illinois for a railroad. The intricacies of the old system and some light upon the general subject may be derived from the decision in the case of the *Peoria and Rock Island R. R. Co. v. Warner*. The opinion of the supreme court, delivered by Justice THORNTON, was filed June 28, 1872. The following syllabus is mainly from the *Chicago Legal News*, of July 13, 1872:

§ 201. "This was an action of trespass against the railroad company. The defendant justified under its charter, and the act of 1845, entitled 'Right of Way.' The only averment in the plea as to notice to the party whose land was condemned was this: 'The defendant avers that said plaintiff was present with said commissoners before their report was signed, and had an opportunity of being heard upon his claim for damages,' and the court held that there was no sufficient averment as to notice.

§ 202. That the party whose land is to be taken has the right to reasonable notice of the time and place where and when application will be made for the appointment of the persons who are to assess the damages.

§ 203. That it was the intention of the legislature

[1] Moses *v.* Pittsburg, Ft. Wayne and Chicago R. R. Co. 21 Ill. 522.

that notice should be given under the act of 1845. The court cites authorities to show that in appeals and similar cases, where the statute giving the right was silent as to notice, that notice was required to be given.

§ 204. That the legislature has repeatedly recognized the validity of the act of 1845; that the act of 1852 contains no express repeal of it, and is amendatory of it. That it was enacted in 1869 that the provisions of both acts should apply to all proceedings for the condemnation of lands; that notice must be given in accordance with the act of 1852.

§ 205. As the sole object of section nineteen was to continue the reservation of power in the legislature to fix the routes and termini of all roads, before the corporations should exercise the right of eminent domain. It has no application to a company whose termini are fixed by its charter."

§ 206. For the convenience of those who may wish to make thorough and original investigation on this subject, the following list of Illinois authorities is appended. The subject has been extensively discussed by many able legists and jurists.[1]

[1] Gillinwater *v.* Mississippi and Atlantic R. R. Co. 13 Ill. 1; Newhall *v.* Galena and Chicago Union R. R. Co. 14 Ill. 273; Illinois Central R. R. Co. *v.* Rucker, 14 Ill. 353; Illinois and Wisconsin R. R. Co. *v.* VanHorn, 18 Ill. 257; Low *v.* Galena and Chicago Union R. R. Co. 18 Ill. 324; Chicago and Milwaukee R. R. Co. *v.* Bull, 20 Ill. 218; Jacksonville and Savannah R. R. Co. Co. *v.* Kidder 21 Ill. 131; Tonica and Petersburg R. R. Co. *v.* Unsicker, 22 Ill. 221; same *v.* Roberts, Ibid. 224; Johnson *v.* Joliet and Chicago R. R. Co. 23 Ill. 203; Rock Island and Alton R. R. Co. *v.* Lynch, 23 Ill. 645; Shute *v.* Chicago and Milwaukee R. R. Co. 26 Ill. 436; Trustees *et al.* *v.* Chicago and Rock Island

R. R. Co. 14 Ill. 314; Johnson *v.* Joliet and Chicago R. R. Co. 23 Ill. 202; City of Chicago *v.* Larned, 34 Ill. 203; Rees *v.* City of Chicago, 38 Ill. 322; City of Chicago *v.* Laflin, 49 Ill. 172; People *v.* Williams, 51 Ill. 63; Harwood *v.* St. Clair Draw Co. 51 Ill. 130; Hessler *v.* Drainage Commissioners, 53 Ill. 105; Cooley on Constitutional Limitations, chap. 15; Potter's Dwarris on Statutes, chap. 11; Redfield on Railway Law, 239.

9

CHAPTER V.

RAILWAY CONSTRUCTION.

I. Construction of the Road.

§ 207. The first step in the way of railway construction is to make a critical survey, and determine the exact route of the road. In ordinary cases such surveying would be trespass. The law provides that a railway company, if duly organized, may cause such examinations and survey for its proposed railway to be made as may be necessary to the selection of the most advantageous route.[1] The officers, agents or servants of the company are authorized to enter upon the lands of any person or corporation, subject, however, to

[1] Gross, vol. ii, page 309, sec. 180.

responsibility for all damages which may be occasioned thereby. This right to hold in abeyance the law of trespass is based on the doctrine of eminent domain.

§ 208. The surveys made, and an exact route agreed upon, the company must, before proceeding to build their line through any county named in their certificate of association, make a map and profile of the route intended to be adopted. The correctness of this map and profile shall be certified by a majority of the board of directors. The same shall then be filed in the office of the county clerk of the county, or with the clerk of the county commissioners court of such county. The whole route need not be profiled and recorded in each county, but only so much as lies in that particular county. All parties interested in the matter can inspect and examine the map and profile, the same as the ordinary public records of a county.[2]

§ 209. The company is empowered to purchase, hold and use all such real estate and other property as shall be necessary for the construction and use of its railway and the stations and other accommodations necessary to accomplish the object of its incorporation. This general power includes the whole subject of eminent domain. It also contemplates purchase in the ordinary way, and donations. No provision peculiar to railroads is made in regard to purchase, and as for donations, the law reads: "The corporation may take and hold such voluntary grants of real estate and other

[2] Gross, vol. i, chap. 81, sec. 58. The survey clause of the law, as found in Gross, vol. ii, makes no mention of filing for public record, but as that provision of the old law is not inconsistent with the new law, it is in force. See repeal clause, Gross, vol. ii, railroads, sec. 196.

property as shall be made to it in aid of the construction and use of its railway, and to convey the same when no longer required for the uses of such railway, not incompatible with the terms of the original grant." [1] The right to convey is the same in the case of purchase. Real estate acquired by the exercise of the right of eminent domain cannot be used for any other than its original purpose.

§ 210. In laying out its road the company must not claim more than 100 feet in width; but for the purposes of cuttings and embankments it may take as much more land as may be necessary for the proper construction and security of the road. If any trees standing hard by would be in danger of falling upon the track, or in any way obstructing the railway, the company may cause them to be cut down. Compensation therefor must be made in the same method and on the same principle as compensation for land.[2] This tree clause is virtually a police regulation, being designed as a safeguard against railway accidents.

§ 211. In the building of a railway it is often necessary to use more earth, stone and gravel in making the road bed, than the land the company has a right to acquire by condemnation furnishes. To facilitate and cheapen construction, the law provides for the taking of the same by the exercise of eminent domain, in case the parties cannot agree on terms. The provision is that "if such owner and corporation cannot agree, then the value of such material taken and the damage occasioned to such real estate may be ascertained, determined and paid in the manner that

[1] Gross, vol. ii, page 309, sec. 181.
[2] Ibid. sec. 182.

may now or hereafter be provided by any law of eminent domain; but the value of such materials and the damages to such real estate shall be ascertained, determined and paid for before such corporation can enter upon and take the same."[1] This latter clause is superfluous, as the law of eminent domain requires pre-payment, or, in case of appeal, a bond equivalent thereto in its certainty of compensation. It should be added that this right to acquire material by condemnation does not extend to fuel and wood.

§ 212. Another construction right specified is the right to "construct its line across, along, or upon any stream of water, water course, street, highway, plank-road, turnpike, or canal, which the route shall intersect or touch."[2] The trustees of the Michigan and Illinois canal once tried to arrest railway construction; but the court held that all grants made by the state, whether to canal trustees or others, although irrevocable, are subject to the right of eminent domain, unless that right is expressly relinquished.[3] We may add that it is an established principle that the right of eminent domain cannot be relinquished.[4]

§ 213. This right is coupled with a duty. The same section adds: "But such corporation shall restore the stream, water course, street, highway, plankroad and turnpike thus intersected or touched to its former state, or to such state as not unnecessarily to have impaired its usefulness, and keep such crossing in

[1] Ibid. sec. 179.

[2] Ibid. sec. 182.

[3] Trustees *v.* Chicago and Rock Island R. R. Co. 14 Ill. 314.

[4] Pollard *v.* Hagan, 3 How. 212; Goodtitle *v.* Kibbe, 9 How. 471; Doe *v.* Beebe, 13 How. 25; Illinois Central R. R. Co. *v* United States, 20 Law Rep. 630.

repair; *provided*, that in no case shall any railroad company construct a road bed without first constructing the necessary culverts or sluices, as the natural lay of the land requires for the necessary drainage thereof." It will be observed that in this restoration clause no mention is made of canals. From the language of the court in the case of the Chicago and Rock Island railroad company, just referred to, it would seem evident that the railroad company may not, in any way or for any length of time, interfere with the actual operations or stability of a canal.

§ 214. A further limitation is placed upon the foregoing right.[1] The construction of a bridge or of any other obstruction over any stream navigated by steamboats is not authorized. Legislation on that subject is provided in a separate statute.[2] Nor is authority given to construct any railroad upon or across any street in any city or incorporated town or village without the assent of the corporation of such city, town, or village. This qualifying section ends by adding: "*Provided*, that in case of the constructing of said railway along highways, plankroads, turnpikes, or canals, such railway shall either first obtain the consent of the lawful authorities having control or jurisdiction of the same, or condemn the same under the provisions of any eminent domain law now or hereafter in force in this state."

§ 215. It is not enough to have the right to acquire the land of private persons and cross highways, streams, etc. It often happens that in the construction of a railroad the new line intersects with existing lines.

[1] Gross, vol. ii, chap. 86.

[2] Gross, vol. ii, p. 100.

The Chicago, Burlington and Quincy, for instance, is crossed in this state by other lines twenty-one times. As these routes, in many cases, are natural rivals, the general assembly has expressly authorized any railroad corporation, in building its line, to cross as often as may be necessary existing railroads; also, upon the grounds of existing railroads, to construct all necessary turnouts, sidings, switches, and other conveniences.

§ 216. The old road is required to unite with the new in constructing the facilities for a mutual interchange of business and convenient transfer of cars. Nothing is allowed on the part of one railroad toward another which would retard its construction and impede its operation. If the two corporations cannot agree upon the amount of compensation to be allowed for the property used, or upon the points at which the crossings shall occur, and the manner thereof, the matter shall be arbitrated on the plan laid down in the law of eminent domain. It should be mentioned in this connection that an act of congress passed July 15, 1862, authorizes and requires railroads to carry passengers and freight from one state to another, and connect with other roads for such purposes. This law is, by its express provisions, repealable at the discretion of congress, but it is still in force. The earliest mention of railways in the legislation of this state is a resolution for the extension of Illinois railroads into Indiana.[1]

§ 217. A road bed is by no means all of a railroad. Besides the rolling stock and the bridges over naviga-

[1] Laws of Illinois, 1839, p. 308.

ble streams, there are side-tracks or switches, station houses for the suitable accommodation of passengers, and warehouses for the fit storage of freight; water tanks and machine shops. Whatever, in fine, a railway company needs for the transaction of its business with expedition, safety, comfort and economy, it is not only allowed but compelled to provide. Lest the provisions previously given should not be ample in their authority, the statute specifies that the company shall have power "to erect and maintain all necessary and convenient buildings and stations, fixtures and machinery for the convenient accommodation and use of passengers, freights and business interests, or which may be necessary for the construction or operation of said railway."[1]

II. Bridges.

§ 218. Bridge statutes of 1872.
219. Bridge companies; articles of incorporation.
220. Filing the same.
221. Board of directors.
222. Powers of the corporation.
223. Navigable rivers; congressional and state legislation.
224. Old bridge charters; time for completion.

§ 218. Three bridge laws were passed in the year 1872, all going into force July 1 of that year. One relates to the time of completing bridges; another to the authority for constructing them, and the last to the formation of bridge companies. We have observed in this enumeration the order of the passage of these statutes, which is the reverse of the proper order of their consideration.[2]

[1] Ibid. sec. 185, clause 2.

[2] Gross, vol. ii, chap. 25, div. xix.

§ 219. Any number of persons, not less than ten, may associate together for the formation of a company for the purpose of constructing and maintaining a bridge over any of the streams of water which are situate, in whole or in part, in the state, or upon the boundary of the state. The bridge must be for public use, including the transference of persons and property. The first thing to do is to make, sign and acknowledge, before some officer authorized to take acknowledgments, articles of association. These articles of association must set forth: 1. The name of the proposed corporation. 2. The number of years the same is to continue.[1] 3. The place at which the bridge is to be constructed. 4. The name of the county or counties in which it is intended to be constructed. 5. The purpose for which it is to be used, whether for railroad or ordinary travel, or both. 6. The amount of the capital stock. 7. Number of shares of the stock. 8. The names and places of residence of the directors of the company. 9. The residence of each subscriber, and the number of shares he has agreed to subscribe for.[2]

§ 220. These articles of association must be filed in the office of the secretary of state, who shall thereon endorse the date when the same was filed, and record the articles in a book to be provided by him for that

[1] The statute places no time limitation, as in the case of ordinary corporations and railroad companies.

[2] It will be observed that the articles of incorporation contemplate a greater degree of completeness in organization prior to public action than is the case in the organization of an ordinary stock company or of a railroad company under Illinois statutory law, although the general principle of organization is the same in all.

purpose, "and," continues the statute, "thereupon, the persons who have so subscribed such articles of association and all persons who shall become stockholders in such company shall be a corporation by the name specified in such articles of association, and shall possess the powers and privileges incident to such corporations.[1]

§ 221. The board of directors named in the articles of incorporation must consist of not less than five nor more than thirteen persons. They shall manage the affairs of the corporation for the first year and until others are chosen in their places. This much the first section of the law provides. The fourth and last adds: "The trustees, managers or directors of such corporation shall be elected and classified in the manner provided by law for the election and classification of the trustees, managers or directors of other incorporated companies, and at least one-third of such directors shall be citizens of this state." The allusion is doubtless to the cumulative method of voting, which under the constitution applies to all corporations in the state, and which is expressly recognized in the statute referred to in the quotation just given.

§ 222. In case of need, the law of eminent domain may be invoked to acquire possession of the private property necessary for the carrying out of the object of the association. The company may issue bonds or other evidences of indebtedness; negotiate loans for the prosecution of its work; secure such indebtedness by deed of trust, or mortgage on the property of the

[1] No provision is made for filing the articles of incorporation in the office of the county clerk.

company. It may, further, consolidate its franchise and property, in the manner provided by general law, with that of any bridge company in the state, or a bridge company organized under the laws of an adjoining state. In fine, it may exercise "any other rights and powers incident to such corporations which may be necessary to carry out the objects contemplated in such organization."

§ 223. The assent of the state is given to any corporation or association organized under the laws of Illinois, and subject thereto, to construct bridges across navigable rivers in this state, and upon boundaries thereof, whenever authorized by congress, "under such restrictions as the congress may impose." This is a plain recognition of the paramount authority of the national government in regulation of inter-state commerce. The doctrine laid down by the supreme court of Illinois is that the power of the state over navigable rivers exclusively within the state to render them useful for domestic purposes was never surrendered.[1]

§ 224. Previous to the adoption of the present constitution some bridge company charters had been granted. One of the three statutes under consideration provides that if any such company had not finished its work within the time specified in its charter it is allowed to go on and complete the enterprise, anything in its charter to the contrary notwithstanding. This extension privilege is qualified by the proviso that "the same shall be constructed and completed within ten years from and after the passage of this act; and, *provided further*, that such corporation shall have been

[1] City of Chicago *v.* McGunn, 51 Ill. 266.

organized and been in operation within ten days from the time the new constitution took effect." It is evident that a railroad company is not obliged to depend upon a bridge company for the means of crossing navigable streams, but simply that the bridge part of railway construction may be under the legislation which has just been stated.

III. Union Depots.

§ 225. No special provision is made for the construction of ordinary depots; but by an act, approved April 3, 1872, and which went into force July 1 of the same year, provision is made for building union depots. The object of this law is, as stated, "to facilitate the public convenience and safety in the transmission of goods and passengers from one railroad to another and to prevent the unnecessary expense, inconvenience and loss attending the accumulation of a number of stations."

§ 226. Any number of persons not less than five may organize themselves into a union depot company. So may three or more railway companies or "joint individuals." The object of this association is defined by statute to be "for the purpose of constructing, establishing and maintaining a union station for passenger or freight depots, or for both, in any city, town or place in this state, with the necessary offices and rooms convenient for the same and appurtenances thereto."

§ 227. The object of the company is further explained in the last section, wherein it is expressly provided that "there shall be no discrimination against or in favor of any railroad company using or desiring to use the said union depot, but the terms, conditions and regulations adopted for the use of the same shall, so far as practicable, be uniform and apply alike to all railroads using or desiring to use said union depot." It may be remarked that all the railway legislation during the present decade is true to the anti-monopoly principle of the constitution.

§ 228. The articles of incorporation must set forth: 1. The number of years the company is to continue. 2. The city, town, or place in which the depot is to be located. 3. The amount of capital stock of the company, which must not exceed $3,000,000. 4. The amount of each share. 5. The names and places of residence of the directors, not less than five nor more than fifteen. 6. The amount of stock taken by each subscriber.

§ 229. These articles of association must be presented first to the circuit court of the county in which the depot is to be located, or to the judge of the same, in vacation. This presentation must be in the form of a petition from the signers for a certificate of incorporation under the provisions of this act. To the petition must be appended a certificate from at least three railroad companies who have tracks leading into the city or place where the depot is to be built, stating its public utility, and that they expect to make arrangements for its use when it shall have been constructed. These certificates must be signed by the presidents of the respective railway companies.

§ 230. The court or judge, if satisfied that these certificates have been actually signed by the companies, shall, upon filing the petition, articles and certificate with the clerk of the court, grant to the association a certificate in the following form:

Whereas, A, B, and C, etc., (stating the names,) have filed in the office of the clerk of the circuit court their articles of association, in compliance with the provisions of an act entitled, "An act authorizing the formation of union depots and stations for railroads in this state," approved April 3, 1872, with their petition of incorporation under the name and style of ......, they are, therefore, hereby declared a body politic and corporate by the name and style aforesaid, with all the powers, privileges and immunities granted in the act above named. By order of the circuit court (or judge thereof.) Attest ....

This, or a certified copy of it, must be filed in the office of the secretary of state when the organization of the company will be complete.

§ 231. In addition to the general powers possessed by joint stock companies existing under the incorporation act of the state, and subject to the limitations specified already, the company has five powers, viz.: 1. To take and hold such real estate as they may acquire either by conveyance or by condemnation. 2. It may acquire by an exercise of the powers of eminent domain as much land as may be necessary to the carrying out of its depot purpose, and hold the same for that purpose, and no other. The necessary approaches to the depot are included, as well as the ground on which the building may stand. 3. It may, with the consent of the local or municipal authorities, lay the track or tracks necessary to connect therewith the railroads proposing to use the depot. If the authorities mentioned give their consent, the company may also construct its building "under, over, or upon any such streets or roads," the track laying being, if necessary, under, over, or upon the streets or roads of "such city, town, or place," the authorities consenting thereto. 4. The company is authorized to borrow money, mortgage its property and franchises, or issue bonds to the extent necessary to complete and maintain its depot. 5. To open, from time to time, books of subscription to the remainder of the capital stock not taken by the subscribers to the articles of association.[1]

§ 232. The first board of directors manage the affairs of the company for the first year, and until others are chosen in their places. After the directors named in the articles of association shall have served for one year, there shall be an annual election of directors, to be conducted on the cumulation plan laid down in the constitution of the state. The directors so elected shall serve one year. Each board shall give notice of the time and place of the election of their successors. The notice shall be given in some newspaper published in the English language at the place where the depot is located. This publication must be at least twenty days prior to the election.

[1] In an ordinary corporation all the stock must be subscribed prior to the completion of the organization of the same.

IV. CONTRACTS AND LIENS.

§ 233. In theory each railway company builds its own road. In practice the work is usually, if not always, done by contract. Often the bonds of the company are turned over to the construction company, and the contractor becomes the owner. There is one act on the statute books of Illinois specially designed to protect contractors in their claims against railroad companies; sub-contractors in their claims against contractors; and laborers in their claims against their employers, whether the same are railroad companies, contractors, or sub-contractors. This three-fold law was approved April, 1872, and went into effect July 1 of the same year.[1]

§ 234. A law on the same subject, passed in 1861,

[1] Gross' Statutes, vol. ii, p. 313.

was thereby repealed, except that all rights and causes of action existing under it were left undisturbed.[1] A still older statute, passed in 1853, is now in force, but has in effect been superseded and annuled.

§ 235. The old legislation provid for actions at law and in chancery, to be brought in any circuit court in any county in the state through which any railroad of the company may be located.[2] The action might be commenced by filing in the clerk's office of the circuit court a declaration or bill in chancery, as the case may be, and by giving notice to the company sued, of such filing, by at least four successive publications of the notice in a weekly newspaper published in the county (or if no newspaper be published in the county, then in the newspaper published in the nearest county.) The first publication had to be at least sixty days previous to the first day of the next succeeding term of the court. The court was obliged to hold such notice sufficient, and treat and determine the case the same as other cases at law or in chancery. The judgment recovered had the same force and effect as other judgments at law or decrees in chancery. The first provision was restricted by the last, which declares that "all actions instituted under the provisions of this act shall be commenced and prosecuted in the counties where the cause of action accrued, and not otherwise."[3]

§ 236. As regards contractors, the statute of 1872

[1] For that dead law, see Gross, vol. ii, chap. 86, div. i. It differed from the new only in being less explicit.

[2] See Ibid. sec. 1 to 5, inclusive.

[3] It is hardly necessary to add that this statute really extended no protection not previously enjoyed under common law.

is so far retroactive as to apply to material supplied or labor performed prior to its passage. It applies to all persons or any person furnishing by contract to railroad companies "fuel, ties, material supplies or any other article or thing necessary for the construction, maintenance, operation or repair" of its road, or who "shall have done and performed, or shall hereafter do or perform any work or labor for such construction, maintenance, operation or repair by like contract." The contractor is entitled to be paid as part of the current expenses of the road. If not so paid he has a lien upon all the property, real, personal and mixed, of the company. This lien shall be not only against the company itself, but against all mortgages or other liens which shall accrue after the commencement of the delivering of the material or the performance of the labor. As a preventive of laches that might work hardship and injustice to innocent parties, it is provided that suit shall be commenced within six months after the maturity of the contract or the performance of the labor or the furnishing of the material.

§ 237. In case the contractor fails to pay his subcontractor, "material-man or laborer" for work done or material supplied on any contract, express or implied, the same shall have a lien upon all the property of the railroad company; "provided such sub-contractor, material-man or laborer shall have complied with the provisions of this act. But the aggregate of all liens hereby authorized shall not in any case exceed the price agreed upon in the original contract by such corporation to the original contractor; and, provided further, that no such lien shall take priority over any existing lien." The eighth section of the act declares that the lien shall continue three months from the time of the performance of the sub-contract, except that the entry of a decree in the case shall bar all liens.

§ 238. The person seeking redress as sub-contractor, material-man or workman must cause notice in writing to be served on the president or secretary of the railroad company substantially as follows:

To........, President (or Secretary, as the case may be) of the........:

You are hereby notified that I am (or have been) employed by........as a laborer (or have furnished supplies, as the case may be) on or for the........, and that I shall hold all the property of said railroad (or railway, as the case may be) company to secure my pay.

§ 239. If a written contract had been made, a copy of it, if obtainable, shall be attached to the notice and form a part of it. This notice must be served within twenty days after the completion of the sub-contract or labor. The same section contains the proviso, no lien shall attach in favor of any person performing such labor or furnishing material until such notice shall have been served as above, or filed for record, as hereinafter provided.

§ 240. If neither the president or the secretary of the railroad company resides in the county in which the sub-contract was made, or the lien accrued, in fact, nor can be found in it, the notice may be filed in the office of the clerk of the circuit court. The clerk shall file the same and keep a record of it; also cause a copy of it to be mailed to the person addressed in the notice. The fee for the same is 25 cents. The clerk must keep a list of the names of the persons so claiming liens and the names of the companies against which such liens are claimed.

§ 241. Ten days are allowed in which to liquidate the claim. If it is not paid within that time the claimant may commence suit therefor, in any court having jurisdiction of the amount claimed, the corporation with which the original contract was made being made defendant in the case. If, however, the claimant prefers, he can bring suit against the railroad company and the contractor jointly, "execution to issue as in other cases." If execution, issued on judgment obtained before a justice of the peace, shall be returned, "not satisfied," a transcript of such judgment may be taken to the circuit court and "spread upon the records thereof, and shall have all the force and effect of judgments obtained in the circuit court, and execution issued thereon as in other cases."

§ 242. In case the claim is established the plaintiff shall be allowed an attorney's fee, $5, if before a justice, and $20 if before a court of record, the same to be taxed as cost.[1]

§ 243. It will be observed that the foregoing applies to completed contracts. Section seven of the law relates to cases in which the original contractor failed to finish his contract. In that event any person entitled to a lien may file his petition in any court of record, in any county through which the road may be constructed, against the railroad corporation and the contractors, setting forth the nature of his claim and the amount due as near as may be, the fact that the

[1] In the railway legislation in regard to extortion, provision is made for attorney's fees. Instead of specific amounts the law says "reasonable attorney's fees."

contractor has failed to complete his contract. The further mode of procedure in such cases is thus: "The clerk of said court shall thereupon cause a notice to be published for four successive weeks in a newspaper printed in the county, setting forth that said petition has been filed, and the time when the writ issued on the same shall have been made returnable, and all persons entitled to liens under this act may enter their appearance and interplead in said cause, and have their claims adjudicated; and it shall be the duty of the court, in case the petitioner or claimant, or either of them, established their claims, to enter a decree against the said corporation and original contractor for the amount to which the persons so establishing their claims are respectively entitled, and such decrees shall have the same force and effect as decrees in other cases."

§ 244. One more statute remains to be noted. It was approved April 26, 1873. It is entitled, "An act to amend an act entitled 'An act to provide for the incorporation of associations that may be organized for the purpose of constructing railways, maintaining and operating the same, for prescribing and defining the duties and limiting the powers of such corporations, when so organized,' approved March 1, 1872." It contains one section and three provisions. The first provision is designed to enable railway companies which had attempted to organize but failed to comply with the terms of the law, to reorganize, or cure the defects in the original organization. The last relates to municipal aid bonds. The intermediate provision is designed to prevent the evasion of contracts. It reads thus:

245. *Provided*, that all corporations to which this

act shall apply shall be held liable for, and shall carry out and fulfill all contracts made by them, or for, or on their behalf, or of which they have received the benefit, whether such corporation, at the time of the making of such contract or contracts, was organized, or had attempted to organize, under the general laws of the state of Illinois, or not; whether said contract was for right of way, work and labor done, or materials furnished, or for the running of trains, or carrying passengers or freight upon such road, or upon any other road in connection therewith. And if such corporation has or does take possession of or use such right of way, labor or material so furnished by other persons or corporations, it shall be evidence of its acceptance of such contract so entered into by such person or corporation with said persons or corporations for its benefit. And upon said corporation failing to pay said sum as it ought equitably to pay for such right of way, labor or materials, or fail to carry out such contracts as aforesaid, so made with persons or corporations, it shall be held liable in an action at law or in chancery for the recovery of the value of said right of way, labor or materials, and for damages for non-fulfillment of such contract, in any court of competent jurisdiction in any county through which the road of such corporation may be located.

§ 246. The subject in hand is now exhausted, so far as concerns statutory law. Only a very few decisions in cases arising out of railway construction contracts present any peculiar phase of the general law of contract. Rarely will a claim arise for which the remedy provided by statute will not be ample.

§ 247. One of the notable railway construction

cases is *Grant v. Green.*[1] A party contracted to construct and equip a railroad, and received on the hypothecated bonds of the road as much money as he had expended in and about the contract. He afterward abandoned the enterprise. The court held that the contract should be decreed rescinded as to such contractor, and that the stock and franchise should revert to the original shareholders, so far as the same had been yielded to the defaulting contractor, except so far as the same could not be done without impairing the rights of innocent holders of the bonds.

§ 248. The general principle, applicable to all contracts, is that the law of the place of performance governs them. It is presumed that both parties to the agreement knew the law of the place.[2] Consequently it matters not where the contract to construct an Illinois railroad, or furnish material for the road, may have been executed, the law as given applies thereto. The general law in regard to the personal property of a railroad company in the possession of the mortgagee is that it is no longer subject to be taken in execution for the debts of the company.[3] But this general law is somewhat modified in the case of construction contracts, as has been shown.[4]

[1] Grant *v.* Green, 46 Ill. 469.

[2] Mason *v.* Dousey, 35 Ill. 424.

[3] Palmer *v.* Forbes, 23 Ill. 301.

[4] In a note to Bradshaw *v.* Newman, Breese 133, occurs the following statement: "The general principle adopted by civilized nations is that the nature, validity and interpretations of contracts are to be governed by the laws of the country where the contracts are made, or are to be performed; but the remedies are to be governed by the laws of the country where the suit is brought." The authorities cited by the editor are Humphrey *v.*

§ 249. Contractors are held to be servants of the company. Whatever they or their subordinates do in the natural course of business the law holds to have been done in the capacity of agent for the corporation.[1] It follows that the latter is subject to the general liability of principal as truly during the construction of its road as afterwards when it is in operation, although the operating of a road is more frequently conducted directly by the company than is its construction.

§ 250. By express statutory provision witnesses may in some railway cases give their opinion, as well as state facts. In an early case an inferior court allowed the witness to give his opinion upon the proper interpretation to put upon a construction contract, although he was not brought on the stand as an expert. The supreme court held that the court, and not the witness, must be the judge of such a point. Several decisions confirm that doctrine.[2]

§ 251. In a case involving the corporate rights of an institution then existing under a state charter the court held that a corporation cannot enter into partnership.[3] It was held, however, that two or more corporations may become jointly bound by the same contract. According to this doctrine, a railroad company cannot form a partnership, in form, at least, with

Collier & Powell, Breese, 297; Stacy *v.* Baker, 1 Scam. 417; Forsyth *et al. v.* Baxter *et al.* 2 Scam. 12; Webster *v.* Massey, 2 Wash. C. C. R. 157; Cox *et al. v.* The United States, 6 Peters, 172; Green *v.* Sarmiento, Peters C. R. R. 74.

[1] Lesher *v.* Wabash Navigation Co. 14 Ill. 85.

[2] Alton, etc. R. R. Co. *v.* Northcote, 15 Ill. 49; Sigsworth *v.* McIntyre, 18 Ill. 128; Taylor *v.* Beck, 13 Ill. 376; McAvoy *v.* Long, 13 Ill. 147.

[3] Marine Bank of Chicago *v.* Ogden, 29 Ill. 248.

a contractor, or a construction company. For an officer of a railroad company to be interested in a construction contract would be a breach of a fiduciary trust, unless he were so with the knowledge and consent of all the stockholders.

CHAPTER VI.

RAILWAY LIABILITIES.

I. Passenger Liabilities.

§ 252. The railway liability fraught with the gravest responsibility is that resulting from the carriage of passengers. This is true whether we consider the importance of personal safety, or the pecuniary risks of the carrier. Illinois has been happily exempt from railway disasters. During the year ending June 30, 1872, only eight passengers in the entire state were killed. A prairie country is less liable to rail accidents than a hilly country, where there are deep cuts, short curves and high embankments. Legislation in this state has done almost nothing to protect the lives of passengers. The common law, although minute, is not sufficient. At the beginning of the final session of the twenty-eighth general assembly a measure designed to lessen the peril of travel by rail was introduced in the senate by Gen. Fuller, chairman of the railroad committee. It passed the senate, but never reached a vote in the house.

§ 253. If railroads were private roads, and the companies *not* common carriers, they could be held liable only for carelessness so gross as to have in it an element of criminality.[1] The theory is, however, that the carrier is not an insurer of personal safety against every accident or injury, save those arising from the act of God or the public enemy, as is the case with freight carriage. An injury may occur by mere mischance, without any fault or negligence on the part of the railroad company or its servants. For such misfortunes the carrier is not deemed responsible. He is liable only for a want of reasonable skill, diligence and care. This difference between freight and passenger

[1] Chicago and Aurora R. R. Co. *v.* Thompson, 19 Ill. 578.

liability is based on the nature of the case. Gooas are entirely in the control of the carrier. The passenger cannot be completely controlled.[1]

§ 254. Passenger and carrier have reciprocal duties. The former is bound to avoid any unnecessary risks, and the latter to take all possible precautions against accident in the provision of suitable coaches and the observance of the most approved methods of conducting his business. The highest degree of caution consistent with proper speed is required. Failure to use the latest appliance, such for example as the "air-brake," would be considered a mark of negligence. Comfort and safety must be considered.[2] But while a carrier is thus obliged to do all that human foresight, care and vigilance can reasonably do, consistent with the mode of conveyance and practical operation of the road, yet he will not be held to a degree of care which would be so expensive as to render it impracticable to continue the business.[3]

§ 255. In case of injury the railroad company is liable for the loss of time; the expense of doctors, nurses, etc. Issue is joined in case of litigation either upon the measure of the responsibility or the amount due on those accounts. In the event of permanent injury the claims allowed are somewhat in the nature of consequential damages. The jury is allowed to estimate the probable pecuniary loss to the person in

[1] Frink *v.* Potter, 17 Ill. 406.

[2] Ohio and Mississippi R. R. Co. *v.* Muhling, 30 Ill. 9; Frink *v.* Potter, I7 Ill. 406; Tuller *v.* Talbot, 23 Ill. 357; Galena and Chicago Union R. R. Co. *v.* Yarwood, 15 Ill. 468; C. B. and Q. R. R. Co. *v.* Hazzard, 26 Ill. 373.

[3] Pittsburgh, Cincinnati and St. Louis R. R Co. *v.* Thompson, 56 Ill. 138.

the course of a lifetime of average length. Awards are so unequal and capricious that no fixed basis of calculation can be said to exist. Sometimes the mind is injured. In a case which arose in this state a few years ago the railroad company contended that a mental injury was not measurable in pecuniary damage. The supreme court held that the court of original jurisdiction was right in instructing the jury to take that injury into account in estimating the liability and assessing the damage.[1]

§ 256. In the case of homicide, whether murder, manslaughter, or justifiable homicide, no action for damages is brought in the interest of those dependent upon the slain for support where the slayer is an individual, and very rarely where the responsibility attaches to a business firm or corporation, except the latter be a common carrier.[2] The law, however, warrants no such conclusion. "Whenever," says the statute, "the death of a person shall be caused by wrongful act, or default, and the act, neglect, or default, is such as would, if death had not ensued, have entitled the party injured to maintain an action and recover damages in respect thereof, then, and in every such case, the person or company or corporation which would have been liable if death had not ensued, shall be liable to an action for damages, notwithstanding the death of the person injured, and although the death shall have been

[1] Toledo, Wabash and Western R. R. Co. *v.* Baddeley, 54 Ill. 20.

[2] In the spring of 1873 four persons in the employ of a pork packing establishment in Chicago were killed by a boiler explosion. The suing of the firm for damages was urged, but no such suits were brought. For some unaccountable reason it seems to be supposed that the law of liability for death applies only to railroads. It will be observed that such is by no means the case.

caused under such circumstances as amount in law to felony." It is only necessary to add that subsequent decisions have recognized the validity of this statute and been governed by it.[1]

§ 257. When the casuality results in death the right of action belongs to the personal representative of the deceased. The amount recovered shall be for the benefit of the widow and next of kin. A statute dating back to 1853, and still operative, provides that this distribution shall be "in the proportion provided by law in relation to the distribution of personal property left by the persons dying intestate; and in every such action the jury may give such damages as they shall deem a fair and just compensation, with reference to the pecuniary injuries resulting from such death to the wife and next of kin of such deceased person, not exceeding the sum of $5,000; *provided*, that every such action shall be commenced within two years after the death of such person."[2]

§ 258. While the statute fixes a maximum of damages in case of death, $5,000, the exact measure thereof is to be determined by the pecuniary injury to those entitled to receive compensation. The law does not attempt to make amends for loss of happiness. As marriage is viewed only as a civil contract, so death is taken cognizance of only from a monetary standpoint. The decisions sustaining this statement are numerous.[3] If a pauper is killed or injured by a railroad company,

[1] Gross' Statutes, vol. i, chap. 17, sec. 5

[2] Ibid. sec. 6.

[3] C. B. & Q. R. R. Co. *v.* Parks, 18 Ill. 460; C. B. & Q. R. R. Co. *v.* Hazzard, 26 Ill. 388; Chicago and Alton R. R. Co. *v.* Roberts, 40 Ill. 503; same *v.* Shannon, 43 Ill. 338; Chicago and

either by an engine, car collision or explosion, the expense of properly caring for the same shall be borne by the company. If injured he shall be cared for by the company; if killed the company shall pay the coroner's fee and all the expense of decent burial.[1]

§ 259. An early decision is sometimes adduced as showing that the dying declaration of the deceased is not to be taken in evidence against the railroad company; but it is now well established that the same rule in regard to dying testimony which applies to other cases does to cases arising under the statute just given. So, too, the testimony of the servants of the railroad is admissible, notwithstanding the peculiar relations they sustain to the company.[2]

§ 260. The liability of a railroad company is entirely financial. In one case the court held that a corporation could commit assault and battery.[3] But this is essentially fictitious. The corporation has no body to imprison. From the very nature of the case its punishment must be in the shape of damages. But the agent or employe of the company is liable to criminal prosecution. If the accident result from gross care-

Northwestern R. R. Co. *v.* Swett, 45 Ill. 197; Illinois Central R. R. Co. *v.* Weldon, 52 Ill. 290; Chicago, Rock Island and Pacific R. R. Co. *v.* Otto, 52 Ill. 416; Chicago and Northwestern R. R. Co. *v.* Peacock, 48 Ill. 253.

[1] Illinois Central R. R. Co. *v.* Weldon, 52 Ill. 290; Gross' Statutes, vol. i, chap. 80.

[2] The tendency of the courts is to allow all the testimony to go before the jury, on the supposition that the latter will make allowance for prejudice and take the evidence at its actual value. That tendency is clearly in the direction of justice, and dictated by common sense. See 1 Greenleaf on Evidence, sec. 156 to 162.

[3] The statutory definition of assault and battery in Illinois is "the unlawful beating of another."

lessness on the part of any person or persons in the employ of the railroad, that person or those persons can be prosecuted for what the law denominates "involuntary manslaughter," and the punishment for which is eight years in the penitentiary.[1]

§ 261. The passenger liabilities of a railroad company are by no means measured by liabilities incident to disasters, resulting in injury or death. The carrier has miscellaneous liabilities of more or less importance.

§ 262. The company is bound to carry all persons at a reasonable and impartial rate. The duty herein is precisely the same as the duty of impartiality in the carriage of freight and the transportation of cars.[2] Several cases have arisen in the inferior courts of the state touching the right of a passenger to be carried at a rate of compensation fixed by statute, but the supreme court has made no declaration on the subject. Every passenger decision up to this time turns upon the construction of common instead of statutory law.

§ 263. The rule in regard to uniformity of charges does not forbid an extra charge for passengers who do not purchase tickets in advance, provided the ticket office is accessable, at reasonable hours.[3] It has been decided that it will be sufficient to justify a railroad company if reasonable opportunity be afforded a passenger to procure a ticket for the train he designs to go upon, and that reasonable opportunity is afforded by keeping a ticket-office open, under the supervision

[1] Gross' Statutes, vol. i, chap. 30, div. 5, secs. 7 and 8.

[2] For a discussion of this general subject see chap. 18.

[3] C. B. & Q. R. R. Co. *v.* Parks, 18 Ill. 460; St. Louis, Alton and Chicago R. R. Co. *v.* Dalby, 19 Ill. 359.

of a competent agent, until the time when the train is advertised to leave.[1]

§ 264. If a passenger refuse to pay his fare he may be required to leave the train at any regular station. Wilfull neglect to purchase a ticket and refusal to pay fare are classed as substantially the same offense, and the passenger offending may always be lawfully ejected from the cars.[2] But this must be done at a regular stopping place.[3] It is decided that the term "usual stopping place" does not mean a mere watering station, but a regular station for passengers to get on and off the train.[4]

§ 265. A person cannot require the railroad company to change its custom, and stop at any particular station for his accommodation. If the person gets on the train and the conductor takes his ticket with the promise to stop at any particular station, this would amount to an agreement to do so. Railroad companies may run trains which only stop at a few stations, provided they also furnish reasonable means of transportation of way passengers.[5]

§ 266. If a passenger holding a ticket for a certain place be carried by without his consent he may recover for whatever damages have accrued to him for non-delivery at his destined place, but he has no right to leap from the cars when the train does not stop. If

[1] St. Louis, Alton and Terre Haute R. R. Co. *v.* South, 43 Ill. 176.

[2] Chicago and Alton R. R. Co. *v.* Flagg, 43 Ill. 364; Illinois Central R. R. Co. *v.* Sutton, 53 Ill. 397; same *v.* Whittemore, 43 Ill. 420; same *v.* Sutton, 42 Ill. 438.

[3] See statute of 1849.

[4] C. B. & Q. R. R. Co. *v.* Parks, 18 Ill. 465; Terre Haute, Alton and St. Louis R. R. *v.* Vanatta, 21 Ill. 188.

[5] Chicago and Alton R. R. Co. *v.* Randolph, 53 Ill. 510.

he does this and thereby receives bodily injury he can not recover from the company, because it shows the absence of proper and ordinary care.[1]

§ 267. A railroad company may attach passenger cars to a freight train. If it regularly does this and holds itself out to the public as doing this, it becomes a common carrier of passengers and is under regular passenger liabilities and regulations. The conductor may expel a passenger in case of disobedience of a reasonable rule the same as a conductor of a regular passenger train; but the company or its agents have no more right to expel a passenger wantonly or without sufficient cause in the one case than in the other.[2] The responsibility of a railroad company for the safety of its passengers will be just as great in the case of freight trains to which passenger cars are accustomed to be attached as in the case of regular passenger trains.[3]

§ 268. This right to carry passengers and freight together is somewhat modified by statute. In making up a passenger train neither baggage, freight, merchandise, or lumber cars shall be placed in the rear of passenger cars. In case of violation of this statute, and the occurrence of any accident, the officer or agent of the company who directed, or knowingly allowed such carelessness, shall be held guilty of intentionally causing the injury, and be punished accordingly. This penalty is applicable also to the conductor and the engineer of the train.[4]

[1] Illinois Central R. R. Co. *v.* Abell, *Legal News*, vol. 4, page 176.
[2] Chicago and Alton R. R. Co. *v.* Flagg, 43 Ill. 364.
[3] Ohio and Mississippi R. R. Co. *v.* Muhling, 30 Ill. 9.
[4] Gross' Statute, vol. i, p. 549.

§ 269. Whatever rules tend to the comfort and safety of passengers on a railroad the company are authorized to make and enforce.[1] But such rules must be reasonable, and uniform in respect to persons, and it is for the court to determine what are reasonable rules.[2] Every railway corporation exercises unchallenged the right to prevent smoking in cars set apart for the use of ladies. While discrimination in freight charges has been common, we find no case in which a passenger has complained of discrimination against himself in the matter of fare. The company has a perfect right to compel holders of second-class tickets to ride in second-class cars. It may also set apart a car for the exclusive use of ladies and gentlemen accompanied by ladies.

§ 270. This right to make and enforce rules extends only to reasonable regulations. An unreasonable rule that effects the comfort and convenience of passengers is unlawful for the reason that it is unreasonable.[3] A railroad company has no right to capriciously discriminate between passengers on account of color. It may not be an unreasonable rule to seat persons so as to preserve order and decorum, and prevent collisions from well-known repugnances, and it might possibly be lawful to require colored persons to occupy separate seats if equally comfortable as those provided for other passengers; but no person can be excluded from a carriage by a public carrier on account of color or any mere prejudice or peculiar belief.[4]

[1] Chicago and Northwestern R. R. Co. *v.* Williams, 55 Ill. 185.

[2] Ibid.

[3] The State *v.* Overton, 4 Zab. 435.

[4] Chicago and Northwestern R. R. Co. *v.* Williams, 55 Ill. 185; West Chester and Philadelphia R. R. Co. *v.* Miles, 55 Penn. 209

§ 271. The railroad company is liable for the baggage of the passenger to a certain amount. It is not liable, however, for merchandise which is not ordinarily carried in a trunk, but only for a reasonable amount of baggage. In an important case the court held that a reasonable amount of bank notes might be carried in a trunk and their value recovered as lost baggage.[1] The cases referred to in the foot note discuss the question of what would be a reasonable amount.[2] In an early case[3] it was held that the carrier could not be held liable for lost baggage, unless it could be shown that he had possession of it or had in some way contracted to carry it. A baggage check would be *prima facie* evidence that the railroad company has the baggage. The whole responsibility for the safe delivery of the same to its final destination rests upon the railroad, and if on a change of passage from one road to another the agent of the road does not find the baggage which is checked, he should at once give notice to the owner, or the company giving the check will be held liable.[4]

§ 272. The statute ordains that baggage may remain in the keeping of a railroad company three months without extra charge for storage. After that time warehouse charges may be made. If after three more months the baggage has not been claimed, it may be sold in the same way and under the same conditions as

[1] Illinois Central R. R. Co. *v.* Copeland, 24 Ill. 332.

[2] Woods *v.* Devin, 13 Ill. 746; Davis *v.* Michigan Southern and Northern Indiana R. R. Co. 22 Ill. 278; Chicago and Aurora R. R. Co. *v.* Thompson, 19 Ill. 578.

[3] Michigan Southern and Northern Indiana R. R. Co. *v.* Meyres, 21 Ill. 631.

[4] Davis *v.* Michigan Southern and Northern Indiana R. R. Co. 22 Ill. 278.

freight, except that notices of the sale must be posted in at least five places. This does not in any way limit or restrict the liability of the company as common carrier.

§ 273. In the issuance of free passes it is customary for railroad companies to specify on the back of the pass that the person accepting and using the same agrees not to hold the company liable for any damage to his person or property under any circumstances whatever. In construing a case arising under such a proviso the court held that the company still remained liable for gross negligence or willful malfeasance, against which good morals and public policy forbid that it should be permitted to stipulate.[1]

§ 274. The rights and liabilities incident to through and lay-over tickets have occasioned no little litigation. The latest Illinois decision was rendered June 23, 1873, in the case of *Churchill v. Chicago and Alton R. R. Co.* The opinion of the court was delivered by Mr. Justice WALKER. It denied the right of a passenger to demand a lay-over ticket. If one was given with conditions, those conditions would be binding. If the lay-over ticket said, "Good for thirty days," the holder must use it within that time or it becomes valueless. No authorities were given by the court for this decision.

§ 275. The law protects the railroad companies in their passenger rights by fixing a special penalty for stealing, embezzling or counterfeiting railway tickets. The punishment fixed by statute is imprisonment in the penitentiary one year. This applies alike to persons in the employ of the company, and to the general public. It includes stamping, printing or signing

[1] Illinois Central R. R. Co. *v.* Read, 37 Ill. 484.

such tickets; or the fraudulent selling or circulating of the same.[1]

§ 276. It is usual for traffic in newspapers, confectionery, fruit and similar commodities to be carried on in a small way on passenger trains. Vendors have rights which the law is bound to respect. In the case of *Barney v. Steamboat D. R. Martin*, which came before the United States circuit court, district of New York, Mr. Justice WARD on the bench, it was held: first, that no passenger, as such, has a right to carry on any business occupation upon the vehicles of a common carrier, and if he attempts so to do, after being requested to desist, he may be ejected; second, a carrier may grant the right to transact a business upon its vehicles, but the right will be limited to the grantee.

II. FREIGHT LIABILITIES.

[1] Gross' Statutes, vol. i, chap. 30, div. vii, sec. 20.

§ 277. It is often a matter of vital moment to determine when the distinctive liability of a common carrier began and ended. A railroad company frequently sustains the relation of warehouseman. Even when there is no storage duty performed there may be a controversy as to when the liability as common carrier really began. For example, hay on the cars of a railroad company for shipment, if detained a day at the request of the shipper, is held during that time by the company in the capacity of warehouseman.[1] In the same case the court made the statement that the distinctive liability of a common carrier attaches when the delivery of the freight to the carrier is complete. When the responsibility of the warehouseman ends, then it is that the technical liability of a common carrier begins, and this liability continues until that of some other person begins. It is only when the goods are deposited in a reasonably safe warehouse that the railroad company can avoid the greater responsibility of a carrier.[2]

[1] St. Louis, Alton and Terre Haute R. R. Co. *v.* Montgomery, 39 Ill. 335.

[2] Illinois Central R. R. Co. *v.* Alexander, 20 Ill. 23; Richards *v.* Michigan Southern and Northern Indiana R. R. Co. Ibid. 404; Chicago and Rock Island R. R. Co. *v.* Warren, 16 Ill. 502; Bartholomew *v.* St. Louis, Jacksonville and Chicago R. R. Co. 53 Ill. 227

§ 278. When it is claimed by the railroad company that its liability in a given case was that of a warehouseman only, the burden of proof rests upon the company. Carrying, rather than storing, being the main business of the corporation, the carrier liability can only be escaped by direct and full proof that the goods were in store. Accordingly a railroad company would be compelled to show not merely the arrival of the freight, but that the same had been separated from the train and placed in the proper or usual place for storage, and in care of a proper person, in order to relieve itself from liability as a common carrier.

§ 279. The first duty of a common carrier is that he must furnish "reasonable and ordinary facilities for doing the business of transportation, such facilities as will meet the ordinary demands of the public; but it is not obliged to provide in advance for or anticipate an unusual influx of freight."[1] If a company has reason to expect a volume of business at certain seasons of the year, if that increase is usual and habitual, then it must be prepared to meet it. The expense of a freight car is so little[2] that the company is bound to be prepared to move the crops in the proper season for the sale of the same, and not to make the minimum of their car demands the measure of their actual supply of facilities.

§ 280. The furnishing of facilities and the transaction of the business must be uniform and impartial. If there is an insufficiency of cars the burden must be

[1] Galena and Chicago Union R. R. Co. *v.* Rae, 18 Ill. 488; Chicago and Alton R. R. Co. *v.* Randolph, 53 Ill. 510. For a fuller discussion of this subject see chapt. 8.

[2] About $700.

shared equally by different points and persons. The accommodations must be uniform, "without favor or prejudice."[1] The court has stated, however, that this doctrine of uniformity allows a difference in charges for different classes of freight, also for different periods of time. Formerly the railroad companies of Illinois claimed the right to bind themselves by contract to deliver grain exclusively to certain elevators.

§ 281. The constitution forbids such monopoly combinations; the courts have pronounced them void, as being contrary to public policy, and the claim has been abandoned. For this reform the state is indebted to the policy inaugurated by the present constitution of Illinois, although the doctrine therein laid down had frequently been proclaimed by the courts.[2] It is worthy of remark that this affords an example of the value of legislation in giving emphasis to common law doctrines of justice.

§ 282. It is conceded that the railroad company may adopt rules for the details of its business which some of its patronage would deem unjust. It is often extremely difficult to decide what is reasonable. If the determination of any given point in this connection is left to the adjudication of the courts, inquiry will be made into previous usages and customs on the

[1] Chicago, Burlington and Quincy R. R. *v.* Parks, 18 Ill. 460; Vincent *v.* Chicago, Alton and St. Louis R. R. Co. 49 Ill. 33; People *v.* Chicago and Alton R. R. Co. 55 Ill. 111; Chicago and Northwestern R. R. Co. *v.* People, 56 Ill. 365; Illinois Central R. R. Co. *v.* Whittemore, 43 Ill. 420.

[2] Notably in Great Western R. R. Co. of 1859 *v.* McComas, 33 Ill. 185; Michigan Southern and Northern Indiana R. R. Co. *v.* Day, 20 Ill. 376; Illinois Central R. R. Co. *v.* Johnson, 34 Ill. 389; Ibid. *v.* Frankenberger, 54 Ill. 88.

presumption that the rules which generally obtain are equitable.[1]

§ 283. This doctrine of uniformity and equity extends to intercourse between railroad companies to all transportation companies and each individual.[2] Indeed, by the statute of 1867, still in force, as well as by the constitution and subsequent legislation, railroad companies are required to provide reasonable accommodations for accepting and carrying consignments from other common carriers. The statute referred to declares that "in case the officers of said companies cannot agree as to the manner and terms upon which such joint business shall be interchanged, said companies shall each choose an impartial person familiar with the management of railroads, and the two thus chosen shall select a third person to act with them, and the award of the persons thus selected, or a majority of them, as to the terms and manner for transacting said joint business, shall be conclusive and binding upon both parties. In case either of said roads shall refuse to select such referee then the county court may select such referee upon application of either party."[3]

§ 284. As to the delivery of freight beyond their own lines it is conceded that railroad companies cannot be obliged to receive goods on the requirement of the consignor that they themselves shall deliver the goods beyond or off their own lines of road. The legal duty of the company in that regard is commensurate with their franchise; confined to their own line

[1] Vincent *v.* Chicago and Alton R. R. Co. 49 Ill. 33.

[2] Gulliver *v.* Adams Express Co. 38 Ill. 502.

[3] Gross' Statutes, vol. i, p. 537.

of road and cannot be made to extend beyond it. Nor can they be compelled to purchase for the accommodation of the public more extended privileges beyond the limits of their franchise. In order to compel a railroad company to deliver grain, shipped in bulk, at a certain elevator, it is necessary that the elevator be connected by some track with the railroad line of the company and so situated as to be considered a part or portion thereof.[1]

§ 285. In determining the extent of the liability of the railroads in this regard, account must be taken of what they have been accustomed to do. If a railroad company has been wont to run its cars upon a side track to a private warehouse to receive or discharge freight, then it must do this whenever and as required.[2] Railroad companies cannot disregard the custom of conveying grain in bulk over the lines of their own roads and delivering it at any elevator thereon to which it may be consigned. If it is consigned to warehouses off or beyond their road they can refuse to receive it in bulk.[3]

§ 286. For unnecessary delay the railroad company will be liable. It is their duty to deliver all goods with reasonable dispatch. If the market value of the shipment was greater on the day the consigment should have reached its destination than it was on the

[1] People et al. *v.* Chicago and Alton R. R. Co. 55 Ill. 95

[2] Galena and Chicago Union R. R. Co. *v.* Rae, 18 Ill. 488; Woodbury *v.* Frink, 14 Ill. 279; Chicago and Rock Island R. R. Co. *v.* Warren, 16 Ill. 502.

[3] People et al. *v.* Chicago and Alton R. R. Co. 55 Ill. 95; Gross' Statutes, vol. i, p. 537.

day of actual arrival, the difference may be recovered from the railroad company.[1]

§ 287. If a delay be caused by an unusual press of business, it will not render the common carrier liable for any incidental loss. All that is required from the carrier is that the delivery be reasonable. The receipt by the owner of a part of the goods *in transitu* does not discharge a railroad company from liability for the remainder.

§ 288. In the case of perishable consignments, fresh peaches for example, the railroads claim the right to exact pre-payment. The freight might lose all its value in transit, and that without any fault on the part of the carrier. Another class of goods, such as eggs and glass, may become valueless in transit, but not if properly carried. The court concedes the justice of exacting pre-payment of freight charges in some cases.[2]

§ 289. A bill of lading is held to be *prima facie* evidence of the actual receipt of the goods and of their receipt in good order. Those presumptions may, however, be rebutted by evidence that the shipper, or previous carrier, practiced deceit and fraud, or that the goods received injury prior to their actual delivery. Testimony to sustain such an allegation is always admissible.[3] But the courts are cautious in allowing excuses.

§ 290. If the carrier takes goods from a bailee he cannot escape liability for negligence on the ground

[1] Lowe *v.* Moss, 12 Ill. 477; Chicago and Mississippi R. R. Co. *v.* Dunbar, 20 Ill. 623; Gross' Statutes, vol. i, p. 549.

[2] Galena and Chicago Union R. R. Co. *v.* Rae, 18 Ill. 488.

[3] Great Western R. R. Co. *v.* McDonald, 18 Ill. 172

that the real title to the goods was in the bailor. This rule has an exception, namely: when the goods had been actually taken out of the possession of the carrier by the bailor, without any injury or injustice to the consignor. "So far as the carrier is concerned, in such case, the consignor is the bailor of the property. Even if the bailor was not the owner of the bailed property the bailee must restore it to him, unless some special reason to the contrary can be shown."[1]

§ 291. Treating of excuses has thus led to a consideration of the relative rights and powers of consignors and consignees. It sometimes happens that while the goods are *in transitu* the consignor wishes to change their destination. The railroad company, being the agent of the consignor, is obliged to obey his order. This has been known to occur even when the consignee first designated had accepted bills drawn on him by the consignor. Of this transaction the carrier knew nothing, being obedient to the command of the consignor up to the time of actual delivery, and so delivered the goods according to direction of the one having absolute control.[2] An action for loss of property, or any injury thereto, may be maintained against the railroad company by anyone having a general or special ownership in the goods lost or damaged. Even a bailee or agent entitled to the possession of the property may bring the suit. The consignor, though only a bailee, would also have this right. The real owner would, of course, have a good cause of action for any loss sustained.[3]

[1] Great Western R. R. Co. (1859,) *v.* McComas, 33 Ill. 185.

[2] Lewis *v.* Galena and Chicago Union R. R. Co. 40 Ill. 282.

[3] St. Louis, Alton and Terre Haute R. R. Co. *v.* Linder, 39 Ill. 433.

§ 292. Notwithstanding the absoluteness of this control on the part of the consignor, the carrier has a lien upon the goods until the freight charges have been paid.[1] A change of consignment often leads to litigation commenced by the consignee first designated against the carrier. If the allegation of non-delivery per consignment is made, the burden of proof rests upon the complainant.[2] If the allegation is that the goods were not delivered in good condition, as the bill of lading called for, the burden of proof is on the carrier. There may have been some special directions in regard to the consignment. If the carrier accepted the goods with those peculiarities, he is bound to carry out the contract in good faith and to the letter.[3]

§ 293. More frequently there is in the bill of lading special exemptions, instead of special obligations, and in the construction and enforcement of these exemptions the policy of the court is somewhat different. The carrier is not allowed to evade the usual obligations of his business, pleading in justification the wording of the bill of lading. "The common law liability of the carrier cannot be evaded by notice." A general notice certainly will not work exemption, nor will it even modify or restrict the common law, although known to the shipper, unless the express acceptance of the exemption can be proved, an acceptance of such a nature as to constitute a special contract.[4]

[1] Galena and Chicago Union R. R. Co. *v.* Rae, 18 Ill. 488.

[2] Woodbury *v.* Frink, 14 Ill. 279.

[3] Michigan Southern and Northern Indiana R. R. Co. *v.* Day, 20 Ill. 375.

[4] American Merchant's Union Express Co. *v.* Schier, 55 Ill. 140; Western Transportation Co. *v.* Newhall, 24 Ill. 466; Illinois Central R. R. *v.* Morrison, 19 Ill. 136.

§ 294. If a special contract is claimed it is then a question for the jury to decide whether the exemption in dispute was actually assented to by the shipper. It is also for the jury to decide whether the goods were shipped under a prior verbal contract which had no such limitations or restrictions. The mere delivery of the receipt with such restrictions is not proof that the shipper assented to them. And even if the assent were complete, the contract is not valid if its scope is to excuse the carrier from gross negligence or willful default, such a contract being contrary to good morals and public policy.[1]

§ 295. The proof that the company is accustomed to give a bill of lading exempting it from certain kinds of loss is not sufficient to work exemption.[2] In a "through freight contract" and in through cars it may be customary to specify in the bill of lading that the carrier is restricted in his liability to loss or damage on his own line and yet he will really be liable to the end of the route.[3]

§ 296. It is quite common to send packages marked "C. O. D."[4] The acceptance of a package so marked is held to be a contract on the part of the carrier to

[1] Baker *v.* Michigan Southern and Northern Indiana R. R. Co. 42 Ill. 73; Adams Express Co. *v.* Haynes, 42 Ill. 89; Illinois Central R. R. Co. *v.* Frankenberger, 54 Ill. 88; Illinois Central R. R. Co. *v.* Adams, 42 Ill. 474.

[2] Illinois Central R. R. Co. *v.* Symser, 38 Ill. 355.

[3] Illinois Central R. R. Co. *v.* Johnson, 34 Ill. 389. The constitutional question touching through freight is discussed in Toledo, Peoria and Warsaw Ry. Co. *v.* Merriman, 52 Ill. 123.

[4] As a matter of fact such consignments are almost always sent by express companies; but the law is equally applicable to railroad companies.

collect on delivery the specified amount due the consignor from the consignee on the package, or return the same.[1] In another case[2] the court held that the mere marking of a package "C. O. D." did not obligate the carrier to collect payment for the same of the consignee. The usage must be shown to be such as to make the acceptance of the consignment so marked an agreement to act as collecting agent of the consignor.

§ 297. In its capacity of warehouseman a railroad company has a lien on the goods for all accrued and unpaid charges, including reasonable storage fee.[3] A warehouseman is liable only for losses occasioned by his failure to exercise ordinary care and diligence.[4] By statute[5] the company is obliged to use due diligence in trying to find the owner of the freight, and must keep the goods six months. After that, or in case the owner has been actually notified of the arrival, three months after the notification the company must send the same to a warehouse if the latter will receive it and pay the charges, and if there is none, or the warehouse refuse to receive the goods, then the company may sell the same at public auction, after giving ten days notice of the time and place of sale by posting up notices of it in at least three conspicuous places within the county. If the goods bring more than the charges, the surplus must be paid to the owner or consignee on demand.

§ 298. In case of wrong delivery by mistake, the party responsible for the blunder must make good the

[1] American Express Co. *v.* Lesem, 39 Ill. 313.

[2] Chicago and Northwestern R. R. Co. *v.* Merrill, 48 Ill. 425.

[3] Low *v.* Martin, 18 Ill. 290.

[4] Chicago and Alton R. R. Co. *v.* Scott, 42 Ill. 132; St. Louis, Alton and Terre Haute R. R. Co. *v.* Montgomery, 39 Ill. 335.

[5] Gross' Statutes, vol. i, page 62.

damage.[1] This is so very plain a proposition that a direct issue on that point is very rarely raised, and never treated by the court as an open question. The only way to escape responsibility is by showing a blunder, inaccuracy or vagueness in the directions given. The liability of the carrier for negligence and his responsibility to make good all losses therefrom is a question of fact to be passed upon by the jury.[2] The carrier is bound to use the same prudence that a cautious man would in the transaction of similar business for himself. In operating its road through the streets of a city a railroad would be held to a very high degree of care and diligence, but it would be only necessary to use every reasonable precaution to avoid an injury and not every possible precaution nor any particular means which it may appear, after the accident, would have avoided it.[3]

§ 299. As a general rule, where both parties are guilty of gross negligence, the plaintiff cannot recover. If the negligence of the plaintiff is equal to that of the defendant he cannot recover, but if the negligence of the defendant is of a higher degree than that of the plaintiff the latter may recover to that extent.[4] It is not only for injury or destruction of property that recovery may be had. If unnecessary delay should occur, the railroad company will be obliged to make

[1] Chicago and Northwestern R. R. Co. *v.* Ames, 40 Ill. 249.

[2] Skelley *v.* Kahn, 17 Ill. 170; Galena and Chicago Union R. R. Co. *v.* Yarwood, 15 Ill. 468; Ibid. 509; Illinois Central R. R. Co. *v.* Nunn, 51 Ill. 78; Toledo, Peoria and Warsaw R. R. Co. *v* Foster, 43 Ill. 415.

[3] C. B. & Q. R. R. Co. *v.* Stumps, 55 Ill. 367.

[4] Illinois Central R. R. Co. *v.* Baches adm'x, 55, Ill. 379.

good the loss occasioned by its negligence.[1] Corporations are usually liable only for compensatory damages, but if the injury is wanton or willful, in addition to actual damages something may be recovered for the vexation and discomfort which may have been suffered by the individual.[2] In general, the law allows no constructive damages, but only actual or compensatory.[3]

§ 300. The measure of damages in case of entire loss of property is the value of the property destroyed.[4] In case of injury to property, the goods, though damaged, must be taken by the owner, and the measure of damages will be the difference in value of goods before and after the injury.[5] Losses occasioned by inherent defects or inevitable leakage cannot be recovered from the carrier.

§ 301. We have thus surveyed the ground of freight liability as suggested by an examination of Illinois statutes and reports. Cases not unfrequently arise which turn upon the true meaning of the term "act of God." The definition of the term given by Sir

[1] Illinois Central R. R. Co. *v.* Owens, 53 Ill. 391; same *v.* Waters, 41 Ill. 73; Michigan Southern and Northern Indiana R. R. Co. *v.* Day, 20 Ill. 375; Galena and Chicago Union R. R. Co. *v.* Rae, 18 Ill. 488; Chicago and Mississippi R. R. Co. *v.* Patchin, 16 Ill. 198; Sangamon and Morgan R. R. Co. *v.* Henry, 14 Ill. 156.

[2] Chicago and Northwestern R. R. Co. *v.* Williams, 55 Ill. 185.

[3] Hayes *v.* Moynihan, 52 Ill. 423; Illinois Central R. R. Co. *v.* McClellan, 54 Ill. 58; Frink *v.* Scroyer, 18 Ill. 416; Priestly *v.* Northern Indiana and Chicago R. R. Co. 26 Ill. 205; Sleuter *v.* Wallbaum, 45 Ill. 43; Deere *v.* Lewis, 51 Ill. 254; Galena and Chicago Union R. R. Co. *v.* Rae, 18 Ill. 488; Illinois Central R. R. Co. *v.* Finnigan, 21 Ill. 648.

[4] Toledo, Peoria and Warsaw R. R. Co. *v.* Arnold, 43 Ill. 418.

[5] Illinois Central R. R. Co. *v.* Finnigan, 21 Ill. 648.

William Jones is "an inevitable accident." But this definition does not prevail in Illinois, nor is it recognized by the best authorities. Parsons, in his work on contracts, defines the term as applying to "an accident which arises from a cause which operates without interference or aid from man." A conflagration is not of that nature unless it was caused by lightning or spontaneous combustion, and not always then. Man may have indirectly caused it by neglect to use due precaution. The doctrine is well expressed by Bouvier in these words: "Where the law casts a duty on a party, the performance shall be excused if it be rendered impossible by the act of God; but where the party, by his own contract, engages to do an act, it is deemed to be his own fault and folly that he did not thereby provide against contingencies and exempt himself from responsibility in certain events; and in such cases (that is, in the instance of an absolute general contract,) the non-performance is not excused by an inevitable accident, or other contingencies, although not foreseen by nor in the control of the party."

III. Car Service.

§ 302. The term car service is used in railway circles to designate the business of hauling the cars of other corporations or persons. The duty to render car service, so far as concerns the cars of other railroad companies, is enjoined in the railroad statute of 1853, also in the supplemental act of 1867.[1] The first statutory recognition and application of this duty in its fullest sense occurs in the railway statute given in full in the chapter on the railroad and warehouse commissioners.

§ 303. The statute of 1853 reads: "All railroad companies incorporated or which may hereafter be incorporated under the authority of this state, the lines or routes of which railroads may connect with or cross each other, shall have power to make contracts and arrangements with each other for the use of each other's engines, machinery, or cars, as also for the mutual transportation of materials, merchandise and passengers upon and along the lines of each other's roads, upon such terms as may be mutually agreed upon between any such corporation."

§ 304. This act was followed fourteen years later by a mandatory act, which has two sections, touching car service. After declaring that the delivery and transfer of freight shall be without favor, prejudice, delay, or extortion, the statute adds, "and it shall be the duty of all such railroad companies to deliver to any warehouse, as directed, any and all cars which may be consigned thereto, and to remove from such warehouse such cars as may be laden thereat for transportation from such warehouse, on the request of the owner or warehouseman, to be shipped within a reasonable time thereafter; and any railroad company shall run the cars of connecting roads over their track

[1] Gross' Statutes, vol. i, 536.

but may charge therefor a reasonable track service, not exceeding the price per mile of the transportation of like articles from local points on the line of such road." The penalty for violation of this law is fixed at twice the value of the consignment, "to be recovered by the agent of such consignment in any action of debt in any court of competent jurisdiction."

§ 305. Of the statute of 1873, given in full elsewhere, it is enough to say in this connection that the railroad companies are required to haul all cars offered them at a reasonable rate and without discrimination of any kind. Precisely the same penalties are attached to extortion and discrimination in car service as in the ordinary carriage of freight and passengers. The law simply recognizes the three branches of railway business as standing upon the same legal basis.

§ 306. Where the use of cars has been hired from a railroad company to be employed in the transportation of freight, to be laden as the hirer may see fit, the company does not incur any risk incident to the mode adopted in loading the same. But a railroad company cannot relieve itself from liability to the public for injuries sustained and for damages resulting from a breach of contract entered into by the lessee, especially where the power to lease is not expressly given by the charter.[1]

§ 307. The law of usage is of great importance in determining the liabilities of a railroad company.[2] The doctrine of the cases cited below[3] is that a rail-

[1] Ohio and Mississippi R. R. Co. *v.* Dunbar, 20 Ill. 623.

[2] Galena Ins. Co. *v.* Kupfer, 28 Ill. 332.

[3] Bissel *v.* Ryan, 23 Ill. 566; Marine Bank *v.* Chandler, 27 Ill. 525; Same *v.* Birney 28 Ill. 90; Byrne *v.* Byrne, 47 Ill. 507;

road company is obliged to take for any person offering that which it has been accustomed to take from others, provided there is no specific and sufficient reason for making an exception. If a railroad company had never been accustomed to haul any cars except those which itself owned, or had leased, it would not be obliged under its common law liability as a carrier to transport freight or passengers in any cars except its own, and it might be questionable, in that event, whether the legislature had a right to require car service. The doing of a thing a few times does not establish a custom. Sometimes, for example, voluntary aid is rendered by a railway agent in recovering lost baggage when the company was not obliged to render any aid. Doing a thing in one case or occasionally does not render the company under obligations to do it always.

§ 308. Such customs as are universally known to exist enter into and form a part of every contract to which they are applicable, although not mentioned or alluded to in the contract.[1] This principle governs the contracts between the state and the railway corporation. In the case of hauling cars, it is only necessary to add that the custom is uniform, long established and so well known as to warrant the belief that all parties to any kind of a transportation contract are familiar with this usage. No case has arisen in which the liability to car service has been denied. The

Dixon *v.* Dunham, 14 Ill. 324; Crawford *v.* Clark, 15 Ill. 561; Munn *v.* Burch, 25 Ill. 35; Fay *v.* Strawn, 32 Ill. 295; Deshler *v.* Beers, 32 Ill. 368; Strong *v.* King, 35 Ill. 9; Turner *v.* Dawson, 50 Ill. 85; Home Ins. Co. *v.* Favorite, 46 Ill. 263.

[1] Michigan Southern and Northern Indiana R. R. Co. *v.* Meyres, 21 Ill. 631; C. B. & Q. R. R. Co. *v.* Hazzard, 26 Ill. 373.

decisions referred to would be of use in substantiating the right, in case it should at any time or in any way be called in question.[1]

§ 309. The statute allows suits at law to be brought against the railroad company in any circuit court through which the railroad extends, only all suits must be brought and prosecuted in the county where the cause of action accrued. In commencing such a suit the prosecution must publish a notice of it four successive times in a weekly newspaper in the county or in the nearest county having a newspaper The first publication must be sixty days prior to the first day of the next succeeding term of court.[2] A railroad company may also be sued in the county where its chief business office is located, though the railroad does not itself pass through such county.[3]

IV. Crossings; Signals; Flags.

[1] For a general discussion of the law of usage see Macomber v. Parker, 13 Pickering 182; United States v. Duval, Gilpin, 356; Ibid. v. Arredondo, 6 Peters, 715; Naylor v. Semmes, 4 Gill & Johns, 274; Knowles v. Dow, 2 Foster, N. H. 387

[2] Gross' Statutes, vol. i, page 536.

[3] Bristol v. Chicago and Aurora R. R. Co. 15 Ill. 436.

§ 310. From a glance at the records of railway casualties, in Illinois, at least, one would be inclined to say that it is safer to be on a train than off. Certain it is that, take the years through, more persons are run over by the cars than killed by collisions and other mishaps to the train. This is especially the case at crossings. The victims are most frequently children. At common law there is redress, on precisely the same principle of liability as in the case of injuries to passengers. While there is no adequate statutory provision to prevent the mismanagement of trains, the legislation on the subject of railway crossings is thorough and greatly beneficial. The statute dates from March 1, 1869. As the requirements are too plain for misunderstanding and their justice has not been called in question by subsequent litigation, it is hardly necessary to do more than to give the law, as found in the statute books.[5]

§ 311. Wherever a railroad crosses the public highway, outside the corporate limits of a city or village, the company is obliged to erect and maintain such crossings and approaches as shall be safe as to persons and property. This in itself is vague, but its very indefiniteness is its chief merit. Had the law attempted

[5] The full text of this act is given in Gross' Statutes, vol. i, chap. 86, div. 10.

to go into particulars in the general proposition, it would have been incomplete. No details, however full, can be absolutely exhaustive while "the whole includes its parts," and by no possibility leaves out anything. The exception of cities and villages is made because the local authorities have jurisdiction over the matter within their respective municipalities. The municipal regulations are usually very strict and minute in details.

§ 312. The enforcement of this law is practically intrusted to the county surveyor. If that officer refuse or neglect to promptly and fully discharge his duty herein he is liable to a fine of not less than $100 nor more than $1,000 for each year of disobedience or negligence. The prosecution for neglect is intrusted to the prosecuting attorney, and the supervisors of the county or county commissioners are required to appoint a competent civil engineer to discharge the duty, in case the surveyor is derelict, the appointee having all the authority, compensation and liability in the premises as the surveyor. It was the evident intention of the general assembly to make sure of the enforcement of the statute.

§ 313. The first specific duty of the surveyor is to notify each railroad company within the county when he will proceed to view and examine any and all railroad crossings in the county upon its line for the purpose of determining what, if anything, shall be done to render them secure. This notice must be given in writing to the superintendent of the road, or some station agent residing in the county. The day named must be at least twenty days subsequent to the notice. The examination must be made once a year. The notice must be transmitted by the person originally notified to the nearest superintendent, and by him turned over to the general superintendent. The original delivery is, however, in itself a complete notification to the company, so far as concerns the surveyor's duties in the case, and makes the same binding upon the company.

§ 314. The company must direct its chief engineer, or some other civil engineer, to meet the county surveyor as notified without unreasonable delay, to determine what is needed, if anything, to render the crossings secure. If they disagree, then they shall select a third civil engineer to act with them, the decision of the majority being final. In the choice of a third party the selection must not be made from the list of civil engineers in the employ of railroad companies. The report made as the result of this investigation shall be made in writing and in duplicate. One copy shall be given to the railroad company for its information. The other copy shall be delivered to and filed with the county clerk. The clerk shall place the same on record. It shall also be laid before the board of supervisors in counties adopting township organization, and the county court in counties not adopting that system of local government.

§ 315. There is no danger that the company will neglect the notice, at least the provision of law is ample, for if no representative of the company appears the county surveyor can proceed alone, and his report will be as absolute and binding as would be the report of the two or three civil engineers acting together. Self-interest would dictate that the company should have an authorized representative on the ground, precisely as in case of litigation the defendant may be trusted to put in a defense.

§ 316. It is not so certain that the report, when made, will be heeded. The company is given sixty days in which to carry out the provisions of the report. If it fail within that time to take due note of the report, then the county supervisors, or judge, as the case may be, shall, without unreasonable delay, "cause to be made all such alterations, repairs, and to have constructed and maintained such improvements upon the railroad crossings with the public highways as may be designated in the report of the county surveyor, at the cost of the railroad company, including the services of the county surveyor, at the rate of ten dollars per day for each day so employed."

§ 317. Besides the report in writing made to the county and the company, the surveyor is required to keep a record of the duties performed and copies of notices served under the provisions of the act. This record must form a part of the records of his office. His compensation from the county shall be a reasonable amount for any service he may render under the statute, "the payment for which is not herein designated." The evident intent of the last clause is to prevent double payment in case the company, by negligence, incurs the expense of the service.

§ 318. In the majority of instances the construction and maintenance of suitable crossings will satisfy the prudential demands of the case, but not always. Sometimes a flagman is required. This statute provides for such cases. If the examiners named recommend that a flagman be placed at any crossing, then the company must incur that expense, the flagman performing the duties usually required of persons acting in that capacity. He shall have authority to stop any and all persons from crossing the track when, in his opinion, there is danger from an approaching train. This stationing of a flagman as recommended must be done within sixty days after the report has been made.

§ 319. The penalty for neglect herein is a fine of one hundred dollars per day for every day of neglect or refusal to do so. The fine, when collected, in due process of law, must be paid to the proper officer of and for the benefit of the school district within which such railroad crossing shall be situated. The enforcement of the provision and collection of the fine is made the duty of the supervisors or county court, as the case may be, in any court of record. The prosecution must be conducted by the prosecuting attorney, under the directions of the county authorities. That there should be no mistake in the details of this part of the law it is added that all moneys so collected shall be "paid into the county treasury, subject to the order of the school directors of the district in which any such crossing is situated."

§ 320. Such are the safeguards thrown around the necessary intersection or ordinary roads and railroads in Illinois. In two cases arising under the common law prior to this legislation the supreme court held that an action could be brought in the name of the people by the prosecuting attorney or by the informer in a *qui tam* action.[1]

§ 321. In a case which arose under the act of 1849

[1] Chicago and Alton R. R. Co. *v.* Howard, 38 Ill. 414; Toledo, Peoria and Warsaw Ry. Co. *v.* Foster, 43 Ill. 480.

not long after its passage, the defense put in the plea that railroad companies created prior to the passage of the law were not amenable thereto. The supreme court held that a statute requiring signals and prescribing their use, was equally applicable to all railroads in the state and must govern them in their signal service.[1] This decision was not only important in itself, but in the principle recognized and enforced is important in its bearing on the recent railway legislation of the state. The decision was, however, only the recognition of a familiar law point.[2]

§ 322. In one case the court held that the track is the exclusive property of the company, on which an unauthorized person cannot go, except at his own hazard, unless it be under special cases.[3] This does not agree with the general drift of decisions. In another case it was held that in passing public highways and streams, railway corporations must exercise the same care, and their liabilities will correspond with those of all others passing and doing business thereon.[4] In still another case, the position taken was that a railroad company and a highway traveler have correlative rights, and each must use proper caution where there is danger of a conflict. Neither has a paramount right, except as the same may result from greater difficulty in avoiding a collision, or the necessities of the case.[5] The conditions of each suit are so peculiar

[1] Galena and Chicago Union R. R. Co. *v.* Loomis, 13 Ill. 548.

[2] See Potter's Dwarris' Statutes.

[3] Galena and Chicago Union R. R. Co. *v.* Jacobs, 20 Ill. 478.

[4] Central Military Tract R. R. Co. *v.* Rockafellow, 17 Ill. 541.

[5] Galena and Chicago Union R. R. Co. *v.* Dill, 22 Ill. 265.

to itself that practically the question of liability for damages is left mainly to the jury.[1]

§ 323. The right of a city to pass and enforce an ordinance to prevent a railroad from blocking up the street unreasonably, as well as to prevent accidents, is now well established. The whole ground was well discussed and adjudicated in a case which arose in Macon county some years ago.[2]

§ 324. We have seen that in certain cases a flag station, or post, must be maintained at a crossing. This is exceptional outside of cities and villages; the almost uniform rule within municipal limits. There is a signal service required at every crossing, under a law dating back to 1849, and amended twenty years later. At every crossing a signal board must be erected, bearing the inscription, "Railroad Crossing—look out while the bell rings, or the whistle sounds." This warning must be painted on each side of the board, in letters at least nine inches in size, and placed at a proper elevation. The bell must be at least 30 pounds in weight, and the ringing or whistling required must begin when the engine is at least eighty rods from the crossing. The penalty for neglect is $100, one-half of which shall go to the prosecuting witness and one-half to the state. This law does not apply to cities and villages; the local ordinances in some cases forbid the ringing and whistling, requiring the flagmen to do all the warning, on the score that the noise would be a serious nuisance.

[1] Besides the cases already given the reader is referred for minute details to Chicago, Burlington and Quincy R. R. Co. *v.* Dewey, 26 Ill. 255; Illinois Central R. R. Co. *v.* Williams, 27 Ill. 48.

[2] Great Western R. R. Co. *v.* City of Decatur, 33 Ill. 381.

§ 325. Failure to give the warning prescribed by law would be held, in case of injury, to constitute *prima facie* evidence of negligence, but not proof positive thereof. The claimant must substantiate his claim to damages by positive evidence of carelessness.[1]

§ 326. A statute, dating in its passage from April 9, 1872, applies to points where two or more railroads intersect. It requires all trains to come to a full stop at a distance of at least 200 feet before reaching a junction, and not more than 1,000 feet from the same, and if practicable within full view of the junction. Any engineer or other person having direction of the train, who disobeys this law, is liable to a fine of $200. Besides this, the engineer or other person responsible for the violation of the law shall be jointly and severally bound with the railroad company which he serves for any and all injuries resulting from such violation. This statute is very generally, if not universally, obeyed.[2]

V. SERVANTS; FIRES.

§ 327. The relations of a railroad servant to his employer are such as the agent in other business sustains to the principal. The former may bind the latter,

[1] Galena and Chicago Union R. R. Co. *v.* Loomis, 13 Ill. 548; Chicago and Rock Island R. R. *v.* Reid, 24 Ill. 144.

[2] Gross' Statutes, vol. ii, page 315.

rendering him liable for contracts made or wrongs committed, even through act contrary to orders. There is no such thing as crime by proxy, but a railroad is held to such a strict responsibility for the just conduct of its business that damages to person or property are assessed against the employer, however contrary to the rules of the company the servant may have acted.

§ 328. The company is not liable for accidents to a servant, when the injury was the fault of his own or that of a fellow-servant, provided reasonable diligence and care was taken to employ competent and trustworthy men.[1] The presumption of law is in favor of the complainant. The company is liable if it select unskilled, incompetent or unreliable men, however careful it may generally be on that point.[2]

§ 329. The railroad company is bound to know the condition of its road, its machinery, etc.; also, the character and reliability of its servants. The only case in which it is practically exempt is when the servant injured was in whole or in part to blame. Even then, if he can show gross carelessness on the part of the company in any respect, he can recover. The company must furnish safe material and appliances of every kind. It may be that the defects were the fault of an agent of the company, rather than an officer thereof; but that fact would not work exemption.[3] The rail-

[1] Illinois Central R. R. Co. *v.* Phillips, 49 Ill. 234; Toledo, Wabash and Western R. R. Co. *v.* Apperson, 49 Ill. 480; Illinois Central R. R. Co. *v.* Welch, 52 Ill. 183; Great Western R. R. Co. *v.* Geddis, 33 Ill. 304.

[2] Honner *v.* Illinois Central R. R. Co. 15 Ill. 550; Ibid. *v.* Cox, 21 Ill. 20; Moss *v.* Johnson, 22 Ill. 633; Chicago and Alton R. R. Co. *v.* Murphy, 53 Ill. 336.

[3] Toledo, Wabash and Western Ry. Co. *v.* Rodrigues, 47 Ill. 188.

road company must defray the expense of doctoring and nursing an employe injured in its service.[1] The general liabilities of the company for injury to or the death of a servant, where it is liable at all, are precisely the same as in the case of passengers.

§ 330. It is a statutory offense for the engineer or conductor of a railroad train to be intoxicated while on duty.[2] The statute characterizes the offense a misdemeanor. The penalty attached is slight. When, however, the crime of drunkenness when in charge of an engine or train result in a fatal accident the guilty party becomes amenable to the penalty attached to the crime of "involuntary manslaughter," which consists in "the killing of a human being without any intention so to do in the commission of an unlawful act, or a lawful act which probably might produce such a consequence in an unlawful manner."[3]

§ 331. Several very extensive fires have occurred in this state which were attributed to sparks from a passing locomotive. The common law doctrine has been supplemented by a statute enacted in 1869. This statute reads: "In all actions against any person, or incorporated company, for the recovery of damages on account of any injury to any property, whether real or

[1] Toledo, Wabash and Western Ry. Co. *v.* Rodrigues, 47 Ill. 188.

[2] Gross' Statutes, vol. i, page 550.

[3] Ibid. page 171. We may add in this connection that the report of the Railroad and Warehouse Commissioners for 1872 gives the total personal accidents by rail in the state for the period covered by that report is 388. Of these 19 were servants. Only eight passengers were killed, or less than half the number murdered on the Chicago and Alton railroad August 16, 1873. The number of persons in Illinois who are employed in railway service, including those dependent upon such service for support, is estimated at 50,000.

13

personal, occasioned by fire, communicated by any locomotive engine while upon, or passing along any railroad in the state, the fact that such fire was so communicated shall be taken as full *prima facie* evidence to charge with negligence the corporation, or person or persons, who shall at the time of such injury by fire, be in the use and occupation of such railroad, either as owners, lessees, or mortgagees, and also those who shall at such time have the care and management of such engine; and it shall not, in any case, be con sidered as negligence on the part of the owner or occupant of the property injured, that he has used the same in the manner, or permitted the same to be used or remain in the condition it would have been used or remained, had no railroad passed through or near the property so injured, except in cases of personal property, which shall be at the time upon the property occupied by such railroad."

§ 332. Prior to this enactment the courts had held that a railroad company is responsible for injuries occasioned by loss of property from fire which is communicated from the sparks of an engine, in case there is any negligence attributable to the railway corporation or its employes. The fact that the fire caught from sparks emitted from the engine is *prima facie* evidence of negligence on the part of the company, and the burden of proof rests on them to rebut this presumption.[1] When dry grass and weeds have accumulated beside the track and caught fire from the sparks of an engine, and this fire has been communicated to other property, causing great loss, the question

[1] Great Western R. R. Co. *v.* Haworth, 39 Ill. 347; Chicago and Northwestern R. R. Co. *v.* McCahill, 56 Ill. 28.

of comparative negligence of the owner of the property and of the railroad company is a question of fact properly left for the jury.[1]

VI. Fences; Obstructions.

§ 334. The subject of railway fences has occasioned a large amount of litigation. For a long time the matter was left to common law regulation. At the present time statutory law is sufficiently minute to reach such cases as have arisen. These enactments date from 1855 and 1869.[2]

[1] Illinois Central R. R. Co. *v.* Nunn, 51 Ill. 78.

[2] For the decisions on this general subject see Illinois Central R. R. Co. *v.* Swearnigen, 33 Ill. 289; Chicago and Alton R. R. Co. *v.* Utley, 38 Ill. 410; Illinois Central R. R. Co. *v.* Whalen, 42 Ill. 396; Galena and Chicago Union R. R. Co. *v.* Appleby, 28 Ill. 284; Headen *v.* Rust, 39 Ill. 186; Toledo, Peoria and Warsaw Ry. Co. *v.* Sweeney, 41 Ill. 226; Ibid. *v.* Miller, 45 Ill. 42; Ohio and Mississippi R. R. Co. *v.* Brubaker, 47 Ill. 462; Toledo, Wabash and Western R. R. Co. *v.* Cole, 50 Ill. 184; St. Louis, Alton and Terre Haute R. R. Co. *v.* Todd, 36 Ill. 409; Illinois Central R. R. Co. *v.* Kanouse, 39 Ill. 272; Toledo, Peoria and Wabash Ry. Co. *v.* Rumbold, 40 Ill. 143.

§ 335. The need of legislation was pressing. In an early case the supreme court held that after the assessment and payment of damages by a railroad company for the right of way the corporation was not bound to make fences on either side of its road bed. The court went so far as to say that after the condemnation of the land and the payment of damages, the proprietor of the adjacent land could not lawfully fence the land at his own expense, or do anything to prevent his cattle from getting on the track.[1]

§ 336. If the railroad had been open to use at the time of the passage of the law, it had to be fenced within six months after the first law was passed, and every road since built must be fenced within six months .after any part of it comes into use, the fence to extend to the part in use. In case of suit for damage under the act the courts rule that the action must state that the road had been in operation the specified length of time.

§ 337. The fence must be sufficient to prevent cattle, horses, sheep and hogs from getting on to the track. This includes mules and asses, also "unruly" cattle, to a reasonable extent. Cattle guards, or ditch fences, at crossings are included in the requirement for fencing. These fences and cattle guards must be kept in good repair. If they are the company is absolved from liability for stock killed, unless negligently or willfully done.[2]

§ 338. This fence requirement entends only to cases

[1] Alton and Sangamon R. R. Co. *v.* Baugh, 14 Ill. 211.

[2] In nearly every suit for cattle killing the real issue is joined on the sufficiency of the fence, or cattle guards, especially the former.

in which it is necessary to keep cattle from straying on the track from adjoining lands. If the adjoining land is unenclosed the requirement does not hold. The third exemption named is where the proprietor of the land has already erected a fence, or agreed with the company to do so.

§ 339. In case the owner of the adjacent land has entered into any such agreement he must carry it out. The six months requirement applies to such a contractor, the same as to the railroad company. If he or his heirs or assigns neglect to do so, the railroad company must, relying for compensation upon a civil action to recover the expense incurred. The statute adds that in case any cattle belonging to a person guilty of such breach of contract should be killed by engine or cars, the company should not be liable for damages therefor, providing they came "upon said road by reason of or on account of the failure of such owner, or owners, their heirs or assigns, to construct or maintain said fence."

§ 340. The same statute provides a penalty of not less than $10 nor more than $100 for riding, leading or driving any animal upon a railroad and within such fences and guards, other than at farm or road crossings, unless permission to do so has been obtained from the corporation. The same penalty is provided for pulling down or in any way impairing the efficiency of the fences or guard. The guilty party must also pay all damages which may result from carelessness or malice. The fine provided is recoverable in an action of debt, before any court having jurisdiction in such cases, in the name of the company and for its use.[1]

[1] At this point the first law ends. The act of 1869, while it leaves the foregoing provisions in force, practically modified somewhat the mode of procedure.

§ 341. Whenever the company is obliged to fence its track, as specified in the foregoing, if it fail to do so the owner or occupant of the adjacent land may give notice in writing to the corporation, or the lessee, or the person using the road, to build the required fence within sixty days, or to repair it within thirty days, as the case may be, after the service of such notice. The notice shall describe the land on which the fence is required to be built or repaired, with a reference to the statute for the information of the agent notified. Notification may be served by delivering the same to any station agent of the company. In case the railroad corporation should refuse or neglect to do its duty in the premises the notifier may make the necessary outlay, and recover the amount thus expended, with interest at one per cent. per month, "together with all costs, fees and disbursements to be taxed." Such notice must be given on some day between the first day of March and the first day of October in any year.

§ 342. In case the stock gets on the track without the fault of the company, the law requires the claimant for damages to show that the train might have been stopped and the injury have been prevented by due care and effort on the part of the servants of the company.[1] It is worthy of remark, however, that in practice it is rarely difficult to satisfy a jury that in the case in hand the railroad company was in some way to blame, and ought to pay for the cattle injured or killed.

§ 343. All casualties by rail are not attributable to

[1] Chicago and Northwestern R. R. Co. *v.* Barrie, 55 Ill. 226; Chicago and Mississippi R. R. Co. *v.* Patchin, 16 Ill. 198; Illinois Central R. R. Co. *v.* Baches, Administratrix, 55 Ill. 379.

the railroad companies and their agents. Occasionally malicious persons, from motive of revenge or for plunder, attempt to wreck a train. Three statutory provisions have been made to guard against such offenses.

§ 344. The forty-fifth section of the railway statute of 1849 provides that "if any person shall willfully do or cause to be done any act or acts whatever, whereby any building, construction or work of a railroad company, or any engines, machine or structure, or any matter or thing pertaining to the same, shall be stopped, obstructed, impaired, weakened, injured or destroyed, the person or persons offending shall be guilty of a misdemeanor, and shall forfeit and pay to the said corporation treble the amount of damages sustained by means of such offense."[1]

§ 345. In 1853 a more stringent act was passed. That statute provides a penalty of imprisonment for not less than one year nor more than five years for placing any obstruction upon any line of any railroad in the state. In case actual injury should result, the penalty is fixed at not less than three years nor more than ten years. If loss of life should result, the offender is to be held guilty of murder.[2]

§ 346. In 1861 the general assembly passed a law to prevent the formation of conspiracies to obstruct railway trains. It was designed as a war measure, but is still in force, and applicable to bandits. It provides the punishment of imprisonment not less than two years nor more than five for entering into such a conspiracy. Attempting to throw a train off the track would subject the conspirators to imprisonment in the

[1] Gross' Statutes, vol. i, page 550.

[2] Gross' Statutes, vol. i, page 540.

penitentiary not less than six months nor more than ten years. The same penalty is prescribed for trying to entice others to join in the conspiracy. The enforcement of this act is enjoined upon all officers, civil and military, of the state, and upon all residents of the state.

VII. Live Stock; Thistles.

§ 347. The usual freight liabilities attach to the transportation of live stock. In addition thereto are certain specific liabilities. Two such additional laws are to be found on the statute books of the state. One of them was dictated by humane considerations, the other was the result of a wholesome fear of the cattle disease, as it is apt to exist in the extreme southwest.

§ 348. Sheep, cattle, swine, and other animals, cannot be kept in the same car more than twenty-eight consecutive hours, unless delayed by storm or some other unavoidable causes. When taken out for food and water an animal must be allowed at least five hours for rest.[1] In estimating the time of confinement the time on connecting roads must be taken into the account. This provision does not apply when the

[1] Gross' Statutes, vol. i, p. 18. The forty-second congress, on the last day of its last session, passed a similar law, which went into force October, 1873.

animals are properly fed and watered on the cars in which they are transported. The expense of the rest and feed, if borne by the railroad company, shall constitute a lien on the freight. The penalty for violating this law is fixed at one hundred dollars for each offense, to be recovered in the name of the people before any justice of the peace in the proper county. It is made the duty of any county officer to prosecute all violations of this humane law brought to his notice, under penalty of one hundred dollars for refusal or neglect so to do.

§ 349. No person, railroad company, or association of persons is allowed to bring Texas and Cherokee cattle into the state, except between the first day of October and the first day of March. The law goes so far as to forbid "any person or persons, railroad company, or other corporation, or any association of persons," owning Texas or Cherokee cattle brought into the state except during the period between October first and March first. This law was passed in 1869, when there was great and just fear of the rinderpest.

§ 350. The penalty provided for violating that statute is a fine of not less than five hundred dollars nor more than ten thousand dollars, and imprisonment in the county jail at the discretion of the court for a period not exceeding six months. The accused may be held to bail on the charge. "Any railroad conductor, agent, or officer of any railroad company who shall haul or ship any such cattle in violation on any railroad in this state shall be deemed to have possession of the same within the meaning of this section." The fines shall be distributed pro rata among the sufferers by the importation by the county supervisors, or commissioners, upon proof of loss, as the board may direct. If such proof is not furnished within a year the money goes to the common school fund of the county, to be used in payment of teachers. Besides, if a cattle owner can prove to the satisfaction of the court that he has suffered loss by reason of such Texas or Cherokee cattle he is entitled to recover specific compensatory damages from the person or persons, individual or corporate, responsible for the same. The disease may not have been communicated while the cattle were in possession of the railroad company, but the statute holds the liability to be the same. Even if the cattle were brought into the state within the allowable period the liability for damage would be the same as just specified. The law contains this clause: "And it shall be competent for the jury to render a verdict and the court to render a judgment, in any such case, upon the opinion of the witness as to whether or not any such Texas or Cherokee cattle caused the injury complained of in any such suit."

§ 351. The definition of "Texas and Cherokee cattle" is elaborate. The term "shall be taken to mean a class or kind of cattle, without reference to where they may have come from, provided it shall not apply when such cattle shall have been introduced into either the states of Kansas, Missouri, Nebraska, Iowa, or Wisconsin, prior to the first of January, before being brought into this state; but the burden of alleging and proving that such cattle were introduced into either of the states above mentioned prior to January first, and wintered there the remainder of the winter, shall be upon the defendant; *provided, further*, that the official certificate of the county clerk of the county where such cattle have been wintered shall be *prima facie* evidence thereof."

§ 352. A railroad company is obliged to keep its cattle pens clean and prevent the generation of noxious gases. It is not responsible for noise and shouting, however, over which it has no control. Nothing which it can do to render its cattle pens less offensive should be omitted [1]

§ 353. By the railway law of 1869 every railway company doing business in Illinois is obliged to cut down all weeds, Canada thistles especially, that may grow upon the lands belonging or appertaining to the railroad. This cutting down must be done in time to prevent the seed from ripening and spreading. The penalty for neglect is one hundred dollars, recoverable before the circuit judge of the county in which the offense occurred, or before any justice of the peace in the county. One-half of the fine goes to the prosecutor, the other half to the school fund of the county.[2]

[1] Illinois Central R. R. Co. *v.* Grabill, 50 Ill. 241

[2] Gross' Statutes, vol. ii, chap. 18.

CHAPTER VII.

RAILROAD AND WAREHOUSE COMMISSIONERS.

I. Law Creating the Commission.

§ 354. Previous to the present constitution the office of Railroad and Warehouse Commissioner was unknown in Illinois. The constitution does not directly contemplate its creation. The authority therefor is precisely the same as that for forming the Penitentiary Commission and similar adjuncts of the state government. The practice of delegating special powers to special commissions is common, and its legality has so often been recognized by the courts as to admit of no controversy.

§ 355. The law creating this board and prescribing its powers and duties was passed April 13, 1871, going into effect July 1 of the same year. No other state has such a board with any real authority. In Massachusetts their functions are simply advisory. The full text of the statute is herewith given:

§ 356. A commission, which shall be styled "Railroad and Warehouse Commission," shall be appointed as follows: Within 20 days after this act shall take effect, the governor shall appoint three persons as such commissioners, who shall hold their office until the next meeting of the general assembly, and until their successors are appointed and qualified. At the next meeting of the general assembly, and every two years thereafter, the governor, by and with the advice and consent of the senate, shall appoint three persons as such commissioners, who shall hold their offices for the term of two years from the 1st day of January, in the year of their appointment, and until their successors are appointed and qualified.[1]

§ 357. No person shall be appointed as such commissioner who is, at the time of his appointment, in

[1] The first board consisted of Gustavus Koerner, Richard P. Morgan and David Hammond, with J. H. Raymond for secretary. They held office until the appointment and confirmation of their successors, in the winter of 1873. There was a long and bitter

any way connected with any railroad company or warehouse, or who is directly or indirectly interested in any stock, bond or other property of, or is in the employment of any railroad company or warehouseman. And no person appointed as such commissioner shall, during the term of his office, become interested in any stock, bond, or other property of any railroad company or warehouse, or in any manner be employed by or connected with any railroad company or warehouse. The governor shall have power to remove any such commissioner at any time, in his discretion.[1]

§ 358. Before entering upon the duties of his office, each of the said commissioners shall make and subscribe and file with the secretary of state, an affidavit in the following form:

"I do solemnly swear (or affirm, as the case may be) that I will support the constitution of the United States and the constitution of the state of Illinois, and that I will faithfully discharge the duties of the office of commissioner of railroads and warehouses, according to the best of my ability."

And shall enter into bonds, with security to be approved

contest over the second board, the original nominees of Gov. Beveridge being rejected by the senate. Finally a selection satisfactory to the governor, the senate and the state was made. The second and present board consists of H. D. Cook, D. A. Brown and J. M. Pierson, and is non-partisan.

[1] The contest just mentioned was largely due to a controversy over the interpretation of this section. The governor conceived that the term "warehouse" referred only to public warehouses, the senate insisting that it equally applies in this connection to a person who stores his own grain in his own warehouse. The latter may now be accepted as the authoritative interpretation of the term, as far as concerns the appointment of railroad and warehouse commissioners, under the statute.

by the governor, in the sum of $20,000, conditioned for the faithful performance of his duty as such commissioner.

§ 359. Each of said commissioners shall receive for his services a sum not exceeding $3,500 per annum, payable quarterly. They shall be furnished with an office, office furniture, and stationery at the expense of the state, and shall have power to appoint a secretary, to perform such duties as they shall assign to him. Said secretary shall receive for his services a sum not exceeding $1,500 per annum. The office of the said commissioners shall be kept at Springfield, and all sums authorized to be paid by this act shall be paid out of the state treasury, and only on the order of the governor: *Provided*, that the total sum to be expended by said commissioners for office-rent and furniture and stationery, shall in no case exceed the total sum of $800 per annum.[1]

§ 360. The said commissioners have the right of passing in the performance of their duties concerning railroads on all railroads and railroad trains in this state.

[1] The incidental expenses of the office from July, 1871, to December, 1872, were $1,612 05. The appropriation made in the ordinary and contingent expense appropriation act of May, 1873, is as follows: "To the railroad and warehouse commissioners, for the incidental expenses of their office, including office rent and care, furniture, stationery, fuel, light and postage, telegraph charges; for the secretary's salary, the same not to exceed fifteen hundred dollars per annnm; extra clerk hire, and the fees of experts employed, which amount shall be fixed by the board, and for all necessary expenditures other than those hereinafter provided for, a sum not to exceed five thousand five hundred ($5,500) dollars per annum. For expenses incurred in suits or investigations commenced by the authority of the state, under any laws

§ 361. Every railroad company incorporated or doing business in this state, or which shall hereafter become incorporated, or do business under any general or special law of this state, shall, on or before the first day of September, A. D. 1871, and on or before the same day in each year thereafter, make and transmit to the commissioners appointed by virtue of this act, at their office in Springfield, a full and true statement, under oath of the proper officers of said corporation, of the affairs of their said corporation as the same existed on the first day of the preceding July, specifying:

1. The amount of capital stock subscribed, and by whom.

2. The names of the owners of its stock, and the amounts owned by them respectively, and the residence of each stockholder, as far as known.

3. The amount of stock paid in, and by whom.

4. The amount of its assets and liabilities.

5. The names and place of residence of its officers.

6. The amount of cash paid to the company on account of the original capital stock.

7. The amount of funded debt.

8. The amount of floating debt.

9. The estimated value of the road-bed, including iron and bridges.

10. The estimated value of rolling stock.

now in force, or hereafter to be enacted, empowering or instructing the board of commissioners, the sum of thirty thousand ($30,000) dollars, or so much thereof as may be necessary for said purpose. The above amounts to be paid upon detailed statements, filed with the auditor, bearing the order of the board and the approval of the governor."

11. The estimated value of stations, buildings, and fixtures.

12. The estimated value of other property.

13. The length of single main track.

14. The length of double main track.

15. The length of branches, stating whether they have single or double track.

16. The aggregate length of siding and other tracks not above enumerated.

17. The number of miles run by passenger trains during the year preceding the making of the report.

18. The number of miles run by freight trains during the same period.

19. The number of tons of through freight carried during the same time.

20. The number of tons of local freight carried during the same time.

21. Its monthly earnings for the transportation of passengers during the same time.

22. Its monthly earnings for the transportation of freight during the same time.

23. Its monthly earnings from all other sources respectively.

24. The amount of expense incurred in the running and management of passenger trains during the same time.

25. The amount of expense incurred in the running and management of freight trains during the same time; also, the amount of expense incurred in the running and management of mixed trains during the same time.

26. All other expenses incurred in the running and management of the road during the same time, includ-

ing the salaries of officers, who shall be reported separately.

27. The amount expended for repairs of road and maintenance of way, including repairs and renewal of bridges and renewal of iron.

28. The amount[s] expended for improvement, and whether the same are estimated as a part of the expenses of operating or repairing the road, and, if either, which.

29. The amount expended for motive power and cars.

30. The amount expended for station houses, buildings, and fixtures.

31. All other expenses for the maintenance of way.

32. All other expenditures, either for management of road, maintenance of way, motive power and cars, or for other purposes.

33. The rate of fare for passengers for each month during the same time, through and way passengers separately.

34. The tariff of freights, showing each change of tariff during the same time.[1]

35. A copy of each published rate of fare for passengers and tariff of freight in force, or issued for the government of its agents during the same time.

36. Whether the rate of fare and tariff of freights in such published lists are the same as those actually received by the company during the same time; if not, what were received.

[1] The information desired by this inquiry and by the thirty-sixth would be of great value, but no details are furnished, so far as the reports show.

37. What express companies run on its roads, and on what terms, and on what conditions; the kind of business done by them, and whether they take their freights at the depots or at the office of such express companies.

38. What freight and transportation companies run on its road, and on what terms.

39. Whether such freight and transportation companies use the cars of the railroad or the cars furnished by themselves.[1]

40. Whether the freight or cars of such companies are given any preference in speed or order of transportation, and if so, in what particular.[2]

41. What running arrangements it has with other railroad companies, setting forth the contracts for the same.[3]

§ 362. The said commissioners may make and propound to such railroad companies any additional interrogatories, which shall be answered by such companies in the same manner as those specified in the foregoing section.

§ 363. Sections 6 and 7 of this act shall apply to the president, directors, and officers of every railroad

[1] The usual answer to this question is, "Both."

[2] The invariable answer to this question is, "None."

[3] The first report made covered the period from July 1, 1871, to December 1 of the same year, and is a volume of one hundred and seventy pages. The second report is for the year following, and contains four hundred and fifty pages. Both are exceedingly valuable, containing as they do a vast amount of information and some pertinent suggestions. The appendix to this volume is mainly based on the information given in those volumes, especially the latter. It is noticeable, however, that on mainly points the answers are evasive.

company now existing, or which shall be incorporated or organized in this state, and to every lessee, manager, and operator of any railroad within this state.

§ 364. It shall be the duty of every owner, lessee, and manager of every public warehouse in this state, to furnish in writing, under oath, at such times as such railroad and warehouse commissioners shall require and prescribe, a statement concerning the condition and management of his business as such warehouseman.

§ 365. Such commissioners shall, on or before the first day of December in each year, and oftener, if required by the governor so to do, make a report to the governor of their doings for the preceding year, containing such facts, statements, and explanations as will disclose the actual workings of the system of railroad transportation and warehouse business in their bearings upon the business and prosperity of the people of this state, and such suggestions in relation thereto, as to them may seem appropriate, and particularly: first, whether in their judgement the railroads can be classified in regard to the rate of fare and freight to be charged upon them, and, if so, in what manner; second, whether a classification of freight can also be made, and, if so, in what manner. They shall also, at such times as the governor shall direct, examine any particular subject connected with the condition and management of such railroads and warehouses, and report to him, in writing, their opinion thereon, with their reasons therefor.

§ 366. Said commissioners shall examine into the condition and management, and all other matters concerning the business of railroads and warehouses in this state, so far as the same pertain to the relation of such roads and warehouses to the public and to the accommodation and security of persons doing business therewith; and whether such railroad companies and warehouses, their officers, directors, managers, lessees, agents and employes, comply with the laws of this state now in force or which shall hereafter be in force concerning them. And whenever it shall come to their knowledge, either upon complaint or otherwise, or they shall have reason to believe that any such law or laws have been or are being violated, they shall prosecute or cause to be prosecuted all corporations or persons guilty of such violation. In order to enable said commissioners efficiently to perform their duties under this act, it is hereby made their duty to cause one of their number, at least once in six months, to visit each county in the state in which is or shall be located a railroad station, and personally inquire into the management of such railroad and warehouse business.[1]

§ 367. Said commissioners are hereby authorized to hear and determine all applications for the cancellation of warehouse licenses in this state, which may be issued in pursuance of any laws of this state, and for that purpose to make and adopt such rules and regulations concerning such hearing and determination as may from time to time by them be deemed proper. And if, upon such hearing, it shall appear that any

[1] Vast good has resulted from the strictly warehouse feature of the law. The business is much more equitably conducted now than formerly, and the oppressive monopoly by which interior shippers were obliged to consign their grain to the elevator designated by the railroad company has been effectually broken up.

public warehouseman has been guilty of violating any law of this state concerning the business of public warehousemen, said commissioners may cancel and revoke the license of said public warehouseman, and immediately notify the officer who issued such license of such revocation and cancellation. And no person whose license as a public warehouseman shall be canceled or revoked, shall be entitled to another license, or to carry on this business in this state of such public warehouseman, until the expiration of six months from the date of such revocation and cancellation, and until he shall have again been licensed: *Provided*, that this section shall not be so construed as to prevent any such warehouseman from delivering any grain on hand at the time of such revocation or cancellation of his said license. And all licenses issued in violation of the provisions of this section shall be deemed null and void.

§ 368. The property, books, records, accounts, papers and proceedings of all such railroad companies, and all public warehousemen, shall at all times, during business hours, be subject to the examination and inspection of such commissioners, and they shall have power to examine, under oath or affirmation, any and all directors, officers, managers, agents and employes of any such railroad corporation, and any and all owners, managers, lessees, agents and employes of such public warehouses, and other persons, concerning any matter relating to the condition and management of such business.

§ 369. In making any examination as contemplated in this act, or for the purpose of obtaining information pursuant to this act, said commissioners shall have the power to issue subpœnas for the attendance of witnesses, and may administer oaths. In case any person shall willfully fail or refuse to obey such subpœna, it shall be the duty of the circuit court of any county, upon application of the said commissioners, to issue an attachment for such witness, and compel such witness to attend before the commissioners and give his testimony upon such matters as shall be lawfully required by such commissioners, and the said court shall have power to punish for contempt, as in other cases of refusal to obey the process and order of such court.

§ 370. Any person who shall willfully neglect or refuse to obey the process of subpœna issued by said commissioners, and appear and testify as therein required, shall be deemed guilty of a misdemeanor, and shall be liable to an indictment in any court of competent jurisdiction, and, on conviction thereof, shall be punished for each offense by a fine of not less than $25 nor more than $500, or by imprisonment of not more than thirty days, or both, in the discretion of the court, before which such conviction shall be had.

§ 371. Every railroad company, and every officer, agent, or employe of any railroad company, and every owner, lessee, manager, or employe of any warehouse who shall willfully neglect to make and furnish any report required in this act, at the time herein required, or who shall willfully and unlawfully hinder, delay or obstruct said commissioners in the discharge of the duties hereby imposed upon them, shall forfeit and pay a sum of not less than $100 nor more than $5,000 for each offense, to be recovered in an action of debt in the name and for the use of the people of the state of Illinois; and every railroad company, and every officer, agent or employe of any such railroad company, and every owner, lessee, manager, or agent or employe of any public warehouse shall be liable to a like penalty for every period of 10 days it or he shall willfully neglect or refuse to make such report.

§ 372. It shall be the duty of the attorney general, and the state's attorney, in every circuit or county, on the request of said commissioners, to institute and prosecute any and all suits and proceedings which they, or either of them, shall be directed by said commissioners to institute and prosecute for a violation of this act, or any law of this state concerning railroad companies or warehouses, or the officers, employes, owners, operators or agents of any such companies or warehouses.[1]

[1] Very little actual litigation has so far been undertaken. In the first annual report of the railroad and warehouse board occurs a sentence which suggests the real difficulty in the way of the law's execution. It is as follows: "It appears, from the very reports of most of the railroad corporations, that the act to prevent unjust discrimination and extortion in the rates for the transportation of freight, is systematically violated, inasmuch as higher rates are charged from local than from competing or terminal points. Many complaints have been received on that head. In every instance have we turned the person complaining to the provision of that law which gives an action for a penalty of one thousand dollars *to the party aggrieved*, but they have steadily declined to prosecute, giving as a reason that they did not want to give offense to the companies who had it in their power to deny them accommodations when most wanted, and could injure them in their business much more than the recovery of many penalties would benefit them. When required to give us an authentic statement of the cause of complaint, verified by affidavits, so that we might proceed under the fifth section of the act which enacts that proceedings for a forfeiture of the charter

§ 373. All such prosecutions shall be in the name of the people of the state of Illinois, and all moneys arising therefrom shall be paid into the state treasury by the sheriff or other officer collecting the same, and the state's attorney shall be entitled to receive for his compensation from the state treasury, on bills to be approved by the governor, a sum not exceeding 10 per cent. of the amount received and paid into the state treasury as aforesaid: *Provided*, this act shall not be construed so as to prevent any person from prosecuting any *qui tam* action as authorized by law, and of receiving such part of the amount recovered in such action, as is or may be provided under any law of this state.

§ 374. This act shall not be so construed as to waive or affect the right of any person injured by the violation of any law in regard to railroad companies or warehouses from prosecuting for his private damages in any manner allowed by law.

II. Warehouse Law.

may be instituted upon any violation of its provisions, they failed to do so, with one exception hereinafter to be mentioned." The present board meets the same difficulty. The commission is simply auxiliary and supplemental. The only way to obviate the difficulty pointed out by the board is for shippers to operate through a corporate organization.

§ 375. On the 25th of April, 1871, the general assembly passed an act to regulate public warehouses, as defined in the thirteenth article of the constitution. The law went into effect July 1 of the same year. That statute was two years later amended as regards grain grading.[1] The full text of the warehouse article of the constitution is as follows, viz.:[2]

§ 376. All elevators or storehouses where grain or other property is stored for a compensation, whether the property stored be kept separate or not, are declared to be public warehouses.

§ 377. The owner, lessee or manager of each and every public warehouse situated in any town or city of not less than 100,000 inhabitants, shall make weekly statements, under oath, before some officer to be designated by law, and keep the same posted in some

[1] For the entire statutes, see Gross, vol. ii, chap. 106; also page 189 of the official copy of the statutes of 1873.

[2] Illinois Constitution, art. xiii.

conspicuous place in the office of such warehouse, and shall also file a copy for public examination in such place as shall be designated by law, which statement shall correctly set forth the amount and grade of each and every kind of grain in such warehouse, together with such other property as may be stored therein, and what warehouse receipts have been issued, and are, at the time of making such statement, outstanding therefor; and shall, on the copy posted in the warehouse, note daily such changes as may be made in the quantity and grade of grain in such warehouse; and the different grades of grain shipped in separate lots, shall not be mixed with inferior or superior grades, without the consent of the owner or consignee thereof.

§ 378. The owners of property stored in any warehouse, or holder of a receipt for the same, shall always be at liberty to examine such property stored, and all the books and records of the warehouse in regard to such property.

§ 379. All railroad companies and other common carriers on railroads shall weigh or measure grain at points where it is shipped, and receipt for the full amount, and shall be responsible for the delivery of such amount to the owner or consignee thereof, at the place of destination.

§ 380. All railroad companies receiving and transporting grain in bulk or otherwise, shall deliver the same to any consignee thereof, or any elevator or public warehouse to which it may be consigned; *provided* such consignee or the elevator or public warehouse can be reached by any track owned, leased or used, or which can be used, by such railroad companies; and all railroad companies shall permit connections to be made with their track, so that any such consignee, and any public warehouse, coal bank or coal yard may be reached by the cars on said railroad.

§ 381. It shall be the duty of the general assembly to pass all necessary laws to prevent the issue of false and fraudulent warehouse receipts, and to give full effect to this article of the constitution, which shall be liberally construed so as to protect producers and shippers. And the enumeration of the remedies herein named shall not be construed to deny to the general assembly the power to prescribe by law such other and further remedies as may be found expedient, or to deprive any person of existing common law remedies.

§ 382. The general assembly shall pass laws for the inspection of grain, for the protection of producers, shippers and receivers of grain and produce.

§ 383. The legislation is in strict accord with these provisions, and has proved of inestimable value in overthrowing storage monopoly and reforming abuses. The Chicago Board of Trade had, by its charter, the inspection authority vested afterwards in the general assembly, and the validity of the constitution on that point has been theoretically questioned, but practically acquiesced in.[1]

§ 384. The power vested in the general assembly to establish grades for grain inspection was delegated to the railroad and warehouse commissioners by the statute of 1873. Upon that board devolves the duty

[1] The directors of the board of trade called upon their official attorney, C. Hitchcock, for an opinion on this subject, and in deference to his advice and to the wishes of the people as expressed through the fundamental law, the vested right in question was not asserted.

of appointing a committee of appeals, and to fix the fees in cases of appeal, except that a maximum is fixed by law, namely: three dollars to each member of the committee for each case.[1]

§ 385. It will be observed that the warehouse article of the constitution aims to correct certain railway abuses in the carriage of grain. The law has not been effective in all its parts, but has proved of great benefit even as partially enforced. The full text of the statute is as follows, viz.:

§ 386. Every railroad corporation, chartered by or organized under the laws of this state, or doing business within the limits of the same, when desired by any person wishing to ship any grain over its road, shall receive and transport such grain in bulk, within a reasonable time, and load the same either upon its track, at its depot, or at any warehouse adjoining its track, or side track, without distinction, discrimination, or favor between one shipper and another, and without distinction or discrimination as to the manner in which such grain is offered to it for transportation,

[1] It is worthy of remark that while the delegation to the commissioners of duties assigned to the general assembly by the constitution in railway matters was pronounced by the enemies of the policy unconstitutional, the adoption of the same policy in grain grading was unchallenged in its validity. The expediency, as well as legality of the policy, is essentially the same in both cases. It is impossible for legislation to adapt itself to the varying demands of different times and occasions. A degree of elasticity in grain inspection and transportation charges if not indispensable, is certainly eminently desirable, provided only it can be obtained without opening wide the door to abuses and injustice.

or as to the person, warehouse or place to whom or to which it may be consigned.[1]

§ 387. And at the time such grain is received by it for transportation, such corporation shall carefully and correctly weigh the same, and issue to the shipper thereof a receipt or bill of lading for such grain, in which shall be stated the true and correct weight. And such corporation shall weigh out and deliver to such shipper, his consignee or other person entitled to receive the same at the place of delivery, the full amount of such grain, without any deduction for leakage, shrinkage or other loss in the quantity of the same. In default of such delivery, the corporation so failing to deliver the full amount of such grain, shall pay to the person entitled thereto the full market value of any such grain not delivered, at the time and place when and where the same should have been delivered.

§ 388. If any such corporation shall, upon the receipt by it of any grain for transportation, neglect or refuse to weigh and receipt for the same, as aforesaid, the sworn statement of the shipper, or his agent having personal knowledge of the amount of grain so shipped, shall be taken as true, as to the amount so shipped; and in case of the neglect or refusal of any such corporation, upon the delivery by them of any grain, to weigh the same as aforesaid, the sworn statement of the person to whom the same was delivered, or his agent having personal knowledge of the weight

[1] It is worthy of note, as showing the value of statutory provisions supplemental to acknowledged common law principles, that while this doctrine has been affirmed often and applied, its violation was habitual and open, prior to the statute. It is now very generally, if not uniformly, respected and obeyed.

thereof, shall be taken as true as to the amount delivered; and if by such statements it shall appear that such corporation has failed to deliver the amount so shown to be shipped, such corporation shall be liable for the shortage, and shall pay to the person entitled thereto the full market value of such shortage, at the time and place when and where the same should have been delivered.[1]

§ 389. At all stations or places from which the shipment of grain by the road of any such corporation shall have amounted, during the previous year, to 50,000 bushels or more, such corporation shall erect and keep in good condition for use, and use in weighing grain to be shipped over its road, true and correct scales, of proper structure and capacity for the weighing of grain by car load, in their cars. After the same shall have been loaded, such corporation shall carefully and correctly weigh each car upon which grain shall be shipped from such place or station, both before and after the same is loaded, and ascertain and receipt for the true amount of grain so shipped. If any such corporation shall neglect or refuse to erect and keep in use such scales, or shall neglect or refuse to weigh, in the manner aforesaid, any grain shipped in bulk from any station or place, the sworn statement of the shipper, or his agent having personal knowledge of the

[1] This provision is designed to cure a very serious evil; but its enforcement has thus far been the exception, rather than the rule. No plan has yet been devised which would be apposite to all cases. The great difficulty seems to be the delay incident to weighing, although the expense would be no inconsiderable item.

amount of grain shipped, shall be taken as true as to the amount so shipped.

§ 390. In case any railroad corporation shall neglect or refuse to comply with any of the requirements of sections 1, 2 and 5 of this act, it shall, in addition to the penalties therein provided, forfeit and pay for every such offense, and for each and every day such refusal or neglect is continued, the sum of $100, to be recovered in an action of debt before any justice of the peace, in the name of the people of the state of Illinois; such penalty or forfeiture to be paid to the county in which the suit is brought, and shall also be required to pay all costs of prosecution, including such reasonable attorney's fees as may be assessed by the justice before whom the case may be tried.

§ 391. Every railroad corporation which shall receive any grain in bulk for transportation to any place within the state, shall transport and deliver the same to any consignee, elevator, warehouse or place to whom or to which it may be consigned or directed: *Provided*, such person, warehouse or place can be reached by any track owned, leased or used, or which can be used by such corporation; and every such corporation shall permit connections to be made and maintained with its track to and from any and all public warehouses where grain is or may be stored.[1]

§ 392. Any such corporation neglecting or refusing to comply with the requirements of this section, shall be liable to all persons injured thereby for all damages which they may sustain on that account, whether such

[1] At first this blow at warehouse monopoly was resisted, but its justice has been judicially recognized, and the desired reform is now an accomplished fact.

damages result from any depreciation in the value of such property by such neglect or refusal to deliver such grain as directed, or in loss to the proprietor or manager of any public warehouse to which it is directed to be delivered, and costs of suit, including such reasonable attorney's fees as shall be taxed by the court.

§ 393. And in case of any second or later refusal of such railroad corporation to comply with the requirements of this section, such corporation shall be, by the court, in the action on which such failure or refusal shall be found, adjudged to pay for the use of the people of this state, a sum of not less than $1,000 nor more than $5,000, for each and every failure or refusal, and this may be a part of the judgment of the court in any second or later proceeding against such corporation.

§ 394. In case any railroad corporation shall be found guilty of having violated, failed, or omitted to observe and comply with the requirements of this section, or any part thereof, three or more times, it shall be lawful for any person interested to apply to a court of chancery, and obtain the appointment of a receiver, to take charge of and manage such railroad corporation, until all damages, penalties, costs, and expenses adjudged against such corporation for any and every violation shall, together with interest, be fully satisfied.[1]

§ 395. All consignments of grain to any elevator or public warehouse shall be held to be temporary, and subject to change by the consignee or consignor at any

[1] This is the only instance in which the appointment of a receiver for a railway company is explicitly contemplated by statute. The subject of injunctions and receivers is treated in chap. ii, division 4.

time previous to the actual unloading of such property from the cars in which it is transported. Notice of any change in consignment may be served by the consignee on any agent of the railroad corporation having the property in possession, who may be in charge of the business of such corporation at the point where such property is to be delivered; and if, after such notice, and while the same remains uncanceled, such property is delivered in any way different from such altered or changed consignment, such railroad corporation shall, at the election of the consignee or person entitled to control such property, be deemed to have illegally appropriated such property to its own use, and shall be liable to pay the owner or consignee of such property double the value of the property so appropriated; and no extra charge shall be permitted by the corporation having the custody of such property, in consequence of such change of consignment.

§ 396. Any consignee or person entitled to receive the delivery of grain transported in bulk by any railroad, shall have 24 hours, free of expense, after actual notice of arrival by the corporation to the consignee, in which to remove the same from the cars of such railroad corporation, if he shall desire to receive it from the cars on the track; which 24 hours shall be held to embrace such time as the car containing such property is placed and kept by such corporation in a convenient and proper place for unloading. And it shall not be held to have been placed in a proper place for unloading, unless it can be reached by the consignee or person entitled to receive it, with teams or other suitable means for removing the property from the cars, and reasonably convenient to the depot of such railroad corporation, at which it is accustomed to receive and unload merchandise consigned to that station or place. Nothing herein contained, however, shall be held to authorize the changing of any consignment of grain, except as to the place at which it is to be delivered or unloaded; nor shall such change of consignment in any degree affect the ownership or control of property in any other way.

§ 397. Every railroad corporation organized or doing business under the laws of this state, or authority thereof, shall receive and deliver all grain consigned to its care for transportation at the crossings and junctions of all other railroads, canals and navigable rivers. Any violation of this section shall render any such railroad corporation subject to the same penalty as contained in section 3 of this act. All laws in conflict with this act are hereby repealed.[1]

III. Railroad Clause Constitution and Legislation of 1873 Based Thereon.

[1] The warehouse legislation under the constitution of 1848 was brief and less specific than the more recent legislation on the subject. In principle and aim the two agree. For the legislation under the constitution which was superseded in 1870, see Gross' Statutes, vol. ii, p. 788.

§ 398. A great many bills were before the twenty-eighth general assembly of Illinois, designed to carry out the railroad clause of the constitution. Only one such measure was passed. It is proposed to give the full text of that law, but prior to doing so its constitutional foundation is submitted, as follows, viz.:[1]

§ 399. Every railroad corporation organized or doing business in this state, under the laws or authority thereof, shall have and maintain a public office or place in this state for the transaction of its business, where transfers of stock shall be made and in which shall be kept, for public inspection, books, in which shall be recorded the amount of capital stock subscribed, and by whom; the names of the owners of its stock, and the amounts owned by them respectively; the amount of stock paid in and by whom; the transfers of said stock; the amount of its assets and liabilities, and the names and place of residence of its officers. The directors of every railroad corporation shall, annually, make a report, under oath, to the auditor of public accounts, or some officer to be designated by law, of all their acts and doings, which report

[1] Ill. Constitution, art. 11, sections 9–15.

shall include such matters relating to railroads as may be prescribed by law. And the general assembly shall pass laws enforcing by suitable penalties the provisions of this section.

§ 400. The rolling stock, and all other movable property belonging to any railroad company or corporation in this state, shall be considered personal property, and shall be liable to execution and sale in the same manner as the personal property of individuals, and the general assembly shall pass no law exempting any such property from execution and sale.

§ 401. No railroad corporation shall consolidate its stock, property or franchises with any other railroad corporation owning a parallel or competing line; and in no case shall any consolidation take place except upon public notice given, of at least sixty days, to all stockholders, in such manner as may be provided by law. A majority of the directors of any railroad corporation, now incorporated or hereafter to be incorporated by the laws of this state, shall be citizens and residents of this state.

§ 402. Railways heretofore constructed or that may hereafter be constructed in this state, are hereby declared public highways, and shall be free to all persons, for the transportation of their persons and property thereon, under such regulations as may be prescribed by law. And the general assembly shall, from time to time, pass laws establishing reasonable maximum rates of charges for the transportation of passengers and freight on the different railroads in this state.

§ 403. No railroad corporation shall issue any stock or bonds, except for money, labor or property, actually received, and applied to the purpose for which such corporation was created; and all stock dividends and other fictitious increase of the capital stock or indebtedness of any such corporation, shall be void. The capital stock of no railroad corporation shall be increased for any purpose, except upon giving sixty days' public notice, in such manner as may be provided by law.

§ 404. The exercise of the power, and the right of eminent domain shall never be so construed or abridged as to prevent the taking, by the general assembly, of the property and franchises of incorporated companies already organized, and subjecting them to the public necessity the same as of individuals. The right of trial by jury shall be held inviolate in all trials of claims for compensation, when, in the exercise of the said right of eminent domain, any incorporated company shall be interested either for or against the exercise of said right.

§ 405. The general assembly shall pass laws to correct abuses and prevent unjust discrimination and extortion in the rates of freight and passenger tariffs on the different railroads in this state, and enforce such laws, by adequate penalties, to the extent, if necessary for that purpose, of forfeiture of their property and franchises.

§ 406. The legislation in regard to the common carrier liability of railroad companies, based on the foregoing, is comprised in three statutes. The original freight act was pronounced void in its main feature by the supreme court, in the Chicago and Alton case. The original passenger act proved inoperative, and has been superseded by the statute of 1873, which makes provision alike for the prevention of freight, passenger and car service abuses.[1] The full text of the law of 1873 is as follows, viz.:

§ 407. *Be it enacted by the People of the State of Illinois, represented in the General Assembly,* If any railroad corporation, organized or doing business in this state under any act of incorporation, or general law of this state, now in force or which may hereafter be enacted, or any railroad corporation organized or which may hereafter be organized under the laws of any other state, and doing business in this state, shall charge, collect, demand or receive more than a fair and reasonable rate of toll or compensation, for the transportation of passengers or freight, of any description, or for the use and transportation of any railroad car upon its track, or any of the branches thereof, or upon any railroad within this state which it has the right, license, or permission to use, operate, or control, the same shall be deemed guilty of extortion, and upon conviction thereof shall be dealt with as hereinafter provided.[2]

§ 408. If any such railroad corporation aforesaid shall make any unjust discrimination in its rates or charges of toll, or compensation, for the transportation of passengers or freight of any description, or for the use and transportation of any railroad car upon its said road, or upon any of the branches thereof, or upon any railroads connected therewith, which it has the

[1] For the full text of the original statutes referred to see Gross, vol. ii, sections 146–157.

[2] The only noticeable feature of this section and the one immediately following is the reference to car service. Previous legislation to prevent railway extortion and discrimination made no direct allusion to this feature of transportation business.

right, license, or permission to operate, control or use, within this state, the same shall be deemed guilty of having violated the provisions of this act, and upon conviction thereof shall be dealt with as hereinafter provided.

§409. If any such railroad corporation shall charge, collect, or receive, for the transportation of any passenger, or freight of any description, upon its railroad, for any distance, within this state, the same, or a greater amount of toll or compensation than is at the same time charged, collected, or received for the transportation, in the same direction, of any passenger, or like quantity of freight of the same class, over a greater distance of the same railroad; or if it shall charge, collect, or receive, at any point upon its railroad, a higher rate of toll or compensation for receiving, handling or delivering freight of the same class and like quantity, than it shall, at the same time, charge, collect, or receive at any other point upon the same railroad; or if it shall charge, collect, or receive for the transportation of any passenger, or freight of any description, over its railroad, a greater amount as toll or compensation than shall, at the same time, be charged, collected, or received by it for the transportation of any passenger, or like quantity of freight of the same class, being transported in the same direction, over any portion of the same railroad, of equal distance; or if it shall charge, collect, or receive from any person or persons, a higher or greater amount of toll or compensation than it shall, at the same time, charge, collect, or receive from any other person or persons for receiving, handling, or delivering freight of the same class and like quantity, at the same point upon its railroad; or if it shall charge, collect, or receive from any person or persons, for the transportation of any freight upon its railroad, a higher or greater rate of toll or compensation than it shall, at the same time, charge, collect, or receive from any other person or persons, for the transportation of the like quantity of freight of the same class, being transported from the same point, in the same direction, over equal distances of the same railroad; or if it shall charge, collect, or receive from any person or persons, for the use and transportation of any railroad car or cars upon its railroad, for any distance, the same or a greater amount of toll or compensation than is at the same time charged, collected, or received from any other person or persons, for the use and transportation of any railroad car of the same class or number, for a like purpose, being transported in the same direction, over a greater distance of the same railroad; or if it shall charge, collect, or receive from any person or persons, for the use and transportation of any railroad car or cars upon its railroad, a higher or greater rate of toll or compensation than it shall, at the same time, charge, collect, or receive from any other person or persons, for the use and transportation of any railroad car or cars of the same class or number, for a like purpose, being transported from the same point, in the same direction, over an equal distance of the same railroad; all such discriminating rates, charges, collections, or receipts, whether made directly, or by means of any rebate, drawback, or other shift or evasion, shall be deemed and taken, against such railroad corporation, as *prima facie* evidence of the unjust discriminations prohibited by the provisions of this act, and it shall not be deemed a sufficient excuse or justification of such discriminations on the part of such railroad corporation, that the railway station or point at which it shall charge, collect, or receive the same or less rates of toll or compensation, for the transportation of such passengers or freight, or for the use and transportation of such railroad car the greater distance, than for the shorter distance, is a railway station or point at which there exists competition with any other railroad or means of transportation. This section shall not be construed so as to exclude other evidence tending to show any unjust discrimination in freight and passenger rates. The provisions of this section shall extend and apply to any railroad, the branches thereof, and any road or roads which any railroad corporation has the right, license, or permission to use, operate, or control, wholly or in part within this state: *Provided, however*, that nothing herein contained shall be so construed as to prevent railroad corporations from issuing commutation, excursion or thousand mile tickets, as the same are now issued by such corporations.[1]

[1] This elaborate section has one idea running through it, viz.: any discrimination in rates is unjust. Herein it joins issue with the Chicago and Alton decision. It is based upon the assumption that the difficulty of allowing any discrimination without practically abandoning the doctrine of uniformity, is such that the only way to render effective the constitutional provision against unjust discrimination is to forbid all discrimination. All legislation, whether state or municipal, to prevent extortion on street cars and in hacks is based on the same assumption. So are laws and regulations designed to prevent the spread of contagious disease. For instance, the state forbids the importation of Texas cattle in certain cases. That law cannot be executed without injustice in a few exceptional cases; neither could it be changed

§ 410. Any such railroad corporation guilty of extortion, or of making any unjust discrimination as to passenger or freight rates, or the rates for the use and transportation of railroad cars, or in receiving, handling, or delivering freights, shall, upon conviction thereof, be fined in any sum not less than one thousand dollars ($1,000), nor more than five thousand dollars ($5,000), for the first offense; and for the second offense not less than five thousand dollars ($5,000), nor more than ten thousand dollars ($10,000), and for the third offense not less than ten thousand dollars ($10,000), nor more than twenty thousand dollars ($20,000); and for every subsequent offense and conviction thereof, shall be liable to a fine of twenty-five thousand dollars ($25,000): *Provided*, that in all cases under this act either party shall have the right of trial by jury.[1]

§ 411. The fines hereinbefore provided for may be recovered in an action of debt, in the name of the

so as to meet those exceptional cases without defeating the object of the statute. The legislature deems the evil of discrimination of such a nature as to call for a similar application of the uniformity doctrine. The power of the legislature over this subject is discussed in chap. x, div. iii.

[1] Neither in this section nor in the act elsewhere is any allusion made to the forfeiture of franchise and property. The absence of legislation does not impair the force of the constitutional provision on that subject. If the penal remedies herein laid down should prove unavailing to secure the object sought, then the forfeiture penalty would be called into requisition. As the statute provides a fourfold grade of penalties, the reasonable presumption is that the general assembly intended the forfeiture penalty for the fifth offense. The passenger act previously referred to provided that extreme penalty for the fifth offense. Such an enforcement of that extreme penalty would be in harmony with the Chicago and Alton decision.

people of the state of Illinois, and there may be several counts joined in the same declaration as to extortion and unjust discrimination, and as to passenger and freight rates, and rates for the use and transportation of railroad cars, and for receiving, handling or delivering freights. If, upon the trial of any cause instituted under this act, the jury shall find for the people, they shall assess and return with their verdict the amount of the fine to be imposed upon the defendant, at any sum not less than one thousand dollars ($1,000), nor more than five thousand dollars ($5,000), and the court shall render judgment accordingly; and if the jury shall find for the people, and that the defendant has been once before convicted of a violation of the provisions of this act, they shall return such finding with their verdict, and shall assess, and return with their verdict the amount of the fine to be imposed upon the defendant, at any sum not less than five thousand dollars ($5,000), nor more than ten thousand dollars ($10,000), and the court shall render judgment accordingly; and if the jury shall find for the people, and that the defendant has been twice before convicted of a violation of the provisions of this act, with respect to extortion or unjust discrimination, they shall return such finding with their verdict, and shall assess and return with their verdict the amount of the fine to be imposed upon the defendant, at any sum not less than ten thousand dollars ($10,000), nor more that twenty thousand dollars ($20,000); and in like manner for every subsequent offense and conviction, such defendant shall be liable to a fine of twenty-five thousand dollars ($25,000): *Provided*, that in all cases under the provisions of this act, a preponderance of evidence in favor of the people shall be sufficient to authorize a verdict and judgment for the people.

§ 412. If any such railroad corporation shall, in violation of any of the provisions of this act, ask, demand, charge or receive of any person or corporation, any extortionate charge or charges for the transportation of any passengers, goods, merchandise or property, or for receiving, handling or delivering freights, or shall make any unjust discrimination against any person or corporation in its charges therefor, the person or corporation so offended against may, for each offense, recover of such railroad corporation, in any form of action, three times the amount of the damages sustained by the party aggrieved, together with cost of suit and a reasonable attorney's fee, to be fixed by the court where the same is heard, on appeal or otherwise, and taxed as a part of the costs of the case.[1]

§ 413. It shall be the duty of the railroad and warehouse commissioners to personally investigate and ascertain whether the provisions of this act are violated by any railroad corporation in this state, and to visit the various stations upon the line of each railroad for that purpose, as often as practicable; and whenever the facts, in any manner ascertained by said commissioners, shall in their judgment warrant such prosecu-

[1] This provision for damage to indemnify the complainant has numerous statutory precedents, and no question as to its constitutionality would be entertained by the courts. It has been observed that in quite a number of cases one-half of the fines attached to the violation of a statute goes to the prosecutor. Experience has shown that *qui tam* actions have proved efficacious, so far, certainly, as applied to the penal features of railway legislation.

tion, it shall be the duty of said commissioners to immediately cause suits to be commenced and prosecuted against any railroad corporations which may violate the provisions of this act. Such suits and prosecutions may be instituted in any county in this state, through or into which the line of the railroad corporation sued for violating this act may extend. And such railroad and warehouse commissioners are hereby authorized, when the facts of the case presented to them shall, in their judgment, warrant the commencement of such action, to employ counsel to assist the attorney-general in conducting such suit on behalf of the state. No such suits commenced by said commissioners shall be dismissed, except said railroad and warehouse commissioners and the attorney-general shall consent thereto.[1]

§ 414. The railroad and warehouse commissioners are hereby directed to make, for each of the railroad corporations doing business in this state, as soon as practicable, a schedule of reasonable maximum rates of charges for the transportation of passengers and freight and cars on each of said railroads; and said schedule shall, in all suits brought against any such

[1] This litigation clause, while it authorizes the Railroad and Warehouse Commissioners to commence suits for violation of the law, is no restriction upon the litigation rights of individuals. Nor is it a section of very much real importance. That board cannot render any considerable aid to the people in the enforcement of the law. It is impossible for the state to stand in the place of the shipper. The commissioners cannot make any shipments in their official capacity. The shipper must furnish all the facts in the case, and that is precisely where the practical difficulty in the way of the law's enforcement arises. (See note to section 372.)

railroad corporations, wherein is in any way involved the charges of any such railroad corporation, for the transportation of any passenger or freight or cars, or unjust discrimination in relation thereto, be deemed and taken, in all courts of this state, as *prima facie* evidence that the rates therein fixed are reasonable maximum rates of charges for the transportation of passengers and freights and cars upon the railroads for which said schedules may have been respectively prepared. Said commissioners shall, from time to time, and as often as circumstances may require, change and revise said schedules. When any schedules shall have been made or revised, as aforesaid, it shall be the duty of said commissioners to cause publication thereof to be made for three successive weeks, in some public newspaper published in the city of Springfield, in this state: *Provided*, that the schedules thus prepared shall not be taken as *prima facie* evidence as herein provided until schedules shall have been prepared and published as aforesaid for all the railroad companies now organized under the laws of this state, and until the fifteenth day of January, A. D. 1874, or until ten days after the meeting of the next session of this general assembly, provided a session of the general assembly shall be held previous to the fifteenth day of January aforesaid. All such schedules, purporting to be printed and published as aforesaid, shall be received and held, in all such suits, as *prima facie* the schedules of said commissioners, without further proof than the production of the paper in which they were published, together with the certificate of the publisher of said paper that the schedule therein contained is a true copy of the schedule furnished for publication by said commissioners, and that it has been published the above specified time; and any such paper, purporting to have been published at said city, and to be a public newspaper, shall be presumed to have been so published at the date thereof, and to be a public newspaper.[1]

§ 415. In all cases under the provisions of this act, the rules of evidence shall be the same as in other civil actions, except as hereinbefore otherwise provided. All fines recovered under the provisions of this act shall be paid into the county treasury of the county in which the suit is tried, by the person collecting the same, in the manner now provided by law, to be used for county purposes. The remedies hereby given shall be regarded as cumulative to the remedies now given by law against railroad corporations, and this act shall not be construed as repealing any statute giving such remedies. Suits commenced under the provisions of

[1] This section contains the delegation of legislative functions to the Railroad and Warehouse Board. In the general assembly the constitutionality of the section was called in question. Diligent and thorough research fails to discover a single authority in denial of the right of the legislature to thus delegate its functions in certain cases to a ministerial body. On the contrary, nothing is more common. It has often been done in this state and in other states. The New York reports contain many decisions recognizing the right of the legislature to thus exercise its functions by proxy, through a board of commissioners. Such boards are clothed with a blending of legislative, executive and judicial authority. They are created to perform certain specified duties, and cannot go beyond the limits prescribed by statute. The general assembly will convene before the 15th of January, 1874, so that in this instance the schedule of the commissioners will amount to a recommendation to the legislature, rather than a landmark for the courts.

this act shall have precedence over all other business, except criminal business.[1]

§ 416. The term "railroad corporation," contained in this act, shall be deemed and taken to mean all corporations, companies or individuals now owning or operating, or which may hereafter own or operate any railroad, in whole or in part, in this state; and the provisions of this act shall apply to all persons, firms and companies, and to all associations of persons, whether incorporated or otherwise, that shall do business as common carriers upon any of the lines of railway in this state (street railways excepted), the same as to railroad corporations hereinbefore mentioned.[2]

§ 417. An act entitled "An act to prevent unjust discriminations and extortions in the rates to be charged by the different railroads in this state for the transportation of freight on said roads," approved April 7, A. D. 1871, is hereby repealed, but such repeal shall not affect nor repeal any penalty incurred or right accrued under said act prior to the time this

[1] The last clause is specially important, as it enables prosecutors under the law, whether acting with or without the aid of the Railroad and Warehouse Commissioners, to push their rights to a speedy recognition. The docket of the courts is so cumbered that this precedence would be of very considerable aid in overcoming the law's delays.

[2] The first half of this section is an exact copy of the definition of the term "railroad corporation," as found in the statute set aside by the Chicago and Alton decision. The second clause is addition. The importance of the amendment is shown under the head of "Transportation Companies."

16

act takes effect, nor any proceedings or prosecutions to enforce such rights or penalties.[1]

[1] The last clause of this section is in accordance with the custom in such cases. Sometimes such qualifying feature of a repeal clause is of very great importance. In this instance it is an empty form, as no cases arising under the repealed act are being prosecuted, or are likely to be. It is entirely safe to say that whatever railway litigation may be further had under the legislation which it is made the especial duty of this commission to enforce will be prosecuted under the statute of 1873, if under any existing act of the general assembly.

CHAPTER VIII.

DOCTRINE OF UNIFORMITY.

§ 418. The distinctive feature of railway law in Illinois is the doctrine of uniformity, which may be termed the underlying principle of the railway clause of the constitution, and of the transportation statutes subsequently enacted. It is this doctrine and the persistent effort to enforce it that has given Illinois preeminence in the railway agitation of the day. In tracing the details of the liabilities of railroads as common carriers, frequent attention has been called to the obligation of the carrier to do business on a reasonable and impartial basis, but the subject is of such importance that it is thought best to present the doctrine as held by the courts generally, in a distinct chapter, and with as much fullness as is consistent with the purpose of this treatise.

§ 419. Some of the earlier railroad charters expressly reserved to the state the right to regulate the freight and passenger tariffs. No railroad was built, however, under any such charter. The greater part of the lines now in operation were constructed under charters in which the corporations themselves are expressly authorized to regulate the matter to suit themselves. No qualifications or restrictions are to be found in a single one of the many charters under which all the railroads were built prior to 1870, and some since. And what is true of existing Illinois railroads holds true of nearly all the railroads of the country. But this does not give to any railroad the right to make exorbitant charges, or to discriminate against any person or locality in violation of the common law as it applies to common carriers. This was the doctrine of the supreme court of Illinois in the case of the *Chicago, Burlington & Quincy R. R. Co. v. Parks*, 18 Ill., 460, in which the duty of railway companies to establish reasonable and uniform tariffs is clearly enunciated, and their right to arbitrarily oppress a citizen by charging him an unusual price is emphatically denied.

§ 420. The language of Mr. Justice CATON upon this point is deserving of more than passing notice. That eminent jurist, in pronouncing the opinion of the court, says, p. 464: "Several questions of considerable public importance arise upon this record, and have been considered by this court. The railroad company has the right, by its charter, to fix the tariff or fare, which it shall receive for carrying passengers and freight upon its road. These charges, however, must be uniform; that is, the charge should be the same for all persons similarly situated, and for all freights of a like kind and quality, for a given service. They may divide passengers and freights into classes, with descriptive distinctions, and charge different rates for different classes, for a given service, but the charge should be uniform upon all persons and freights embraced within each class. Thus may every one know what he has to pay, beforehand, for passage or freight, by inspecting the table of classes and charges fixed by the company. They may not say that they will charge A twice as much as they do the public in general. While they show favor to individuals or classes, by carrying them free or for half price, if they choose, they cannot be allowed to arbitrarily oppress an individual, by charging him an unusual price, simply because it is him."

§ 421. Thus was announced, in a judicial opinion of the supreme court of this state, delivered as long ago as 1857, the obligation of railways to observe the rule of uniformity in their charges, and to avoid unjust discriminations. And while, it is true, the question of discrimination is passed upon only as between persons, and not as between localities, in other respects the opinion of the court establishes the same doctrine as a common law principle, which has been incorporated into the recent legislation, viz.: the rule of uniformity and the prohibition of unjust discriminations in the carriage of freight or passengers. It is also worthy of note that this opinion was rendered in a case where the railway company was vested, by its charter, with full control over its freight and passenger rates.

§ 422. The duties incumbent by the common law upon all carriers, whether by land or water, whether railways, steamboats or stage lines, are plain. Foremost of these is their duty to receive passengers and goods, and to carry them *for a reasonable reward*. The question of the reasonableness of the rate charged is of the very essence of the relation between the parties. And the common law doctrine may be regarded as too well established to admit of controversy, that the carrier can charge only a reasonable compensation for services rendered.[1]

§ 423. A brief review of some of the leading cases in support of the principle above enunciated may not be amiss, and will certainly serve to fix the principle itself more clearly in the mind of the reader. In *Harris v. Packwood*, 3 Taunt., 264, we have the high authority of Lord Chief Justice MANSFIELD in support of the proposition that carriers have not an unlimited discretion to charge such rates as they may see fit, but that the rates established must be uniform. He says: "It would, however, be useless to pass any such statutes to limit the price of carriage, if the carrier be at liberty to charge what he pleases; the price must be reasonable."[2] And Mr. Justice LAWRENCE, in the same case, while conceding the right of carriers to charge a greater price for transporting goods of greater value, says: "I would not, however, have it understood that carriers are at liberty by law to charge

[1] See in support of this proposition, 2 Kent's Com. 599; Story on Bailments, § 508; Harris *v.* Packwood, 3 Taunt. 264; Riley *v.* Horne, 5 Bing. 217; Cole *v.* Goodwin, 19 Wend. 261, opinion of Mr. Justice COWEN; Parker *v.* Bristol and Exeter Ry. Co. 6 Exch. 702; Parker *v.* Great Western Ry. Co. 7 Manning & Granger, 253; Lamar *v.* New York and Savannah Steamship Co. 16 Ga. 558; Sanford *v.* The Catawissa R. R. Co. 24 Pa. St. (12 Harris), 378; Shipper *v.* The Pennsylvania R. R. Co. 47 Pa. St. 338.

[2] Harris *v.* Packwood, 3 Taunt. 264.

whatever they please: a carrier is liable by law to carry everything which is brought to him, for a reasonable sum to be paid for the same carriage; and not to extort what he will."

§ 424. Indeed, both in England and America, the question of determining whether a carrier has made reasonable charges has repeatedly been before the courts, and their jurisdiction[1] to pass upon the reasonableness of the rates charged is well established. Thus in *Parker v. The Bristol & Exeter Ry. Co.*, 6 Exch., 702, the question involved was whether plaintiff had been overcharged by the railway company, and this question was left to the decision of a jury.[2] In this case the company was required by its charter to charge all persons equally under the same circumstances. By the scale bill of the company certain rates were fixed for the transportation of freight, and the bill contained a foot note to the effect that where goods were collected and delivered by the parties themselves, a deduction would be made of a specific sum per ton. Plaintiff collected and delivered his own goods; and demanded a larger deduction than that mentioned in the scale bill, and had invariably paid the amount demanded by the company under protest, and brought his action to recover the excess. It was objected by the defendant, among other things, that the action for money had and received would not lie; but the court held that the plaintiff was entitled to maintain the action for such amount as the jury should think had been overpaid by

[1] By this is not meant that the courts have exclusive jurisdiction. That is a point to be discussed under the head of "Legislative Jurisdiction."

[2] Parker *v.* Bristol and Exeter R. R. Co. 6 Exch. 702.

him. And the court refused to disturb the finding of the jury upon this point, and denied a new trial.

§ 425. And in *Parker v. The Great Western Ry. Co.*, 7 Manning & Granger, 253, the jurisdiction of the court over the question of the reasonableness of the charges made, and whether unjust discrimination was shown in the rates, was recognized, and the whole question was passed upon by the court as a judicial question, although the company was empowered by its charter to fix its own charges.[1] So in *Parker v. The Great Western Ry. Co.*, 8 Eng. L. & Eq., 426, and *Edwards v. same*, Ib. 447, both of which cases were decided by Lord Chief Justice JERVIS, the reasonableness of charges and the justice of discrimination were the chief points determined by the court.[2]

§ 426. One of the earliest American cases in which the same doctrine is recognized, is *Lamar v. New York & Savannah Steamship Co.*, 16 Ga., 558. Here the object of inquiry was, whether the freight asked was the usual freight, and whether the carrier might, in case of packages of extra value, charge an extra price. And the decision of the court is based expressly upon the fact that they find the price asked to be a reasonable and the usual price for the transportation of the particular kind of goods in question.[3]

§ 427. It is to be observed, however, with reference to the English cases above cited, that the charters of the companies, as is the case with most English railway charters, limit the right of the companies in fixing their rates to the establishing of reasonable charges,

[1] Parker *v.* Great Western R. R. Co. 7 Manning & Granger, 253.
[2] Ibid. and Eng. L. & Eq. 426; Edwards *v.* same, Ibid. 447.
[3] Lamar *v.* New York and Savannah Steamship Co. 16 Ga. 558.

and provide, also, that no unjust discriminations shall be made. Similar provisions have in some instances been inserted in the charters of railway companies in this country, especially in Pennsylvania. It is proposed, therefore, to consider in brief the effect of such provisions as bearing upon the common law liabilities of the railways.

§ 428. So far from changing or modifying the common law doctrine, it is believed that the only effect of these limitations in the charter is to recognize and declare as law principles which derive their origin from the common law and exist independent of statutes. The case of *Sandford v. The Catawissa R. R. Co.*, 24 Pa. St. (12 Harris,) 378, is a case of great importance in illustration of the doctrine contended for, and recognizes in clear and unmistakable terms the common law duty of railways to transport for all alike and without distinction. In this case the charter of the railroad expressly provided that it should be the duty of the company to transport all freight "so that equal and impartial justice shall be done to all owners of property by the said company." But the court held that this clause of the charter was merely declaratory of the common law. The language of Chief Justice Lewis upon this point is as follows: * * * "But wherever a charter is granted for the purpose of constructing a railway, and the corporation is clothed with the power to take private property, in order to carry out the object, it is an inference of law from the extent of the power conferred, and the subject matter of the grant, that the road is for the public accommodation. The right to take tolls is a compensation to be received for the benefits conferred.

If the public are entitled to these advantages, it results from the nature of the right, that the benefits should be extended to all alike, and that no special privileges should be granted to one man or set of men, but denied to others. The special stipulations inserted in charters for the purpose of securing these rights, are placed there in abundance of caution, and affirm nothing more than the common right to equal justice which exists independent of such provisions. Of this character is the declaration in the charter of the railway company before us, which requires it to transport articles 'in the order in which' it 'shall be requested to transport the same,' 'so that equal and impartial justice shall be done to all owners of property,' 'who shall pay or tender the toll and freight due under this act.' The supposed necessity for such provisions in charters granted in this country and in England proves nothing more than that the law-makers in both countries were aware of the difficulty in holding large corporations to those common obligations of justice which individuals feel bound to acknowledge without legislative enactment."[1]

§ 429. The same doctrine is affirmed in *Shipper v. The Pennsylvania R. R. Co.*, 47 Pa. St. 338. In this case, Mr. Justice STRONG, now on the national bench, pronouncing the opinion of the court, says: "The charter of the defendants, authorizes them, from time

[1] Sandford *v.* Catawissa R. R. Co. 24 Pa. St. (12 Harris.) Here we have enunciated in clear and unmistakable terms the doctrine that railways are incorporated for the use and in the interests of the public; in other words, that they are *quasi* public corporations, with the performance of public functions and duties incumbent upon them.

to time, to establish, demand and receive such rates of toll or other compensation for the use of their road and for the motive power, and for the transportation of passengers, merchandise and commodities, as to the president and directors shall seem reasonable, not exceeding a maximum prescribed. There is no express stipulation that the rates and charges shall be equal to all who may offer goods for transportation over the road. Such stipulations are common in English railway charters, and they are found in some charters of railway companies in this country. They are, however, but declaratory of what the common law is. It was so said in *Sandford v. The Catawissa R. R. Co.*, 12 Harris, 378, and there is certainly good reason for denying such companies the power of discriminating between persons offering goods for transportation. It seems to be implied in the power given them to establish reasonable rates that the rates must be fixed equal and impartial."[1]

§ 430. It is thus manifest, from an examination of the authorities, both English and American, that railway companies, in their capacity as common carriers, are hedged about by certain definite limitations, subject to which they hold and exercise their franchise, and beyond which they dare not pass without rendering themselves amenable to the process of the courts. Foremost of these limitations is their obligation to carry for reasonable rates and without unjust discrimination, either as to persons or localities. It is an obligation ante-dating charters and statutes, and finding its origin only in the common law. Statutes (and

Ibid.; Shipper *v.* Pennsylvania R. R. Co. 47 Pa. St. 338.

charters) have simply declared and emphasized what already existed.

§ 431. From all this it follows that every railroad, whatever its charter on the one hand, or the statutory law on the other hand, is entitled to receive only a fair and equitable compensation for the business transacted as common carriers. Oppression, whether by a corporation or by an individual, is not to be tolerated. All our railroads, then, are upon essentially the same basis. The new companies can claim under common law all that really belongs to the old companies, under their charters. When subjected to close judicial analysis it is found that, while the charters emphasize the rights of the railroads, and the constitution the rights of the people, neither does more than to recognize and bring out conspicuously a feature of the common law. One is the counterpart of the other, so far, at least, as concerns the principle of justice on which railway tariffs must be based to be lawful. However variant with this interested parties may maintain, no intelligent controversy upon this fundamental point is possible. The doctrine, as laid down in the decisions quoted, has never been denied in any decision, English or American.

CHAPTER IX.

CHICAGO AND ALTON CASE.

I. Preliminary Statements and Argument of Counsel.

§ 432. No railroad company in Illinois so much as pretended to pay any heed to either the passenger or freight statutes of 1871. There is some semblance of respect for the statute of 1873. The difficulty in the way of enforcing those laws was stated by the Railroad and Warehouse Commissioners in their first report.[1] The only case which reached final adjudica-

[1] See note to section 372

tion was that of the *Chicago & Alton R. R. Co. v. The People.* The opinion filed in that case attracted more attention than any state decision ever rendered in this country. It was, or rather is, essentially national in the range of its importance. The issue of law joined was so broad and vital that the case might fitly be called *Railroad v. People.* Popular interest had not been so generally drawn to and centered in a judicial utterance since the rendering of the Dred Scott decision of nearly twenty years ago.

§ 433. With the exception of the Dartmouth College decision, no case was ever more thoroughly misunderstood and misrepresented, and that without being at all obscure in its utterances. The scope of its positive declarations is narrow, as compared with the propositions enunciated by counsel.

§ 434. The opinion of the court was delivered by Chief Justice LAWRENCE. It was filed on the 22d day of February, 1873, the full bench concurring. The court as then constituted consisted of CHARLES B. LAWRENCE, PINKNEY H. WALKER, SIDNEY BREESE, WILLIAM K. MCALLISTER, ANTHONY THORNTON, BENJAMIN R. SHELDON and JOHN M. SCOTT.[1] The complete title of the case is "*The Chicago and Alton Railroad Company* vs. *The People*, ex. rel. *Gustavus Koerner, Richard P. Morgan, Jr., and David S. Hammond, Railroad and Warehouse Commissioners.*"

§ 435. As the facts in the case are given in the decision, it is only necessary in presenting the arguments of counsel to state the propositions laid down

[1] Hon. SIDNEY BREESE is at the present time Chief Justice, and the places of Messrs. LAWRENCE and THORNTON are now filled by ALFRED M. CRAIG and JOHN M. SCHOFIELD.

and the authorities cited, as given in the *Chicago Legal News*. It was contended by the counsel for the appellants as follows, viz.: [1]

§ 436. The appellant, by the several acts of the general assembly set forth in its plea, was expressly authorized to fix, charge and receive such rates of toll for all passengers and property transported, as its president and directors should from time to time establish. Cases were cited in the court below to show that legislative grants are strictly construed—a proposition not denied but having no application in a case where nothing is claimed by construction or implication.[2]

§ 437. The authority granted to the appellant to charge and receive such rates of toll for the transportation of freight and passengers as its president and directors should from time to time establish, was a contract between the state and the appellant.[3]

§ 438. Charging a greater compensation for trans-

[1] The counsel for the company was Hon. Corodon Beckwith.

[2] Billings *v.* The Providence Bank, 4 Peters, 514; Charles River Bridge *v.* Warren Bridge, 11 Peters, 548; The Binghampton Bridge Case, 3 Wallace, 51.

[3] Fletcher *v.* Peck, 6 Cranch, 87; New Jersey *v.* Wilson, 7 Cranch, 164; Dartmouth College *v.* Woodward, 4 Wheaton, 518; Richmond, etc. R. R. Co. *v.* Louisa R. R. Co. 13 Howard, 71; Binghamnot Bridge Case, 3 Wallace, 73; Home of the Friendless *v.* Rouse, 8 Wallace, 430; 3 Parsons on Contracts, p. 527, 531 *et seq.;* Boston and Lowell R. R. Co. *v.* Salem and Lowell R. R. Co. *et al.* 2 Gray, 1–32; Sweatt *v.* Boston, Hartford and Erie R. R. Co. *et al. Am. Law Review*, Oct. 1871, p. 169; 1 Redfield on Railways, p. 53; Whiting *v.* Sheboygan and Fond du Lac R. R. Co. 15 Wis. 181; Talbot *v.* Hudson, 16 Gray, 417; Reddall *v.* Bryan, 14 Md. 444; People *v.* Salem, 20 Mich. 496; Railroad Co. *v.* McClure, 10 Wallace, 511.

porting persons and property a shorter distance than for a longer one, is not necessarily unreasonable nor an unjust discrimination.[1]

§ 439. The judicial department of the government has the sole authority to determine between the public and the appellant what rates are reasonable, and what are unreasonable, and what discriminations are just and what are unjust.[2]

§ 440. The power of the general assembly to pass all such laws as are necessary to promote the health, safety, morals, good order and general welfare of the inhabitants of the state, did not authorize the passage of the act of April 7, 1871.[3]

§ 441. The counsel for the respondent submitted the following propositions and authorities, viz.: [4]

§ 442. Corporations are subject to government and

[1] Attorney General *v.* Birmingham and Derby Junction R. R. Co. 2 English Railway Cases, 124; Ransome's Case, 1 C. B. (N. S.) 437; Oxlade's Case, 1 C. B. (N. S.) 454; *in re* Caterham Ry. Co. 1 C. B. (N. S.) 410; *in re* Harris and the Cockermouth R. R. Co. 3 C. B. (N. S.) 692; *in re* Jones and Eastern Counties R. R. Co. 3 C. B. (N. S.) 718; Hozier *v.* Caledonian R. R. Co. Scotch Sessions Cases, 17 vol. (N. S.) 302; Strick *v.* Swansea Canal Co. 16 C. B. (N. S.) 245; act of 8 and 9 Vict. c. 28; *in re* Oxlade and N. E. R. R. Co. 15 C. B. (N. S.) 80; *in re* Nicholson and G. W. R. R. Co. 5 C. B. (N. S.) 366; Baxendale *v.* The London and S. W. R. R. Co. 1 L. R. Exch. 137.

[2] Commonwealth *v.* Proprietors of N. B. Bridge Co. 2 Gray, 339; State *v.* Noyes, 47 Me. 204; Washington Bridge Co. *v.* State, 18 Conn. 53.

[3] Cooley on Con. Lim. pp. 85, 86, 87; Live Stock, etc. Association *v.* Crescent City, etc. Co. 1 Abbott Cir. Ct. R. 388, s. c. 3 *Chicago Legal News*, 17; Commonwealth *v.* Alger, 7 Cush. 84; Yates *v.* Milwaukee, 10 Wall. 497.

[4] The counsel for the people were Hon. J. H. Rowell, State's Attorney, Hon. R. M. Benjamin and Hamilton Spencer, Esq.

subordinate to legislation, precisely the same as an individual or natural person.[1]

§ 443. Legislative authority is a trust which the legislature cannot irrevocably delegate or abandon. It may authorize its exercise through agents of the public, but such agents must of necessity remain subject to public control.[2]

§ 444. This legislative authority which cannot be delegated or abandoned—which is a trust confided by the people to the legislature—has the same extent and is the same unlimited power in regard to legislation which resides in the British Parliament, except where restrained by written constitutions.[3]

§ 445. The prevention of unjust discrimination and

[1] Providence Bank *v.* Billings, 4 Peters, 563; Thorp *v.* R. & B. R. R. Co. 27 Vermont, 145; W. River Bridge Co. *v.* Dix, 6 Howard, 553; Bank of Republic *v.* Co. of Hamilton, 21 Ill. 58.

[2] Fletcher *v.* Peck, 6 Cranch, 87; Goszler *v.* Corporation of Georgetown, 6 Wheaton, 597; Charles River Bridge Co. *v.* Warren Bridge Co. 11 Peters, 420; East Hartford *v.* Hartford Bridge Co. 10 Howard, 534; Richmond, etc. R. R. Co. *v.* Louisa R. R. Co. 13 Howard, 90; Piscataqua Bridge *v.* N. H. Bridge, 7 N. H. 35; Brewster *v.* Hough, 10 N. H. 138; Presbyterian Church *v.* City of N. Y. 5 Cowen, 538; Stuyvesant *v.* Mayor, etc. of N. Y. 7 Cowen, 606; Mott. *v.* Penn. R. R. Co. 30 Pa. St. 35; Toledo Bank *v.* Bond, 1 Ohio St. 659; Ohio L. Ins. and T. Co. *v.* Debalt, 16 Howard, 431; Cooley's Cons. Lim. 283; New Jersey *v.* Wilson, 7 Cranch, 164; Washington University *v.* Rouse, 8 Wallace, 442, 12 Wallace, 551.

[3] Calder *v.* Bull, 3 Dallas, 386; Cochrane *v.* VanSurlay, 20 Wend. 382; Braddee *v.* Brounfield, 2 Watts. and Serg. 271; Harvey *v.* Thomas, 10 Watts. 63: Blanchamp *v.* The State, 6 Blackf. 299; Doe *v.* Douglas, 8 Blackf. 10; Thorpe *v.* R. & B. R. R. Co. 27 Vt. 142; 1 Kent, Comm. 448; Cooley Const. Lim. 87; Commonwealth *v.* Duane, 98 Mass. 1.

17

extortion comes within the legitimate exercise of the police powers of the state.[1]

§ 446. It cannot be presumed that the legislature intended irrevocably to part with the power of preventing by legislative enactment unjust discrimination between communities or individuals.[2]

§ 447. Railways are improved public highways, and therefore can be constructed by the aid of the right of eminent domain. Railroad companies are public agents created for the practical administration of the public property (right of way) put into their hands as such agents to be administered to subserve public interests and therefore must remain subject to public control.[3]

[1] Thorpe *v.* R. & B. R. R. Co. 27 Vt. 150; Mayor of Baltimore *v.* State, 15 Maryland, 389, 5 Howard, 583; Commonwealth *v.* Alger, 7 Cushing, 84; People *v.* Mayor of N. Y. 32 Barbour, 102; Miss. R. R. Co. *v.* McClelland, 25 Ill. 142; G. & C. U. R. R. Co. *v.* Appleby, 28 Ill. 282; same *v.* Dill, 22 Ill. 264, 269; same *v.* Loomis, 13 Ill. 548, 550; I. & C. R. R. Co. *v.* Kercheval, 16 Ind. 85; People *v.* Draper, 25 Barbour, 374; Veazie *v.* Mayo, 45 Me. 560; Commonwealth *v.* Tewksbury, 11 Met. 55, 57; Dingman *v.* People, 51 Ill. 272.

[2] 16 Howard, 435; 4 Peters, 514; 11 Ib. 548; 25 Ill. 142; Bradley *v.* N. Y. & N. H. R. R. Co. 21 Conn. 294; Mohawk Bridge Co. *v.* U. & S. R. R. Co. 6 Paige, 554; 27 Vt. 149; 2 Redf. on Railways, 408; 2 Greenleaf's Cruse, 67.

[3] Dyer *v.* Tuskaloosa Bridge Co. 2 Porter (Ala.), 303; Vattel Lib. i, Cap. 20 S. 249; Bynkershock, Lib. i, Cap. 15; Domat Book i, Tit. 8; S. I. R. R. Co. *v.* Davis, 2 Dev. and Bat. (N. C.) 469; Sanford *v.* R. R. Co. 34 Penn. St. 380; Vedder *v.* Fellows, 20 N. Y. 131; 1 Rice (S. C.), 398; 6 Howard (U. S.), 556; Whiting *v.* Sheboygan R. R. Co. 18 *Am. Law Register*, 165; People *ex rel.* *v.* Salem, 20 Mich. 483; The Chicago, Danville and Vincennes R. R. Co. *v.* Smith, at Ottawa, Ill. Jan. T. 1872; 4 Wheaton, 627.

II. Opinion of the Court.

448. Facts in the case.
449. Charter pleaded in defense; Verdict court below.
450. The statute on which the case was based.
451. Argument for the railroad.
452. Argument for the people.
453. Points not passed upon.
454. How the same might be brought in issue.
455. Legislature may prohibit unjust discrimination.
456. Such legislation consistent with railway charters.
457. English authorities cited.
458. Deductions therefrom.
459. Admission of counsel for appellant
460. Former state decisions.
461. Application of them to this case.
462. The presumption of injustice.
463. Right of the legislature reaffirmed.
464. Difficulty of its exercise.
465. Discrimination not necessarily unjust.
466. Trial by jury; Legislative control.
467. Supposable case of just discrimination.
468. Transportation reform demand stated.
469. Amendments to the statute suggested.
470. Forfeiture; In what case just and how effected.
471. English law of 1854.
472. Summing up of the case.

§ 448. The opinion of the court is as follows, viz., Lawrence C. J.: This record brings before us the proceedings upon an information in the nature of a *quo warranto*[1] filed by the Railroad Commissioners of the state against the Chicago and Alton Railroad Company, under the act which went into operation July 1, 1871, entitled "An act to prevent unjust discriminations and extortions in the rates to be charged by the different railroads in this state for the transpor-

[1] For a discussion of *quo warranto* see chap. x, div. 1.

tation of freight on said roads."[1] The information set forth that the company, in violation of this act, had repeatedly charged and received for transporting lumber from Chicago to Lexington, a distance of one hundred and ten miles, the sum of five dollars and sixty-five cents per one thousand feet, while at the same time it had only charged for transportation of like lumber from Chicago to Bloomington, a distance of one hundred and twenty-six miles, the sum of five dollars per one thousand feet.

§ 449. The company, by way of defense, pleaded its charter, and alleged that the rates of toll from Chicago to Lexington were in fact reasonable, while the rates from Chicago to Bloomington were unreasonably low, and were established because of the competition, at the latter point, with the Illinois Central railroad company. To this plea the relators demurred. The demurrer was sustained, a judgment of ouster was pronounced against the company, and its franchise was declared forfeited. From this judgment the company has prosecuted an appeal to this court. The question involved in this record is the constitutionality of the act of the legislature under which the information was filed. The object of the general assembly in passing the law is indicated by its title, which we have already given.

§ 450. The substance of the first section of the act is, that no railroad corporation in this state shall charge a larger compensation for the transportation of freight over any distance than it is charging at the same time for freight of the same class over a less distance, nor shall it charge the same amount that it

[1] For the full text of this law see Gross, vol. ii, chap. 86.

charges over a less distance. Another clause of the same section provides that no railroad company in this state shall charge a larger compensation for freight over any portion of its road than is charged for freight of the same class over any other portion of equal length. The second section of the act merely defines what is meant by the phrase "railroad corporation." The third section makes the rates of the year 1870 the standard for freight charges. This section is not brought before us by this record. The fourth section provides for the recovery of a penalty of one thousand dollars, in an action of debt, together with a reasonable attorney's fee, by any person aggrieved by the violation of this act. The fifth and last section provides, that any willful violation of this act by any railroad corporation, "shall be deemed and taken a forfeiture of its franchises," and authorizes a proceeding to that end, such as is before us in the present record.

§ 451. Very elaborate arguments have been filed by counsel, but they are chiefly devoted to a discussion of the power of the legislature to control the rate of railway charges or to fix their maximum limit. It is urged by counsel for the company that its charter is a contract with the state, by which the latter has irrevocably granted to the corporation the right to establish its rates of toll, subject only to an implied condition, which is admitted by counsel, that they shall not be unreasonable or excessive. It is further urged that this charter, with all the privileges it granted, is protected under that clause of the constitution of the United States which prohibits the states from enacting any law impairing the obligation of contracts.

§ 452. On the other hand it is contended by counsel for the relators, that railroad corporations, which obtain their right of way through the exercise of the right of eminent domain — a right belonging only to the sovereign power of the state, and to be delegated by that power only for public purposes — must be regarded as *quasi* public corporations, and, therefore, subject to legislative control, so far as may be necessary for the public welfare, of which the legislature must necessarily be the judge. It is further contended that the right to control and regulate their tolls is a species of police power, which the legislature cannot alienate from the state even if it should so desire, because essential to the proper sovereignty of the state.[1]

§ 453. These propositions of counsel invite us to a wide field of discussion, upon which we do not at present propose to enter. We have stated them for the purpose of saying, in terms, that we express no opinion in regard to them, and do not propose to do so until a case shall come before us demanding their discussion.

§ 454. There are laws upon our statute book involving their consideration, but the act before us does not necessarily do so in its application to the present case, and the expression of an opinion in regard to legislation not involved in this record would be obviously improper.

§ 455. Conceding, for the purposes of this appeal, all that is claimed by counsel for the appellant in regard to the inviolability of railroad charters, regarded in the light of contracts, we are still of opinion that the legislature has the clearest right to pass an act for

[1] See legislative jurisdiction.

the purpose of preventing an unjust discrimination in railway freights, whether as between individuals or communities, and to enforce its observance by appropriate penalties. The grounds of this opinion may be briefly stated, and they are as follows:

§ 456. A railroad company is chartered, and is chartered solely for the purpose of exercising the functions and performing the duties of a common carrier. The duties and liabilities of common carriers are clearly defined by the common law, and have been so defined for centuries. In all commercial countries the law upon this subject is one of the most important branches of legal science, and its leading principles were established by the courts of England at an early day. One of these principles is, that nothing excuses the carrier for the non-delivery of the goods received by him for carriage, except the act of God, or the public enemy. We do not find it written in the charters of railroad corporations in this state, that they shall exercise their franchises subject to this stringent liability, yet, nevertheless, this court has firmly held them to it, not permitting them to evade it even by a notice, or by any means short of a special contract with the shipper, to which his free assent must be shown to have been given.

§ 457. Another perfectly well settled rule of the common law in regard to common carriers is, that they shall not exercise any unjust and injurious discrimination between individuals in their rates of toll. In the language of Chief Justice Holt, when delivering the opinion of the court of king's bench, in the celebrated case of *Coggs v. Bernard*, decided in 1703,[1]

[1] Coggs *v.* Bernard, 2 Ld. Raymond.

the common carrier "exercises a public employment," and it necessarily follows that he must deal with the public fairly and without unjust discrimination. This common law duty of common carriers is not prescribed in the charters of railroad corporations, but, like the other duty of delivering goods in safety, unless prevented by the act of God or the public enemy, it attaches to them, by virtue of their function as common carriers, the moment they commence the transportation of freight. In accepting their charters, which gave them an artificial existence as common carriers, they necessarily accepted them with all the duties and liabilities attached, by the existing law, to the function of a common carrier. This proposition seems, to our minds, so plain as hardly to admit of more argument than an axiom in mathematics.

§ 458. While the law now imposes, and always has imposed, upon individuals exercising the vocation of a common carrier, the obligation of rendering service to all persons, without injustice to any, how utterly unreasonable it is, to claim that a corporation is to be permitted to discriminate in its tolls, at its own discretion, and without regard to justice, merely because the legislature, in the charter that created it for the purpose of exercising a like vocation, has authorized it to establish rates of toll, without, in terms, providing that they shall be free from unjust discrimination. What was the import of that grant, made, as it was, in broad and general terms? Clearly nothing more than that the corporation should have the same right of establishing tolls that a natural person has, when acting as a common carrier — a right to be exercised within the same limitations that the common law, in behalf of justice and public policy, imposes upon the natural man.

§ 459. This case has been argued on both sides with commendable ability and candor, and we avail ourselves of an admission made by counsel for the company, to illustrate the position we are enforcing. It is conceded by counsel, in express terms, that "a natural person is not allowed to make unreasonable and excessive charges as a common carrier, and an artificial person is subject to the same restrictions." It is of course contended by counsel that the legislature has no power to determine what charges are reasonable or unreasonable, but with that branch of the question we have, in this case, no concern. It is undoubtedly true, as conceded by counsel, that the artificial person has no more right than the natural person to make unreasonable and excessive charges as a common carrier. And why? This restriction is not found in railway charters as generally framed, and certainly not in the charter presented by this record, in regard to which counsel are speaking. The obvious reason is the principle we have already stated. The rule forbidding unreasonable charges was a common law rule when these charters were granted, and the companies accepted their charters with this implied limitation upon the power granted, in general terms, to establish their rates of freight. If this implied condition against unreasonable rates of freight attached by the existing law to their charters, at the date of their acceptance, on what ground can it be held that the corresponding condition against unjust discrimination did not equally attach? There is no ground for the distinction. The charters were granted for the purpose of furnishing improved means of transportation and travel to all persons alike, without unjust discrimination between individuals or communities, and they were accepted with the knowledge that the nature of the grant imposed that obligation.

§ 460. This question of unjust discrimination is not before this court for the first time. In the case of Vincent against this same company,[1] we held that railway companies can make no injurious discrimination between individuals, and therefore could not charge one rate for delivering grain at a certain elevator in Chicago and a higher rate for delivering at another elevator in the same city, and equally accessible upon its line. The same rule was recognized in *The People v. C. & A. R. R. Co.*,[2] though the facts of that case were found not to require its application. The rule was again declared in *C. & N. W. R. R. Co. v. The People.*[3] The opinion in that case cites several English and American cases in which it was held that railway companies could not be permitted to practice an injurious and arbitrary discrimination between different persons, and we now refer to them without further citation.

§ 461. If, then, an unjust discrimination is not to be permitted as between individuals, in regard to freights, is it any more permissible as between different communities or localities? We are wholly at a loss to discover the slightest difference, in reason or principle. If a farmer, living three miles from the Springfield station, upon this company's road, is

[1] Vincent *v.* Chicago and Alton R. R. Co. 49 Ill. 33.

[2] People *v.* Ibid. 55 Ill. 111.

[3] Chicago and Northwestern R. R. Co. *v.* People, 56 Ill. 365

charged fifteen cents per bushel for shipping his corn to Chicago, is it just that the farmer who lives twenty miles nearer Chicago, should be charged a higher sum? Certainly not, unless the railway company can show a peculiar state of affairs to justify the discrimination, and this must be something more than the mere fact that there are competing lines at one point, and not at the other. The discrimination in such a case is as much a discrimination between individuals as it would be in reference to two persons living in the same locality, and shipping at the same station, unless, as before stated, a satisfactory reason can be given for discrimination between the points of shipment, and such a reason, in the case supposed, it is not very easy to conceive.

§ 462. So, too, in the case before us. The resident of Bloomington, who sends to Chicago for a car of lumber, is charged by the company at the rate of five dollars per thousand feet for transportation. The resident of Lexington, who orders the same lumber at the same time, is charged five dollars and sixty-five cents per thousand feet for a transportation sixteen miles less in distance. Is there not here, unless an explanation can be furnished by the company, an unjust discrimination between individuals, quite as much within the prohibition of the principles of the common law, as would be an unjust discrimination between individuals of the same town? We have endeavored to show on what a firm foundation rests the constitutional power of the legislature to prohibit unjust discrimination in railway freights, even conceding what is claimed for their charters as contracts.

§ 463. We should, however, be doing the counsel

for appellant an injustice, if it were to be inferred, from what we have said, that they distinctly assert a right, on the part of the company, to make unjust discriminations. We understand them to concede, in the conclusion of their argument, the power of the legislature to prohibit such discriminations, but they insist that no discrimination is unjust, if the person against whom it is made is not himself charged an unreasonable rate.[1] They therefore averred, in their plea to the information, that the charges for freight to Lexington were, in fact, reasonable, and those to Bloomington were unreasonably low. But in our opinion, if the act of the legislature had directed its penalties, as it should have done, not against all discriminations, but only against unjust discriminations, and had made *that* the issue to be tried, it would have been no answer to aver, in the plea, that the larger rates for the less distance were reasonable rates. That would have had only an argumentative bearing upon the issue to be tried, to-wit: the existence of an unjust discrimination

[1] In other words, the right to provide a general remedy is denied. Practically, the difference is all important. If each case had to be acted upon separately, then no feasible remedy for extortion would be possible, and statutory aid would be inoperative and void. It is exceedingly difficult to allow *any* discrimination without shutting the door against any effective means of reaching the evil, and it is by no means certain that discrimination under any circumstance is allowable. If it would not directly lead to injustice, it might indirectly, and while the law of tort allows no compensation for "consequental damages," it is entirely competent for law to guard the approaches to wrong and danger. For example, quarantine laws are based on the assumption that all vessels must be treated alike, and that any discrimination would be unjust. This subject will be further discussed in the next chapter.

between neighboring towns. What is a reasonable rate of freight over a railroad is at best a mere matter of opinion, depending on a great variety of complicated facts, which but few persons could intelligently investigate, and which it would be wholly in the power of the company to furnish or withhold. Railroad experts might be produced, who would testify that, in their opinion, the rate to Lexington, in the present case, was a reasonable rate, but the fact that a less rate was charged for the greater distance to Bloomington, if the difference was a permanently established, and not a casual difference, and if it could be explained only by the fact that there was a competing line at one place and not at the other, might be well accepted as conclusive proof that the rate to Lexington was not a reasonable rate. The only issue to be made, under a law properly framed, would be, whether there was an unjust discrimination or not. If on the trial of such an issue the prosecutor proves a permanently established discrimination like that disclosed by the present record, and the company can show no other reason for it than the existence of a competing line at the favored point, the defense must be held unsatisfactory, notwithstanding witnesses may testify that they believe, as a matter of theoretical opinion, that the rates to Lexington are reasonable. They cannot be reasonable, and the discrimination must be unjust, if the lesser rates for the greater distance have been established merely because the company has ceased to exercise at that point a practical monopoly. It cannot be supposed that either of the competing lines would establish a permanent rate of charges upon a scale that would not furnish a remunerative profit. The rates to

Bloomington would be established under the influence of a fair competition, which, by the ordinary laws that govern commerce, might be relied upon as establishing a rate not unreasonably low. At Lexington, the rates would be established by the uncontrolled discretion of the company, and it should not cause surprise if they were fixed unreasonably high. If the rates are not unreasonably low at Bloomington, they are unreasonably high at Lexington. If they are unreasonably low at Bloomington and at all other points touched by competing lines, is it not certain that the company will indemnify itself by charging at the stations where there is no competition, a rate unreasonably high? And will not a discrimination arising solely from such cause be necessarily an unjust and injurious discrimination, as to all persons shipping or receiving freights at the non-competing stations?

§ 464. If Lexington is a town where a considerable business is done, it is evident that this discrimination of rates, if permanently established, will diminish its business and check its growth. It was never intended or expected that these corporations should use their power to benefit particular individuals, or build up particular localities, by arbitrary discriminations in their favor that must cause injury to other persons or places engaged in rival pursuits or occupying rival positions. It is in vain to say, in defense of such discriminations, made without just cause, that the rate of charges against the injured person or locality, is a reasonable rate, and therefore no injury is done. An injury, as a matter of fact, is committed, in the manner just suggested, and the legislature has the right to require the corporation to show a sufficient cause for the discrimination which produces the injury, and it cannot be permitted to evade the issue by raising the speculative inquiry as to whether the rates charged against the injured parties or localities are not, after all, reasonable rates. Even if reasonable, when regarded in reference to the profit upon the capital invested in the road, they are not reasonable in the true sense of the term, if no satisfactory reason can be given for charging less rates for the same or for greater services rendered to persons doing business with the company at neighboring stations. From what we have said, it will be seen that the object of the law under which these proceedings were instituted, was, in our opinion, clearly within the power of the legislature. The law was intended to prescribe the methods by which to enforce a common law duty that the railways of the state voluntarily assume whenever they exercise the functions of a common carrier, and it is in no respect a violation of their charters. It remains to be considered, whether there are defects in the details of the law which need to be amended, before it can be executed. We are of opinion that there are such defects, but they are susceptible of easy amendment.

§ 165. The discrimination forbidden by the common law to common carriers, is an unjust or unreasonable discrimination. The provision in our new constitution is also against unjust discrimination. It is in the following words: "The general assembly shall pass laws to correct abuses and prevent unjust discrimination and extortion in the rates of freight and passenger tariffs on the different roads in the state, and enforce such laws by adequate penalties, to the extent, if necessary for that purpose, of forfeiture of their property and franchises."[1] This provision, expressly directing the legislature to pass laws to prevent *unjust* discrimination, is a recognition of the palpable fact that there may be discriminations which are not unjust, and, by implication, it restrains the power of the legislature to a prohibition of those which are unjust. That was, undoubtedly, the object of the legislature in passing the existing law. This is clearly shown by its title. But the act itself goes further.[2] It forbids any discrimination whatever, under any circumstances, and whether just or unjust, in the charges for transporting the same classes of freight over equal distances, even though moving in opposite directions, and does not permit the companies to show that the discrimination is not unjust. The mere proof of the discrimination makes out a case against the railway companies, which they are not allowed to meet by evidence showing the reason or propriety of the discrimination; and then, upon this sort of *ex parte* trial, imposes as a penalty for the offense a forfeiture of the franchise, which would often be equivalent to a fine of millions of dollars. The object of the law is commendable, but such a proceeding, to be followed by such a penalty for the first offense, cannot be sustained. It could only have been authorized through the inadvertence of the legislature. The law, as it now stands, makes an offense out of an act which might be shown not to be an

[1] Art. xi, sec. 15.

[2] The constitution makes the legislature judge of what constitutes unjust discrimination. Should the final verdict of statutory law be that any discrimination is indirectly, if not immediately, unjust, that finding would be final on the principle of the constitution and of this very decision.

offense, but an exercise of a wise discretion, really beneficial to the people of the state, and while debarring the companies from all right of explanation, confiscates their franchises upon the first conviction.

§ 466. The legislature cannot raise a conclusive presumption of guilt against a natural person from an act that may be innocent in itself, taking from him the privilege of showing the actual innocence or propriety of the act, and confiscating his property as a penalty for the supposed offense. Those provisions of our constitution which forbid the deprivation of life, liberty or property, except by due process of law, and which guaranty the right of trial by jury "as heretofore enjoyed," and the right in all criminal prosecutions to appear and defend in person and by counsel, would all be violated by such a law. These provisions, it is true, are designed to apply only to natural persons; but artificial persons must be permitted to invoke the spirit of justice which prompted them, so far as may be necessary to protect their property and franchises against the operation of a law that substantially condemns without a trial.

§ 467. That the naked fact that a railway company charges a larger sum for transporting freight of the same class over a given distance than it is charging for the same distance over another part of its road, or in the opposite direction, is not, of itself, conclusive evidence of an unjust discrimination, will be manifest on a moment's consideration. Take for instance the road of the appellant, with one terminus at Chicago and the other at East St. Louis. At one season of the year more freights are moving from Chicago towards East St. Louis than in the opposite direction. The consequence, of course, is, that the supply of empty cars at the latter point will be in excess of the demand. There is a water route between these points which also touches several intermediate stations upon the road. Now, unless the railway company is permitted, under such circumstances, to induce shipments over its line by lowering its freights, it is evident that a portion of its cars will return empty. This would, of course, necessitate a higher charge for freight running towards St. Louis than it would be necessary to impose if return freights could be secured by lowering the rates on the return trip. To forbid the company to lower the rates of return freight would thus benefit no one, and would work an injury both to the company and to the people along the line. At other seasons of the year, the larger amount of freights is moving in the opposite direction, and then the operation must be reversed. We give this illustration for the purpose of showing that a difference of price for the same distance of transportation is not necessarily an unjust discrimination, and that any law must be fatally defective which infers guilt as a conclusive presumption from the mere fact of difference of rates without permitting the companies to show why the different rates were adopted.

§ 468. We may so far take judicial notice of the course of public affairs in this state, as to say, that the real abuse which the legislature was endeavoring, by this act, to prevent, was not such proper discrimination as those we have just been supposing; but the practice, which had become general among the railways, of charging a higher compensation for carrying the agricultural products of the state to market when shipped at a station where there was no competing line, than when shipped where there was such competition, although the distance over which the freight was carried in the latter case might greatly exceed the distance in the former. The same system also prevailed in regard to the freight from Chicago to points in the interior, although probably not felt to be so great an evil. For discriminations of this character, when adopted as a system, we can certainly perceive neither justification or excuse, but, nevertheless, it is the right of a company, when prosecuted on the ground of unjust discrimination, to offer what evidence it can by way of explanation. It might, for example, show in the present case, that the lumber shipped to Lexington had caused a greater expense in loading or unloading than that shipped to Bloomington. This may not be a very probable defense, but defenses may, nevertheless, exist, and if they do, the companies should not be deprived of the right to make them.

§ 469. Before this act can be enforced, it should be so amended as to correspond with the requirements of the constitution, by directing its prohibitions against *unjust* discriminations. It should make the charging of a greater compensation for a less distance or for the same distance, merely *prima facie* evidence of unjust discrimination, instead of conclusive evidence, as it now is; and it should give to the railway companies the right of trial by jury, not only on the fact of discrimination, but upon the issue whether such discrimination is just or not.

§ 470. There is another feature in this law to which we deem it our duty to advert. As the act now stands, a forfeiture of all franchises is the only penalty that can be imposed upon a company in a prosecution instituted on behalf of the people, and it is imposed for the first offense. This, as already remarked, in some cases would amount to a fine of millions of dollars. Is not this a violation of the spirit of that constitutional provision which says, in terms, that "all penalties shall be proportioned to the nature of the offense?" Is it not also a violation of the spirit of the very clause of the constitution under which this act was framed, and which requires the legislature to pass laws to prevent unjust discrimination and extortion by railroad corporations, "and enforce such laws by adequate penalties, to the extent, *if necessary for that purpose*, of forfeiture of their property and franchises?" Would it not be better to enforce the law by a series of considerable and increasing fines, before imposing the final penalty of forfeiture? A law admitting of but one penalty, and that of the hardest possible character, will necessarily be subjected by the courts to close criticism and a strict construction.[1]

§ 471. The English parliament passed a law in 1854 prohibiting the giving of undue or unreasonable preferences or advantages by railway companies in the

[1] The justice of this stricture is conceded. The law of 1873 went to the other extreme of omitting any reference to forfeiture, an evident oversight, and one which will probably be remedied at an early day. Indirectly it fixes the limit. Twenty-five thousand dollars is the extreme limit of damages. In the event that even this penalty should fail to have the desired restraining effect, the court would be in duty bound to inflict the final punishment contemplated by the constitution. An omission on the part of the general assembly to exercise its full authority would not relieve the court from obligation to consider whether the circumstances of the case demanded the extreme punishment or not. That penalty would be just in case the offender had shown that milder treatment was ineffective.

management of their business. Under this act various cases have arisen in the English courts, which have been cited by counsel. It is unnecessary to comment upon them. They hold, as we do, that a discrimination is not necessarily an unjust discrimination; that is to be determined upon the evidence.

§ 472. The opinion of the court is, that while the legislature has an unquestionable power to prohibit unjust discrimination in railway freights, no prosecution can be maintained under the existing act until amended, because it does not prohibit unjust discrimination merely, but discrimination of any character, and because it does not allow the companies to explain the reason of the discrimination, but forfeits their franchise upon an arbitrary and conclusive presumption of guilt to be drawn from the proof of an act that might be shown to be perfectly innocent. In these particulars, the existing act violates the spirit of the constitution.[1] The judgment of the circuit court ousting the appellant of its franchises, must therefore be reversed.

[1] It is a settled principle of jurisprudence that a decision setting aside certain features of a law as unconstitutional leaves the other features of the statute in force. In this case there was nothing of any consequence left of the act after this decision.

CHAPTER X.

CONSTITUTIONAL LAW.

I. Contracts and Charters.

§ 473. In no government that exists, or that has existed, is the opinion of the hour more effectively curbed than in the United States. Our constitutional system is a constant restraint. The past guides and checks the impulses of the present. The people do indeed rule, but popular sovereignty is a limited monarchy. In England whatever legislation parliament ordains the crown sanctions, and the courts enforce, unquestioningly. With all the British deference to the past there is only one legal way to escape the enforcement of an act of parliament, and that is to repeal it. Under our system of constitutional government it is always competent for the courts to question the validity of a statute. For this reason the present treatise demands an inquiry into the constitutionality of the railway policy of Illinois.

§ 474. The main reliance of the enemies of this policy for its judicial overthrow is the clause of the national constitution, which reads: "No state shall pass any law impairing the obligations of contracts."[1] In this brief sentence is contained the most characteristic feature of our government.

§ 475. In the republics after which our form of government was modeled, and under the common law, which is the foundation of all jurisprudence, both in this country and in England, we find suggestions of the need of such a prohibition, rather than proofs of its utility. The history of English rule in America is, in its general legal outlines, the history of contracts made only to be broken. Among the many charters granted and then violated was one ceding a vast area, including the entire state of Illinois, to a company composed of Francis Bacon, Oliver Cromwell and about fifty other British subjects. A few years later the contract was not only "impaired," but wholly abrogated. Had every commercial and real estate contract made by the English government been observed in good faith not an element of England's prosperity would have survived in freedom. It is equally true that had it not been for the bad charter faith of the English government the thirteen American

[1] U. S. Constitution, art. i, sec. 9.

colonies would have remained loyal. Fresh from a war provoked by impairment of the obligations of contracts, the founders of this republic were impressed with the importance of governmental good faith. Never having had experience of the peril of allowing men in power to bind their successors and the country forever, they had no very lively sense of the danger of collusion between public officers and corrupt cabals.

§ 476. It would be difficult to balance the good and evil of the two systems—the British and the American. Absolute popular sovereignty, restrained only by habitual reverence for the past, is liable to gross abuse; and so are constitutional limitations. The interpretation of the constitution is left, in its ultimate and binding form, to the courts, and there is more or less danger that personal opinion will usurp the place of organic law, consciously or unconsciously.

§ 477. The term "contract" has been frequently defined by the courts. Chief Justice MARSHALL's definition in the Dartmouth College case is, "an agreement in which a party undertakes to do or not to do a particular thing."[1] His successor, Chief Justice TANEY, explained a contract to be "an agreement between two or more parties to do or not to do a particular thing."[2] Parsons, in his work on contract, calls it, "an agreement between two or more parties for the doing or not doing of some specified thing."[3] These definitions are identical. Blackstone, and after him Kent, are more complete. They say, "a contract is an agreement upon sufficient consideration to do or

[1] 4 Wheaton, 197.

[2] 11 Peters, 420, 572.

[3] 1 Parsons on Contracts, 5.

not to do a particular thing."[1] Mr. Justice STORY is still more explicit: "A contract is a deliberate agreement between competent parties upon a legal consideration to do to abstain from doing some act."[2]

§ 478. The question involved in the clause of the constitution already quoted, namely, whether a charter is or is not a contract, was discussed, and decided in the affirmative, in the Dartmouth College case. The discussion was so thorough and the decision so able, and accordant with the letter and purpose of the constitution, that the correctness of its deductions have not been authoritatively disputed. The only controversy admissible pertains to the application of the doctrine therein laid down. No decision more eminently just was ever rendered; no decision was ever so persistently misrepresented and pervented.

§ 479. In the year 1769 Dartmouth College was created by charter. It grew out of an attempt to educate the Indians. John Eliot, the great apostle of modern missions, the illustrious founder of a family preëminently honorable in the annals of the country, had undertaken the civilization of the Indians, and Eleazor Wheelock supplemented Eliot by establishing a school for their training. It was first started at Lebanon, Connecticut. It was afterwards thought best to remove it to what is now Hanover, New Hampshire, where it received a land grant subsidy of 44,000 acres. A liberal fund was raised in England for the institution. Lord Dartmouth gave more than any one else, and after him the college, as it now became, was named. A board of trustees was organized in accord-

[1] 2 Blackstone, 446; 2 Kent, 449.

[2] Story Contr. sec. 1.

ance with the provisions of the charter, with Lord Dartmouth president of the board.

§ 480. Nothing worthy of note in this connection occurred in the history of the college until 1815. At that time the institution was presided over by John Wheelock, son and immediate successor of the first president. His administration gave some dissatisfaction, and the trustees removed him. The year following the legislature of New Hampshire took part in the controversy by passing statutes legislating the old board of trustees out of office, and creating a new corporation. Among other things this legislation made the governors of New Hampshire and of Vermont *ex-officio* members of the board of management. In addition to this entire change in the control of the institution its name was changed from Dartmouth College to Dartmouth University. Some other alterations hardly less fundamental were made.

§ 481. The immediate occasion of litigation was the demand by the new board of trustees upon the old board for the records of the college. There was no issue of fact raised. The controversy was over the validity of the state legislation. The old board of trustees denied the right of the state government to enact such legislation, basing the denial upon the clause of the constitution of the United States which has been quoted. The state courts sustained the validity of the legislation. The case reached its final adjudication in the supreme court of the United States, to which tribunal it was appealed on the strength of another clause of the constitution, which gives the federal judiciary jurisdiction over all cases in law and equity arising under the constitution of the United States.[1]

§ 482. Daniel Webster, for the old board, made the great argument of the case. With him were associated as counsel Jeremiah Smith and Jeremiah Mason. Opposed to them were William Wirt, William Pinkney and John Holmes. Messrs. Wirt and Pinkney were eminent lawyers. The names of both of them appear in the list of the attorney generals of the United States. Chief Justice MARSHALL was then on the bench, and Mr. Justice STORY one of the associate justices at the time.

§ 483. The legal points of the Dartmouth college case have been frequently restated by the courts. The latest statement thereof by the supreme court of the United States was in the case of *Miller v. The State of Pennsylvania*. The decision in this case has been rendered, but not officially published. That summary of the law as established in this important case is as follows, viz.: "Much consideration was given to the question under consideration in the case of *Dartmouth College v. Woodward*, 4 Wheat. 175, in which the right of the state was denied to amend the charter granted to the college by the crown before the revolution, and to modify and restrict the same without the consent of the trustees under the charter. Four propositions were decided by the court in that case, the opinion being given by the chief justice: 1. That the charter was a contract within the meaning of that clause of the constitution which ordains that no state shall pass any law impairing the obligation of contracts. 2. That the charter was not dissolved by the

[1] United States Constitution, art. iii, sec. 2.

revolution. 3. That the acts of the state legislature altering the charter in a material respect, without the consent of the corporation, was an act impairing the obligation of the charter, and was unconstitutional and void. 4. That the college, under its charter, was a private and not a public corporation."

§ 484. This latest statement has the merit of brevity, without the omission of a single point, and the principles therein laid down are now axioms, and need no argumentation. The reasoning of the court in that case is regarded as one of the masterpieces of judicial literature.

§ 485. No legislation, in Illinois, at least none relating to railroads, is at all analogous to the New Hampshire legislation in regard to Dartmouth college. It is easy to suppose an analogous case.

§ 486. There is one railroad in the state — the Illinois Central — which was built in part by a land subsidy and largely by English capital, thus resembling Darmouth college. Supposing the general assembly should abolish the existing board of directors; create a new one, of which the governors of Illinois and of Iowa should be *ex officio* members; change the name to Prairie Central railroad company; compel the construction of a double track from Chicago and Dunleith to Cairo. *That* would be "impairing the obligations of contracts," within the contemplation of the constitution of the United States as defined and applied by the court in the Dartmouth college case. Again: had the legislature of New Hampshire passed a general law for the regulation of colleges, to prevent the abuse of rights and privileges enjoyed under their charters, said legislation being simply declaratory of common law principles as applied to public institutions of learning, that would have been legislation analogous to Illinois railway law, as found in the constitution and statute books of the state.

II. Commerce between States by Rail.

§ 487. One other feature of the national constitution demands consideration, namely, that relating to the means of commercial intercourse. It is contained in two clauses. The first reads: "The congress shall have power to regulate commerce with foreign nations, and among the several states and with the Indian tribes."[1] The other clause referred to reads: "The congress shall have power to establish post offices and post roads."[2]

[1] United States Constitution, art. i, sec. 8, clause 3.

[2] Ibid. clause 7.

§ 488. The clause last quoted gave rise to a great deal of discussion in congress before the days of railroads. The contest was over the construction of the term "establish." It was contended by Benton and others that it meant simply the designation of routes by which the mails should be conveyed. STORY, in his great work on the constitution, shows conclusively that the right to construct post roads is vested in congress. Its exercise has never been attempted in the case of railways, although the mail service is mainly conducted by rail. The objection to its exercise rests on a question of expediency, rather than an interpretation of the constitution. The nearest approach to an exercise of this reserved right, since the construction and final abandonment to the states of the Cumberland turnpike, was in the passage by congress of a general railway incorporation act. That statute applies, however, only to territories. It has never been called into operation, nor is it likely to be.[1]

§ 489. The first clause in the foregoing quotation from the constitution of the United States is suggestive of the origin of the present organic law of the nation, in distinction from the articles of confederation. The evils of a Union in which each part was greater than the whole, in point of actual authority, was first felt by the commerce of the country. Intercourse with foreign nations and between citizens of different states was seriously hampered by the sovereignty of the state, and the necessarily diverse exercise of that sovereignty. At the suggestion of the legislatures of

[1] For a discussion of this subject of post roads, see 2 Story on the Constitution, chap. 17; Benton's Thirty Years in the Senate, vol. ii, 167.

the states of New York, Pennsylvania, Virginia, New Jersey and Delaware, a commercial convention was held at Annapolis, Maryland, commencing Sept. 11, 1786. The states named were represented, and no others. That convention, after a session of three days, embodied its conclusions in a report unanimously adopted, in which they said: "Deeply impressed, however, with the magnitude and importance of the object confided to them on this occasion, your commissioners cannot forbear to indulge an expression of their earnest and unanimous wish, that speedy measures may be taken to effect a general meeting of the states in a future convention, for the same and such other purposes as the situation of public affairs may be found to require." The report concluded with the recommendation that all the states appoint commissioners, "to meet at Philadelphia on the second Monday in May next, to take into consideration the situation of the United States."

§ 490. No little discussion was had in the convention over the phrasing of the commercial clause of the constitution. It does not include any commerce which is entirely within the limits of one state. Every railroad forms a link in a national chain, and a shipment from one point in a state to another point in the same state may, ultimately, go through several states; but it is none the less true that the strictly internal commerce of a state is under state, rather than national control.[1] This rule has one generic exception: The bridging of a navigable river is not allowable without

[1] Gibbons *v.* Ogden, 9 Wheat. 194; Brown *v.* Maryland, 12 Wheat. 446; Veazie *v.* Moor, 14 Howard, S. C. R. 568.

permission from congress.[1] In some states this feature of national sovereignty is denied; but it is distinctly recognized in Illinois.

§ 491. The completeness of congressional authority in some cases does not forbid the exercise of state control over all roads in numerous respects, provided state legislation does not conflict with the authority vested in and exercised by congress. Cooley on Constitutional Limitations cites a large array of cases to show that the state may exercise police authority. Very many of these citations are from the Illinois reports. Jeremy Bentham's definition of police power restricts it to a "system of precautions, either for the prevention of crime or calamities." In applying the doctrine to state control of railroads, Chief Justice REDFIELD adds: "there is also the general police power of the state, by which persons and property are subject to all kinds of restraints and burdens, in order to secure the general comfort, health and prosperity of the state."[2] Having given this enlarged definition of police power, the same learned jurist immediately added: "of the perfect right in the legislature to do which no question ever was, or upon acknowledged general principles, ever can be made, so far as natural persons are concerned. And it is certainly calculated to excite surprise and alarm that the right to do the same in regard to railways should be made a serious question."[3] The

[1] The Daniel Ball, 10 Wallace, 558; Pennsylvania *v.* Wheeling and Belmont Bridge Co. 13 How. 518.

[2] Thorpe *v.* Rutland and Burlington R. R. Co. 27 Vt. 140.

[3] In support of this doctrine of state control Cooley quotes, among others, Galena and Chicago U. R. R. Co. *v.* Loomis, 13 Ill. 548; Ib. *v.* Appleby, 28 Ill. 283; Suydan *v.* Moore, 8 Barber, 358; Fitchburg R. R. *v.* G'd Junction R. R. and Depot Co. 1 Allen, 552.

reports of the different states and of the United States show that the police authority of the state has frequently been challenged, but always maintained, the only difference being in the range of meaning given to the term "police power."

§ 492. The Redfield definition of the term includes measures to prevent extortionate charges and unjust discrimination. The question on this subject remaining to be considered is this: Does the right extend to through freight, or is it limited to freight starting from a point within the state, and destined to a point without the same state? This issue of law has never been directly raised in the supreme court of Illinois. Its immediate pertinence is due to inquiry growing out of the distinctive railway legislation of Illinois, as witnesses the following official circular.

§ 493. The Illinois railway law of 1873 went into effect July 1, and on the same day the Railroad and Warehouse Commissioners issued a circular setting forth their understanding of the statute in several relations, but more especially in its relations to interstate commerce. It reads as follows, viz.:

§ 494. State of Illinois, Office of Railroad and Warehouse Commissioners, July 1, 1873.—To the Public: Some important questions having arisen under the act of May 2, 1873, to prevent extortion and unjust discrimination, we deem it proper to make known to the public our construction of certain portions of the act. We would first direct attention to the first section, which declares that if any railroad corporation doing business in this state shall charge or receive more than a fair or reasonable rate of toll or compensation for the transportation of passengers or freight, the same shall be deemed guilty of extortion, and upon conviction be punished by specific penalties. The avowed object of the statute is to prevent extortion as well as unjust discrimination. In making their rates of charges conform to the requirements of the third section, defining what would be *prima facie* evidence of unjust discriminations, the railroad companies must not ignore the first section forbidding extortion. In our judgment the rates of charges prior to this date have been in the main unreasonably high, and any increase thereof would be a clear violation of the law.

§ 495. The following are the questions above referred to: 1. Does the act apply to through freights as well as local freights? 2. Does the act admit of any discrimination in freight tariffs based upon the quantity shipped; or must the railroad companies, to comply with the act, adopt one uniform rate per hundred pounds, per ton, or per car load, regardless of the quantity or the amount of the shipment? 3. Where two or more railroads operated by different companies are so connected as to form in fact one continuous line, and shipments are made from a point on one line to a point on the other, may the charge be at the rate applicable to the distance over both roads, or at the aggregate of the local rates on each road? 4. Can railroad corporations hereafter issue excursion tickets? After due consideration of the questions we have arrived at the following conclusion:

§ 496. 1. The provisions of the act are applicable as well to through as to local freights, so far, at least, as to require that less should be charged for the transportation of domestic or local freights from one point to another within this state, than the sum charged for the transportation of through or foreign freights the same distance within the state, and for its transportation from or to a point without the state. Thus, the charges from a point west of the state to a point within the state must not be the same as, or less than, the charges from the west line of the state over the same road to the same point of destination. So the charges from a point within the state to a point east of the state must not be the same as, or less than, the charges from the same point of departure over the same road to the east line of the state. So, also, the charges from a point west of the state to a point east of the state must not be the same as, or less than, the charges over the same road from the west line to the east line of the state. The general principle is that the charges for any distance within this state must not be the same or greater than the charges for a greater distance.

§ 497. 2. A reasonably less rate may be charged per one hundred pounds, per ton, or per car, where large amounts of freight are shipped by the same person, than where small shipments are made, without violating the act. Discriminations of this character, as upon fair business principles, were just and reasonable before the passage of the act; are not prohibited thereby, but seem to be recognized therein by the words "like quantity" frequently occurring in the third section of the act.

§ 498. 3. Where two or more railroads are owned and operated by different companies, and are connected so as to form in fact one continuous line, and either of such companies receives freight upon its road to be shipped to some point upon the other road, the same may be treated for purposes of such shipment as one entire line, and the same rate may be charged as if one company owned the road upon which the freight was shipped for the entire distance, instead of charging the aggregate of the local rate on each road for the distance shipped thereon.

§ 499. 4. The act expressly provides that nothing therein contained shall be so construed as to prevent railroad corporations from issuing commutation, excursion, or one thousand mile tickets, as the same hitherto have been issued by such corporation.

H. D. Cook,
D. A. Brown,
John M. Pearson,
Commissioners.

§ 500. The limitation of state control over railway commerce was discussed in some of its phases by the supreme court of the United States in the case of *Reading R. R. Co. v. Pennsylvania.* The right of a state to tax gross receipts of railroad companies was affirmed. The receipts may be made up in part of business belonging under the designation of commerce between the states; but the tax would not, on that account, be a regulation of inter-state commerce.[1] In the same decision the court held that a statute of a state imposing a tax upon freight, taken up within the state and carried out of it, or taken up without the state and brought within it, is repugnant to that provision of the constitution of the United States which ordains[2] that "congress shall have power to regulate

[1] 15 Wall. 248.
[2] Ibid. 232.

commerce with foreign nations and among the several states, and with the Indian tribes."

§ 501. This subject was passed upon again by the same court in another, yet substantially the identical case, *Philadelphia and Reading R. R. Co. v. Pennsylvania.* The validity of the tax mentioned in the foregoing section was in issue. Omitting so much of the opinion as is irrelevant in this connection, we have the following as the latest utterance upon the subject of commerce between states by the only court which is competent to make an authoritative declaration thereupon:

§ 502. If, then, this is a tax upon freight carried between states, and a tax because of its transportation, and if such a tax is in effect a regulation of inter-state commerce, the conclusion seems to be inevitable, that it is in conflict with the constitution of the United States. It is not necessary to the present case to go at large into the much debated question whether the power given to congress by the constitution to regulate commerce among the states is exclusive. In the earlier decisions of this court, it was said to have been so entirely vested in congress, that no part of it can be exercised by a state. *Gibbons v. Ogden*, 9 Wheaton, 1; *Passenger Cases*, 7 How. 283. It has, indeed, often been argued, and sometimes intimated by the court, that so far as congress has not legislated on the subject, the states may legislate respecting inter-state commerce. Yet, if they can, why may they not add regulations to commerce with foreign nations beyond those made by congress, if not inconsistent with them, for the power over both foreign and inter-state commerce is conferred upon the federal legislature by the same words. And certainly it has never yet been decided by this court, that the power to regulate inter-state, as well as foreign commerce, is not exclusively in congress. Cases that have sustained state laws alleged to be regulations of commerce among the states, have been such as related to bridges or dams across streams wholly within a state, police or health laws, or subjects of a kindred nature, not strictly commercial regulations. The subjects were such as in *Gilman v. Philadelphia*, 3 Wall. 713, it was said, "can be best regulated by rules and provisions suggested by the varying circumstances of different localities, and limited in their operation to such localities respectively." However this may be, the rule has been asserted with great clearness, that whenever the subjects over which a power to regulate commerce is asserted, are in their nature national, or admit of one uniform system or plan of regulation, they may justly be said to be of such a nature as to require exclusive legislation by congress. *Cooley v. Port Wardens*, 12 How. 299; *Gilman v. Philadelphia, supra; Crandall v. The State of Nevada*, 6 Wall. 42. Surely transportation of passengers or merchandise through a state, or from one state to another, is of this nature. It is of national importance that over that subject there should be but one regulating power, for if one state can directly tax persons or property passing through it, or tax them indirectly by levying a tax upon their transportation, every other may, and thus commercial intercourse between states remote from each other may be destroyed. The produce of western states may thus be effectually excluded from eastern markets, for though it might bear the imposition of a single tax, it would be crushed under the load of many. It was to guard against the possibility of such commercial embarrassments, no doubt, that the power of regulating commerce among the states was conferred upon the federal government.

* * * * * * * * *

§ 503. A state cannot tax persons for passing through or out of it. Inter-state transportation of passengers is beyond the reach of a state legislature. And if state taxation of persons passing from one state to another, or a state tax upon inter-state transportation of passengers is unconstitutional, *a fortiori*, if possible, is a state tax upon the carriage of merchandise from state to state, in conflict with the federal constitution. Merchandise is the subject of commerce. Transportation is essential to commerce; and every burden laid upon it is *pro tanto* a restriction. Whatever, therefore, may be the true doctrine respecting the exclusiveness of the power vested in congress to regulate commerce among the states, we regard it as established that no state can impose a tax upon freight transported from state to state, or upon the transporter, because of such transportation. But while holding this, we recognize fully the power of each state to tax at its discretion its own internal commerce, and the franchises, property, or business of its own corporations, so that inter-state intercourse, trade or commerce, be not embarrassed or restricted. That must remain free.[1]

§ 504. This opinion comes the nearest to being

[1] This opinion was delivered by Mr. Justice STRONG. The court was divided. For the full text, see Chicago Legal News, vol. v, No. 45.

apposite to the question of through freight, and the regulation by a state of the charges for its transportation, of any decision yet rendered. The exact limitation of state control over inter-state commerce will not have been authoritatively defined until the tribunal of last resort has rendered a decision in a case arising under the peculiar legislation of Illinois, or similar legislation in other states, should there be such legislation elsewhere.

§ 505. The Hon. ISAAC REDFIELD is so far an authority on railway law that his opinion on this subject is given. It is as follows, viz.:[1] "The fact that the entire subject of regulating all commerce among the different states, including all the means and appliances by which it was carried on, was committed to congress, and that, thereafter, the states were to have no concurrent action in the regulation of the same, would seem to reduce the question of congress having the power of regulating inter-state railway traffic to the single inquiry, whether it forms any portion of the commerce of the country, which requires to be regulated at all. Those who assume to argue that congress has no power to regulate the traffic upon these extended lines of railway reaching from one end of the Union to the other, must, if they would meet the question fairly, either say, the traffic on these extended lines of railway, amounting to many millions annually, probably ten times as much as the entire commerce of the country at the time of the adoption of the constitution, is not commerce at all, or, if it be, is not subject to any regulation or control whatever. For it is certain the states have neither the power or capacity to regu-

[1] Redfield, vol. 1, p. 723, fifth edition.

late, to any purpose, or with any efficiency, this inter-state railway traffic. It must then come under the control of congress or be left to its own devices and impulses, — an experiment never yet tried in any other country. * * * It will not be important here to enumerate the exceptions to the regulation of commerce by congress. It does not, of course, extend to that commerce which is exclusively within the limits of a single state; which begins and ends within the same state.[1] Hence, a state law conferring an exclusive right to the navigation of the upper waters of a river wholly within the limits of such state, and separated from tide water by falls, which are impassable for purposes of navigation, and not forming a continuous line of commerce between two or more states, or with a foreign country, is not unconstitutional.[2] And it seems to have been considered, by the later decisions, that so long as congress wholly abstains from all attempts to regulate any particular department of commerce, either foreign or inter-state, state laws in regard to the same will not be declared void.[3] There are some subjects of state cognizance which in their operation and enforcement produce an effect, incidentally, upon commerce beyond the limits of a single state, such as pilotage, ferries, health regulations, the support of paupers, police, and crime, which,

[1] Passaic Bridges, 3 Wall. 782; Heldeman v. Beckwith, 4 McLean (C. C.) 286.

[2] Veazie v. Moore, 14 How. 568.

[3] United States v. Railroad Bridge Co. 6 McLean (C. C.) 517; Woodman v. Kilbourne Man. Co. 6 Am. Law. Reg. (N. S.) 238; Cooley v. Board of Wardens, 12 How. (U. S.) 299; Gilman v. Philadelphia, 3 Wall. 713.

nevertheless, must be left to the control of the states, and whose legislation, if fairly kept within necessary limits, must be upheld."

III. Legislative and Judicial Authority.

§ 506. The object aimed at in the railway section of the constitution of Illinois, and the legislation thereunder is to prevent unjust charges and discrimination. The power of the state to exercise that authority has been shown to rest alike on the written and unwritten law. The final question is: How far is the exercise of that right vested in the legislature?

§ 507. The Chicago and Alton case gave to the supreme court its first and thus far its only opportunity to define its position herein. That opportunity was not improved, except indirectly. The only allusion to it was in connection with the forfeiture of franchise. No authorities were quoted by the learned Chief Justice. It is, however, a well established principle that even when the forfeiture of a franchise is the inevitable sequence of legislation, a judicial verdict on a writ of *quo warranto* or *scire facias* is necessary.

§ 508. In an early Illinois case the court held that "the legislative power cannot directly reach the property or vested rights of the citizen by providing for their forfeiture or transfer to another without trial and judgment in the court; for to do so would be the exercise of a power which belongs to another branch of the government, and is forbidden to the legislature." [1] This sentence fairly states the law as held by Illinois, in common with the other states of the Union.

§ 509. A corporation may, by willful malfeasance or nonfeasance, forfeit its franchises, which may be seized by the state on a judgment upon and information filed and prosecuted by the state, or its proper agent. At common law, at the dissolution of a corporation its property reverts to the grantor, except that in this country the creditors have, in effect, a first mortgage upon the same. Many charters in this country have been declared forfeited.

§ 510. The question as to the forfeiture of a charter, and the property acquired thereunder, may be tried by a writ of *quo warranto* or *scire facias*. The former is the more usual method. The supreme court holds that a proceeding by *quo warranto* is a "prosecution," within the intent of statute, and must therefore be carried on "in the manner and by the authority of the people of the state of Illinois." [2]

[1] Newland *v.* Marsh, 19 Ill. 382.

[2] For a thorough discussion of this subject see Wilmans *v.* Bank of Illinois, 1 Gilm. 667; People *v.* Mississippi and Atlantic R. R. Co. 13 Ill. 66; Wright *v.* People, 15 Ill. 417; People *v.* Ridgely, 21 Ill. 65; Curran *v.* Arkansas, 15 How. 312; Bacon *v.* Robertson, 18 How. 480; State *v.* Bailey, 16 Ind. 46; Silver Lake

§ 511. While it is too plain for doubt that the forfeiture of the franchises and property of a corporate body cannot be effected without judicial proceedings, it by no means follows that the legislature has not the power to lay down general rules for the conduct of corporate business. On the contrary, the authorities are

Bank *v.* North, 4 Johns' ch. N. Y. 370; Bank of Marietta *v.* Pindall, 2 Rand. Va. 465; Clarke *v.* New Jersey Co. 1 Stor. C. C. 531· British Co. *v.* Ames, 6 Met. Mass. 391; Savage Manuf. Co. *v.* Armstrong, 24 Me. 34; Day *v.* Essex Bank, 13 Vt. 97; Terret *v.* Taylor, 9 Cranch. 43; Commonwealth *v.* Commercial Bank, 28 Penn. St. 383; Aurora Co. *v.* Holthouse, 7 Ind. 59; Guaga Iron Co. *v.* Dawson, 4 Blackf. 202; Libby *v.* Hodges, 9 N. H. 394· Bank of Augusta *v.* Earle, 13 Peters, 519; Lucas *v.* Bank of Georgia, 2 Stew. 147; Vermont *v.* Turnpike Co. 11 Vt. 431; Commonwealth *v.* U. S. Bank, 2 Ashmead, 349. No legislation making detail provision for the enforcement of the right to exact this extreme corporate penalty exists. A bill was before the twenty-eighth general assembly in the winter of 1873, entitled, "An act to prevent unjust discrimination in the rates charged by railroads in this state for the tranportation of freight cars, and to encourage competition in freighting," containing the following provision: Any railroad corporation which shall be five times consecutively convicted of a violation of this act shall be deemed and held to have forfeited its franchises and property; and such corporation, so offending, may be proceeded against by the state's attorney in any circuit or county through or into which its road may run, either by *scire facias*, or upon an information in the nature of a *quo warranto*, to judgment of ouster. And in case of forfeiture of property and franchise, and judgment of ouster, the court shall fix the time, place and conditions for the sale of the same, at which time and place said corporate property and franchise shall be sold to the highest bidder giving security satisfactory to the court for the proper management of said road and the lawful conduct of all the business pertaining to said corporation. The proceeds of such sale, after defraying the costs and expenses of the suit or suits for forfeiture, shall be paid into the treasury of the state.

a unit in asserting that power. It is conceded that the courts, in the absence of specific legislation, have the power to prevent extortion and unjust discrimination on the part of common carriers. It was claimed by the counsel for the company in the Chicago and Alton case that this power is exclusively enjoyed by the judiciary. The court did not distinctly admit or deny the claim, nor give any authorities bearing upon it. This issue of law has often been raised, but never before in a connection of such transcendent importance.

§ 512. The most prominent state in adjudication on the question under consideration is New York. This issue has been often presented in the courts of that state, and learnedly discussed. The now well established doctrine of that commonwealth is correctly stated in these words: "The legislature possesses the whole legislative power of the people, except so far as limited by the constitution. In a judicial sense, and so far as the courts are concerned with its application and construction, their authority is absolute and unlimited, except by the express restrictions of the fundamental law. The state legislature is not restricted in power, any more than the British parliament, except by the state and federal constitution." [1]

§ 513. There is nothing whatever in the constitu-

[1] For authorities see Abbott's Digest, every volume of which contains some citations in support of this doctrine. The following are among the more important cases: Appeals, 1863—Bank of Chenango *v.* Brown, 26 N. Y. 467; S. P. Cathcart *v.* Fire Department of N. Y. Id. 529. Supreme court, 1864—Clark *v.* Miller, 42 Barber, 255; Luke *v.* City of Brooklyn, 43 Id. 54; People *v.* Morrell, 21 Wend. 563; Butler *v.* Palmer, 1 Hill, 324; Bloodgood *v.* Mohawk and Hudson R. R. Co. 18 Wend. 9; Leggett *v.* Hunter, 19 N. Y. 445.

tion of the United States, nor in the organic law of Illinois, which by any possible construction could be made to support the assumption of paramount judicial authority. The national constitution makes no attempt to define the relative functions of different branches of a state government, and the constitution of Illinois not only affords no ground for asserting that the judiciary has exclusive jurisdiction in the premises, but on the contrary, it expressly confers that jurisdiction upon the legislature. Its language is: "The general assembly shall, from time to time, pass laws establishing reasonable maximum rates of charges for the transportation of passengers and freight on the different railroads in this state."[1] Not content with this, the same organic law adds in another section: "The general assembly shall pass laws to correct abuses and prevent unjust discrimination and extortion in the rates of freight and passenger tariffs on the different railroads in this state, and enforce such laws, by adequate penalties, to the extent, if necessary for that purpose, of forfeiture of their property and franchises."[2]

§ 514. The decisions of Illinois on legislative and judicial jurisdiction are explicit and harmonious. They entirely agree in every essential feature with the doctrine of New York. So very plain were the early decisions that of late years there has been no room for doubt, and it is only the supreme importance of the subject in its bearing upon practical results that has induced a reopening of the question.[3] The only

[1] Ill. Constitution, art. xi, sec. 12.

[2] Ibid. sec. 15.

[3] The following are the more important Illinois decisions on this issue: Field *v.* People, 2 Scam. 79; Mason *v.* Wait, 4 Scam. 127;

inquiry for the courts is, "Does the will of the representatives, as expressed in the law, conflict with the will of the people, as expressed in the constitution?" Of the cases cited it is only necessary to particularize one. The first is selected for this purpose, because that has been uniformly referred to as a just and binding precedent.

§ 515. At the December term, 1839, the supreme court was called upon to decide whether A. P. Field or J. A. McClernand was entitled to the office of Secretary of State. The former had been elected to the office. The Governor of the state, Thomas Carlin, attempted his removal, and the appointment in his place of Mr. McClernand. The case resolved itself into the single question: Does the Governor possess the constitutional power of removing from office the Secretary of State, and appointing a successor at will? The decision was in the negative, and that because no specific grant of such power to the executive could be adduced from the constitution of the state. In its very elaborate and learned decision the court said: "The constitution is a limitation upon the powers of the legislative department of the government; but it is to be regarded as a grant of powers to the other departments. Neither the executive or the judiciary, therefore, can exercise any authority or power, except such as is clearly granted by the constitution." It will be observed that the judiciary and executive are

People *v.* Marshall, 1 Gilm. 672; People *et al.* *v.* Reynolds, 5 Gilm. 1; Nelson *v.* People, 33 Ill. 390; Turney *v.* Wilton, 36 Ill. 385; St. Louis, Jacksonville and Chicago R. R. Co. *v.* Trustees, 43 Ill. 303; Chicago and Alton R. R. Co. *v.* Shannon, Ibid. 338; People *v.* Solomon, 51 Ill. 38.

classed together, and broadly distinguished from the legislature. The court continued: "Upon the principle of our government, that the sovereign power of the state resides in the people, and that only such powers as they have delegated to their functionaries can be exercised, where a claim of power is advanced by the executive (judiciary), the question is, not whether the power in question has been granted to the people, but whether it has been granted to the executive, (judiciary); and if the grant cannot be shown, he has no title to the exercise of the power."[1]

§ 516. In his essay on Crimes and Punishment, a treatise which bore a conspicuous part in the reform of the judicial system of France, Voltaire insists that "there is nothing more dangerous than the common axiom: *the spirit of the laws is to be considered.* To adopt it is to give way to the torrent of opinion. When the code of laws is once fixed it should be observed in the literal sense, and nothing more is left to the judge than to determine whether an action be or be not conformable to the written law."[2] This statement is simply the opinion of the author as to what ought to be the law.

§ 517. In Potter's Dwarris occurs the following quotation credited to Cushing on Jurisprudence, section 40: "Legislation, though general, may, nevertheless, descend to minute details and particulars. When this is the case, it so far occupies the place which would otherwise be filled with jurisprudence." In the ninth chapter of Potter's Dwarris the relative

[1] Field *v.* People, 2 Scam. 79.

[2] Beccoria on Crime, commentary by Voltaire, chap. 5.

functions of legislation and jurisprudence are discussed and succinctly stated as follows: "The great and essential difference between legislation and jurisprudence, that which separates one from the other distinctly, is the manner in which they respectively become established. The former takes the place where the law-making power discovers occasion for it, and its provisions are framed prospectively for such classes of cases as the legislation thinks most likely to occur. The latter is only called into being when an actual case arises for its exercise, and is then adapted to the particular circumstances of the case.[1] Legislation, when once established, becomes fixed and unalterable, and it receives no additions but by subsequent legislation. Jurisprudence is constantly progressive, and continually enlarging and extending itself, as cases occur for its exercise, and adapting its principles to the social and political changes which are perpetually going on in society." To this the American editor adds: "Under the American theory, the powers of the legislature are limited by written constitutions, beyond the bounds of which they may not pass; and it is conferred upon the courts of justice to declare all legislation void which is in excess of the fundamental law."[2]

[1] This fact explains the practical importance of the question of jurisdiction under discussion.

[2] As the authority to regulate railway charges and prevent extortion and discrimination is expressly conferred by the fundamental law of Illinois upon the legislature, its exercise is not only admissible, but imperatively binding upon that body. It could not, if it would, leave its exercise to the exclusive jurisdiction of the courts. To do so would be unconstitutional.

§ 518. This subject is discussed still more thorougly by Chief Justice COOLEY in his work on Constitutional Limitations, and summed up in the statement, "the law is applied by the judiciary and made by the legislature."[1] Speaking of the danger from the abuse of judicial power, the same writer remarks: "No rule can be laid down in terms which may not contain the germ of great mischief to society by giving to private opinion and speculation a license to oppose themselves to the just and legitimate powers of government." In this connection he refers to *Wynehamer v. People.*[2]

§ 519. From his seat on the supreme bench of Vermont Chief Justice REDFIELD asserted and maintained as follows: "It has never been questioned, so far as I know, that the American legislatures have the same unlimited power in regard to legislation which resides in the British parliament, except where they are restrained by written constitution. That must be conceded, I think, to be a fundamental principle in the political organization of the American states. We cannot well comprehend how, upon principle, it should be otherwise. The people must, of course, possess all legislative power, originally. They have committed this in the most general and unlimited manner to the several state legislatures, saving only such restrictions as are imposed by the constitution of the United States, or of the particular states."[3] If the learned judge had been aiming to meet the question in dis-

[1] Cooley, on Constitutional Limitations, 91.

[2] 13 N. Y. 391.

[3] Thorpe *v.* Rutland and Burlington R. R. Co. 27 Vt. 142.

cussion, as presented by Illinois law, he could not have been more apposite.[1]

[1] The following are the citations made in the opinion to support the foregoing doctrine: Leggett *v.* Hunter, 19 N. Y. 445; Cochran *v.* Van Surlay, 20 Wend. 365; People *v.* Morrill, 21 Wend. 563; Sears *v.* Cottrell, 5 Mich. 251; Mason *v.* Wait, 4 Scam. 134; People *v.* Supervisors of Orange, 27 Barb. 593; Taylor *v.* Porter, 4 Hill, 144.

APPENDIX.

THE RAILWAYS OF ILLINOIS.

§ 520. The facts herein given are almost wholly condensed from the second annual report of the Railroad and Warehouse Commissioners, for the year ending December 1, 1872, a volume of 450 pages. For the sources of their information see sections 361–365. The usual gauge of Illinois railroads is 4 feet 8½ inches. The gauge will be mentioned only when it varies from that rule. Of the general policy of the roads as regards deference to the statute intended to prevent extortion and discrimination, it may be remarked that while a new schedule of rates was adopted on the first of July, 1873, the policy was to equalize, somewhat, the rates, making an aggregate increase, and that, not unfrequently of 20 per cent. The increase then made was adopted for the purpose of making the law odious. Since then the rates have been somewhat modified. The answers given to the questions touching car services or transportation companies will be given in full, except where the reply is simply that no discrimination is shown.

§ 521. Chicago and Alton.—Capital stock, $11,-355,300.00; all paid in. Total funded debt, $3,698,-000.00. No floating debt. Total length of track, 624½ miles. Intersects with other railroads at 19 different points. Gives no exclusive privileges or preference to any transportation company, person or corporation. Hauls 12 sleeping cars and 5 dining cars for the Pullman Palace Company. No stock dividends ever issued. During 1872 no passengers were killed; but August 16, 1873, a collision occurred near Lemont, in which 20 persons were killed. It was the most appalling casualty that ever occurred on an Illinois railroad. The company promises to lay a double track. Its business warrants the outlay, and the police power of the state could compel the construction, if necessary. It is estimated that the catastrophe will cost the company $500,000.

§ 522. Chicago, Burlington and Quincy.—Capital stock, $18,652,910; all paid in. Total funded debt, $12,996,956.95. Floating debt, none. Length of track, 972½ miles. Intersects with other roads at 15 points. Average charge per mile per 100 pounds through freight, 0.071–1 cts.; for local freight, 0.0159–1 cts. Annual amount through freight, 584,432 tons; of local freight, 1,144,130 tons. As regards transportation companies, the answer is: "The Merchants' Dispatch and Empire Line do business on the road at rates of commission agreed upon from time to time, and the usual mileage for use of cars. A cent and a half per mile, loaded or empty. Transportation companies repair their own cars. Business of no line is given a preference as to speed or order of transportation. This company is also owner in the Blue Line and Continental Line, each of which lines has a central management, maintained by each company comprising the lines, contributing proportionately to business done. Each road comprising the line seeks to place in the line its own proper proportion of cars, and in case of their actually doing so, the mileage of cars is practically paid for in kind. In case any road is over or short, the difference is made up at the usual rate of mileage."

§ 523. CHICAGO, DANVILLE AND VINCENNES.—Funded debt, $2,500,000. Value of road and equipments, $2,311,000. Length of track, 102 miles. Gauge, 4 feet 9 inches. Average rate per mile per 100 pounds for through freight, $\frac{3}{4}$ mills; for local freight, $2\frac{3}{35}$.

§ 524. CHICAGO AND IOWA.—Total funded and floating debt, $1,850,000. Value of road and equipments, $2,283,000. Length of track, 88 miles. Amount of municipal aid, $380,000. All cars are treated alike. The company owns no freight cars nor interest in any.

§ 525. CHICAGO AND NORTHWESTERN.—Refused to give present ownership of the stock, alleging the illegality of the statutory and constitutional requirement of information on that point; also, the impracticability of doing so, if the company were so inclined. Funded debt, $20,474,000. Total paid up stock and debt, $35,878,643.82. Cost of construction and equipment, $56,646,922.34. Length of track, 485 miles. Crossed at five different points in the state by other railroads. The company is made up of numerous companies. The report furnishes the following information on this point:

Illinois and Wisconsin Railroad Company, organized December 30, 1851, under act of the legislature of Illinois, of February 12, 1857; extends from Chicago north to Wisconsin state line; consolidated March 30, 1855, with the Rock River Valley Union Railroad Company (of Wisconsin), formerly the Chicago, St. Paul and Fond du Lac Railroad Company. This company, during its existence (retaining its corporate name), received by consolidations the following named companies, to-wit: 1. Wisconsin Superior Railroad Company (of Wisconsin), consolidated March 5, 1857. 2. Marquette State Line Railroad Company (of Michigan), consolidated March 21, 1857. 3. Ontonogan and State Line Railroad Company (of Michigan), consolidated March 27, 1857.

The Chicago, St. Paul and Fond du Lac Railroad Company was reorganized under the act of the leislature of Illinois, February 19, 1859, and the act of the legislature of Wisconsin, of March 14, 1859, and was incorporated June 6, 1859, by the name of the Chicago and Northwestern Railway Company, under which name it still exists, and has, since its incorporation, received by consolidations the following named companies, to-wit: Dixon, Rockford and Kenosha Railroad Company (of Illinois and Wisconsin), organized January 16, 1864; consolidated January 19, 1864.

The last named company was formed by consolidations of the "Kenosha and State Line Railroad Company," and the "Dixon, Rockford and State Line Railroad Company."

Galena and Chicago Union Railroad Company (of Illinois), incorporated January 16, 1836; amended March 4, 1837; amended February 24, 1847; consolidated June 2, 1864.

The Mississippi and Rock River Junction Railroad Company, incorporated February 13, 1851; amended February 28, 1854; was consolidated with the Galena and Chicago Union Railroad Company January 9, 1855, and confirmed by act of February 15, 1855.

The Elgin and State Line Railroad Company, incorporated February 12, 1859, (originally called the "Fox

River Valley Railroad Company," incorporated June 18, 1852,) was leased to the Galena and Chicago Union Railroad Company November 11, 1858.

The Chicago, St. Charles and Mississippi Air Line Railroad Company, incorporated January 31, 1849, as the St. Charles Branch Railroad Company; charter amended and name changed January 3, 1853, was also leased to the Galena and Chicago Union Railroad Company before the consolidation.

Peninsular Railroad Company (of Michigan), incorporated February 12, 1855; consolidated October 21, 1864.

Beloit and Madison Railroad Company (of Wisconsin), organized September, 1862; consolidated March, 1871.

Baraboo Air Line Railroad Company (of Wisconsin), incorporated March 8, 1870; amended February 2, 1871; consolidated March 10, 1871.

§ 526. Chicago, Rock Island and Pacific.—This company now consists of the consolidation of the Chicago and Rock Island, organized February 17, 1847, and the Chicago, Rock Island and Pacific, of Iowa, organized May 28, 1866. Capital stock, $18,999,200. Funded debt, $8,702,000. Floating debt, $70,672.92. Value of road and equipment, $28,761,315.65. Track in Illinois, 301¾ miles. Points at which other roads cross it, 6. Passenger earnings for the year in Illinois, $765,944.93; freight, $3,008,026.60; earnings from other sources, $189,206.29. Company hauls cars of all transportation companies who desire that service, and receives the going or tariff rates. The company owns and runs its own sleeping cars.

§ 527. Chicago and Rock River.—Capital stock

subscribed, $916,660; the amount paid in, $579,850. Nearly one-half made up from municipal aid bonds. Funded debt, $900,000. Cost of construction per mile, $36,000. Length of line to be 108 miles. Crosses Illinois Central once. Chartered March 4, 1869. Principal stockholders and contractors, Wicker, Mechling & Co., Chicago.

§ 528. COLUMBUS, CHICAGO AND INDIANA.—Capital stock, $13,328,568.96, all paid in. Funded debt, $24,221,374. Floating debt, $130,974. Value, $36,-919,288.13. Length of track in Illinois, $32\frac{2}{10}$ miles. Gauge, 4 feet 9½ inches. Intersects other roads at four points. Hauls cars for National Transportation Company, which uses its own cars, bears all expense of forwarding, receiving and billing freight, except hauling trains, "paying therefor rates which are regulated by current traffic." These cars are given no preference in any particular.

§ 529. GILMAN, CLINTON AND SPRINGFIELD.—Stock, $2,000,000, All paid in. Funded debt the same as stock. Total trackage, 116½ miles. Railroad intersections, 5. Municipal aid, $635,500. A note adds: "Stock subscriptions were tendered for these subscriptions. Town officers refused to issue bonds. Said stock is entered as paid, for the reason that the subscribed stock was to be turned over to the construction company in bonds or stock." Amount of stock outstanding, $2,000,000. Company chartered April, 1869.

HANNIBAL AND NAPLES.—Paid up stock and funded debt, $1,357,000. Value, the same. Trackage, 53 miles. Gauge, 4 feet 8½ inches. Has no equipments. Total earnings for the year, $95,397.47. Aided by

Pike county, $150,000. The road leased by the Toledo, Wabash and Western.

§ 530. Illinois Central.—Stock subscribed, $25,-448,900. Amount paid in, $25,447,140. Funded debt, $8,390,500. Cost of construction and equipment, $33,902,987.55. Trackage, 818$\frac{38}{100}$ miles. Intersects with 19 different railroads in Illinois. Any freight and transportation company can have its cars hauled over the road at an impartial rate; no preference or favoritism shown. Company owns the sleeping cars, and charges less than the usual rate for berths. Charter granted February 10, 1851. Charter amended three years later, and again in the year following. No consolidation in this state. Ten per cent. cash dividends declared on the stock of the original company for the past seven years. Road completed 1856.

§ 531. Illinois and St. Louis.—Gives full list stock subscribers. Total subscribed and paid in, $618,000. Funded debt, $660,000. Floating debt, $260,260. Debts equal value. Length of line, 15 miles. Aided by city of Belleville, $25,000. The original charter was granted February 28, 1841, under another name. Present name dates from February 16, 1865. Mainly a coal road.

§ 532. Indianapolis, Bloomington and Western.—Stock subscribed, $5,003,700. Proportion for Illinois, $3,052,331. All paid in. Debt proportioned to Illinois, $4,095,000. Cost of road and equipments in Illinois, $7,341,502.54. Trackage in Illinois, 147$\frac{4}{10}$ miles. Gauge, 4 feet 8$\frac{1}{2}$ inches. Intersects at six points. Municipal aid, $842,000. Road put in operation in 1870. The company is pushing several branches.

§ 533. Indianapolis and St. Louis.—Value, $2,945,-000. Length of track, 212 miles. Intersections with other lines, 5. Hauls cars for several transportation companies, to none of whom is any preference given in terms or facilities. This company is lessee of the

§ 534. St. Louis, Alton and Terre Haute.—The latter has a stock of $4,768,400. Funded debt, $7,000,000. Cost and value of road, $3,057,390. Trackage, 264 miles. Original charter granted January 28, 1851. Several lines consolidated 1856. Property foreclosed and sold under mortgage 1862, by order of the U. S. Circuit Court, Southern District, Illinois.

§ 535. St. Louis and Southeastern.—Capital stock subscribed and paid in, $758,300. Cost of construction, $1,325,614.51. Considerable right of way donated. Organization effected March, 1869. Construction began in May following. Municipal aid, $825,000. Length of road, 197 miles, including side tracks. Gauge, 4 feet 9 inches. Cost of construction and equipment, per mile, $21,176. Railway intersection at five points.

§ 536. Toledo, Peoria and Warsaw.—Capital stock paid up, $5,700,000. Funded debt, $6,450,000. Floating debt, $204,793.96. Cost per mile, $45,500, making a total of $12,150,000. Railway crossings, 7. Cars hauled for National Transportation Company. They furnish their own cars and receive 1½ cents per mile mileage. Company organized February 14, 1863, and is successor to the Mississippi and Wabash, chartered ten years before. In operation since October, 1868.

§ 537. Toledo, Wabash and Western.—Stock paid in, $16,000,000. Funded debt, $10,404,000. Cost.

$19,879,779.60, or $55,685.66 per mile. Competes with other roads at 14 points. Has 10 miles of effective Osage orange hedge fencing. It has no special conditions as to use of track for hauling the cars of transportation companies. The Red Line, Globe Line, South Shore Line and Great Western Dispatch patronize the road, the cars being furnished by the railroad.

§ 538. CHICAGO AND CANADA SOUTHERN.—Chartered March 31, 1869. The company has charters from Indiana, Michigan, Ohio and Illinois. None of the Illinois part of the line constructed. Capital stock, $10,000,000.

CHICAGO AND ILLINOIS SOUTHERN.—This corporation is a consolidation of the Chicago and Illinois Southern Railroad Company with the Decatur, Sullivan and Mattoon Railroad Company. The former company transacted no business prior to the consolidation, and the latter transferred to the present company no books or accounts upon which to base a full report. The road was reported as so far completed that mixed trains have been run from Mattoon to Dalton, 29 miles; it intersects the Indianapolis and St. Louis Railway one mile west of Mattoon, runs in upon that track and uses the depot of that road at Mattoon. The intention is to build a road from Mattoon to Decatur, 40 miles.

§ 539. CHICAGO, MILWAUKEE AND ST. PAUL.—Articles of association under the general railroad law of the state were made and filed April 2, 1872. By agreement the Chicago and Milwaukee Railway Construction Company took all the stock, $2,000,000. Russell Sage, New York, President. At the time the report was made four only of the nine directors resided in Chicago.

§ 540. Chicago and Muscatine.—Organized in the fall of 1871. Total subscription to date, $200,000; 10 per cent. paid in. No work begun.

§ 541. Chicago and Pacific.—Exists by the provisions of a charter granted by the state to the Atlantic and Pacific Railroad Company, dated February 16, 1865, the name of which was changed to that of the Chicago and Pacific Railroad Company. Its eastern terminus was fixed at a point, to be selected by the company, on a line between the states of Indiana and Illinois, in Cook county; and its western terminus at any point on the Mississippi river, to be hereafter selected, at or north of Savanna, Ill. The company has commenced the construction of the railroad at Chicago, and is progressing westward. Definite construction arrangements extend only to Elgin.

§ 542. Chicago and Paducah.—Is a consolidation of the Fairbury, Pontiac and Northwestern Railway Company, and the Bloomington and Ohio River Railroad Company. The consolidation was effected on the 22d day of March, 1872. The proposed line of road wil. extend from Streator, in LaSalle county, to Flora, in Clay county, a distance of about 200 miles. On the 30th of June, 1872, there was completed from Streator to Fairbury 32 miles, and from Bement to Windsor 35 miles; total, 67 miles. The capital stock is $5,000,000; paid in, $1,350,000. Municipal aid, $540,000. Cash man, Plumb & Co., Chicago, contractors.

§ 543. Chicago, Pekin and Southwestern. — Is designed to run from Chicago to Pekin, 160 miles. Expended to date for construction, $345,474.49. Stock subscribed, $519,500. Actually paid, $240,000. Municipal aid subscribed, $290,000. Principal office at Streator.

§ 544. GRAND TOWER MANUFACTURING AND TRANSPORTATION CO.—The total length of track of this road road is $30\frac{24}{100}$. Under the head of "miscellaneous exhibits" is found only this item: "Coal, 13,305,460 tons." This road comes the nearest to not being a highway of any railroad in Illinois.

§ 545. INDIANA AND ILLINOIS CENTRAL.—This road is in process of construction from Indianapolis, Indiana, to Decatur, Illinois. It is 152 miles in length, and connects at termini with the extensive network of railways which converge to these points. The expenditure to date were about $1,400,000. Capital stock subscribed and paid in, $4,500,000. Municipal aid in Illinois, $330,000.

§ 546. JACKSONVILLE, NORTHWESTERN AND SOUTHEASTERN.—Debt secured by mortgage, $100,000. Municipal aid, $8000.00. Length, 17¼ miles.

§ 547. KANKAKEE AND INDIANA.—Chartered April 19, 1869. Construction began August 20, 1871. Capital stock subscribed, $92,400; paid in, $67,300. Funded debt, $220,000. Length of road, 11 miles. Guage, 4 feet 8½ inches. Cost of road per mile, $6,000. Municipal aid, $66,500. Designed to intersect the Chicago Branch of Illinois Central Railroad at Kankakee, 56 miles south of Chicago, and the Cincinnati, Lafayette and Chicago Railroad at St. Ann, making in connection with these lines a through route from Chicago, via Kankakee, to Cincinnati.

§ 548. LAFAYETTE, BLOOMINGTON AND MISSISSIPPI.—Chartered February 28, 1867. Municipal aid, $467,000. Length, $82\frac{3}{10}$ miles. Capital stock, $1,000,000, all paid in. Funded debt, $1,300,000. Has four railway intersections.

§ 549. LOUISVILLE, NEW ALBANY AND ST. LOUIS AIR LINE.—Capital stock depends upon completion of the road. The intention is to build a line from New Albany, Ind., to East St. Louis, Ill., 250 miles, this company in connection with other railroad companies forming the line. Their cars or freight give no special preference of any kind. The railroad companies forming the T. W. W. Co. were consolidated July 1, 1865. Original construction began 1850.

§ 550. WESTERN UNION.—The report of this company is for the entire line in Illinois and Wisconsin. Paid up stock and debt, $7,723,654.32, nearly all expended in building and equipping the line, which is 207 miles long. Crossing the Chicago and Northwestern twice and the Chicago, Burlington and Quincy once. Company formed by the consolidation of eight different companies, the oldest dating back to January 21, 1851. The road is now held under mortgage foreclosures.

§ 551. CAIRO AND ST. LOUIS.—Capital stock subscribed, $950,000, all by municipal subscriptions. Road chartered February 16, 1865; charter amended April 16, 1869. Mortgaged October 2, 1871, to the amount of $2,500,000. Its only peculiarity is its gauge, 3 feet.

§ 552. CARBONDALE AND SHAWNEETOWN.—Original charter granted March 7, 1867; present name taken March 10, 1869. Capital stock outstanding, $355,500. Municipal aid, $100,000. Funded debt, $200,000. Length of road in Illinois, 18 miles.

§ 553. CHESTER AND TAMAOROA.—Organized June 15,

1869. Began construction a year later. Stock, $1,000,-000; paid in. Municipal aid, $315,000. Intersects other railroads at two points. Trackage, 44½ miles. Finished March, 1872.

§ 554. MUSCATINE, KEWANEE AND EASTERN.—Capital stock, $110,000, all municipal aid. This road commences on the east bank of the Mississippi river, opposite the city of Muscatine, Iowa; is to run eastward through Kewanee, Henry county, to a point on the east line of the state of Illinois not yet designated. The entire length of the main track will be about 200 miles. No right of way had been obtained, nor any grading done at the time the report was made.

§ 555. PARIS AND DECATUR.—Chartered February 18, 1861. Stock paid in, $1,600,000. Robt. G. Hervey & Co. contracted to build the road for this amount. Municipal aid, $463,000. Construction began August, 1870.

§ 556. PLYMOUTH, KANKAKEE AND PACIFIC.—Has 101 miles in Illinois, terminating in this state at Bureau. Is a branch, virtually, of the Pennsylvania Central. Municipal aid in Illinois, $543,000. Average cost of construction, $4,531.60.

§ 557. SPRINGFIELD AND SOUTHERN ILLINOIS. Capital stock, $3,776,500. Funded debt, $4,400,000. Floating debt, $140,000. Length of main track, 228 miles.

§ 558. ST. LOUIS, JERSEYVILLE AND SPRINGFIELD.—Organized March 20, 1872. No subscriptions or expenditures, except for surveys. General offices at Jerseyville.

§ 559. ROCKFORD, ROCK ISLAND AND ST. LOUIS.—Total stock paid in, $6,490,579.41, including municipal aid to the amount of $1,043,000. Total funded debt, $9,000,000. Length of the road, 344 miles. Only about three-fourths of the road is fenced. It has seventeen railway intersections.

§ 560. Pekin, Lincoln and Decatur.—Amount of stock $1,500,000, all paid in. Of this stock county and township aid covers $625,000, and individual aid $75,000. Total funded debt, $1,076,000. The road cost $38,333.33 per mile, and is 67 miles long. The road is leased to the Toledo, Wabash and Western.

§ 561. Peoria and Rock Island.—Total stock paid in, $1,857,950. Debt of the company, $1,665,277. The road is 91 miles long, and reports four hundred bridges. General offices at Peoria. The total estimated value of the road, with its equipments, is $3,623,558.

§ 562. Peoria, Pekin and Jacksonville.—President resides in Connecticut, and draws $10,000 salary. The funded debt is $2,000,000. The stock is $1,000,000. The total estimated value of road and equipment is $427,136. It is 83 miles long. The municipal aid was $70,000.

§ 563. Ohio and Mississippi.—Total stock, $24,030,000. Debt, $10,440,751. Length of the road, 393 miles, of which 147½ miles are in Illinois. Gauge, 57 inches.

§ 564. Michigan Central.—This is the only railroad company doing business in Illinois which has no corporate existence in the state. On a capital stock of $17,987,048 its net earnings for the last fiscal year were $1,808,957. Its main line extends from Chicago to Detroit, 285 miles. The company operates, under lease, 430 miles more.

§ 565. Lake Shore and Michigan Southern.—Capital stock, $35,000,000, all paid in. The total cost of construction and equipment was $62,053,600, and the total length of the road is 1,023 miles, only 14 miles being in this state. The gauge of the road is 4 feet 9½ inches. Six transportation companies do a through freight business on that line. They are paid the usual mileage on cars, 1½ cents per mile, whether loaded or empty, and receive a commission on freight, but the nature of that commission arrangement is kept secret.

§ 566. PITTSBURGH, FORT WAYNE AND CHICAGO.—Total stock subscribed, $21,614,285, of which only $1,614,285 paid in. The funded debt amounts to $13,623,000. Gauge of the road, 4 feet 9½ inches. The road is 468 miles long, and cost, with equipments, $26,288,122. Only 14½ miles of the road are in Illinois. The fullest report in regard to transportation companies is given by this company. It is as follows: "The transportation companies are to establish and maintain, at their own expense, independent and efficient agencies in the principal cities of the east and west, and, generally, to co-operate with the officers of the company in establishing the line in public favor; furnish their own cars, and keep them in repair, subject to the approval of the car inspector of the railway company; pay all expenses, including loss and damage of freight, connected with the shipment and delivery of freight, and pay to railway company certain specified rates, which rates are based upon an average of prevailing rates charged by the railway company for similar freight. The railway company pay to the transportation company three mills per ton per mile for the use of their cars, and have a general supervision of the rates and business."

We have thus been at the labor of sifting from the mass of facts given by the railroad companies such items as give the best idea of each road in Illinois.

GENERAL SUMMARY.

§ 567. ACREAGE.—The report makes the following exhibit of the area of the state with reference to railroads: The number of acres within five miles, 25,621,-778; between five and ten miles, 6,603,007; between ten and fifteen miles, 1,629,931; between fifteen and twenty miles and over, 708,800. Total area in acres, 34,563,516. This summary is based on details furnished by Mr. T. J. Nicholl.

§ 568. CAPITAL STOCK.—The paid in capital of all the railroad companies of Illinois foots up $140,126,-064.28; their funded debt, $111,456,325.97; floating debt, $3,330,173.20. Amount of paid in stock and debts, $254,912,563.45. These last figures represent the actual capital invested up to July, 1872, in railroads existing under Illinois legislation, although the official statement of the cost of road and equipment up to that date, and for those railways, foots up $238,584,541.24. We have here an excess of paid up stock and debts over cost of building and equipping of $20,328,022.21.

§ 569. COST.—The average cost per mile of constructing and equipping the roads completed July, 1872, was $42,264.48. Total miles of road at that date were 6,360$\frac{60}{100}$; main line, 4,709$\frac{12}{100}$; branches, 1,549$\frac{68}{100}$.

§ 570. Rolling Stock.—The total equipments reported: Locomotives of twenty to thirty tons weight, 1,305; of ten to twenty, 822; of less weight, 76. Total, 2,203. Passenger cars, 984; other cars, 48,114. Total, 49,098.

§ 571. Mileage.—The mileage of trains during the year ending July, 1872: Passenger, 9,109,549; freight, 18,290,187; other trains, 4,777,438. Total, 32,301,174.

Tonnage of Completed Roads.—Through freight, 1,789,046$\frac{3}{8}$; local freight, 3,513,589$\frac{1}{4}$.

Accidents.—Passengers killed, 8; injured, 21; employes killed, 65; injured, 126. Accidents to others: Killed, 75; injured, 93.

§ 572. Earnings.—The gross earnings for all railroads operated in Illinois were $43,227,128.04; the gross expenses were $45,249,968.55. Excess of expenses over earnings, $2,022,840.51. These figures are based upon the sworn statements of the railway managers, which statements are summarized by the railroad and warehouse commissioners in their annual report, dated December 1, 1872, as follows:

EARNINGS—IN DETAIL.

	Names of Companies.	Passenger.	Freight.	Miscellaneous.	Total.
1.	Chicago and Alton	$1,325,723 07	$3,609,525 68	$232,863 40	$5,168,112 15
2.	Chicago, Burlington and Quincy	1,742,181 47	5,124,831 97	726,664 74	7,593,678 18
3.	§ Chicago, Danville and Vincennes	38,307 97	234,360 39	14,801 98	287,470 34
4.	† Chicago and Iowa	15,192 63	56,830 30	1,239 42	73,262 35
5.	* Chicago and Northwestern	1,056,473 41	2,426,222 43	203,615 04	3,686,310 88
6.	Chicago, Rock Island and Pacific	765,944 93	3,008,026 60	189,206 29	3,963,177 82
7.	Chicago and Rock River	840 85	6,581 38	300 00	7,722 23
8.	* Columbus, Chicago and Indiana Central	45,167 64	121,802 75	6,278 85	173,249 24
9.	Grand Tower and Carbondale	10,722 65	28,861 29	1,000 00	40,583 94
10.	‡ Gilman, Clinton and Springfield	30,656 40	122,118 50	3,975 19	156,750 09
11.	Hannibal and Naples	34,159 26	55,533 25	5,704 96	95,397 47
12.	Illinois Central	1,341,667 13	4,728,247 18	383,670 86	6,453,585 17
13.	Illinois and St. Louis	12,808 50	57,126 60	6,420 72	76,355 82
14.	Indianapolis, Bloomington and Western	243,273 00	500,529 78	33,325 22	777,128 00
15.	Indianapolis and St. Louis	344,283 05	953,252 83	125,361 12	1,422,897 00
16.	Lake Shore and Michigan Southern	7,000 00	126,000 00	28,000 00	224,000 00
17.	Ohio and Mississippi	382,208 85	809,273 25	59,080 91	1,250,563 01
18.	Peoria, Pekin and Jacksonville	75,367 16	195,801 60	49,907 60	321,076 36
19.	§ Peoria and Rock Island	33,110 56	84,257 62	20,376 07	437,477 92
20.	Pekin, Lincoln and Decatur	20,499 56	45,871 30	4,945 60	71,316 46
2 .	Pittsburgh, Ft. Wayne and Chicago	117,713 64	302,621 00	17,143 28	437,744 25
22.	* Rockford, Rock Island and St. Louis	252,635 32	760,236 22	54,877 15	1,067,748 69
23.	St. Louis, Alton and Terra Haute	136,470 64	157,452 32	214,384 09	508,306 96
24.	St. Louis and Southeastern	123,004 87	218,881 88	15,965 85	357,852 60
25.	St. Louis, Vandalia and Terra Haute, by T. H. & I. Co.	358,641 63	730,502 57	21,305 86	1,110,450 06
26.	Toledo, Peoria and Warsaw	250,698 26	961,899 87	64,712 33	1,277,310 46
27.	Toledo, Wabash and Western	1,209,334 38	4,304,493 38	492,900 67	6,006,728 43
28.	* Western Union	118,077 22	343,452 48	19,642 46	481,172 16
	Totals,	$10,155,164 05	$30,074,594 42	$2,997,669 57	$43,227,428 04

§ Being for six months from 1st of January, 1872.
† Being for nine months from 9th October, 1871.
‡ Being for ten months from November, 1871.
* See page 27, Secretary's Report.

GROSS EARNINGS COMPARED WITH EXPENSES.

	Names of Companies.	Gross Earnings.	Amount of Operating and General Expenses.	Excess of Earnings.	Excess of Expenses.
1.	Chicago and Alton	$5,168,112 15	$3,171,725 98	$1,996,386 17	
2.	Chicago, Burlington and Quincy	7,593,678 18	5,550,586 17	2,043,102 01	
3.	Chicago, Danville and Vincennes	287,470 34	163,544 40	123,925 94	
4.	Chicago and Iowa	73,262 35	155,000 00		$81,737 65
5.	Chicago and Northwestern	3,686,310 88	2,168,810 20	1,517,500 68	
6.	Chicago, Rock Island and Pacific	3,963,177 82	1,753,746 78	2,209,431 04	
7.	Chicago and Rock River	7,422 22	5,085 43	2,336 80	
8.	Columbus, Chicago and Indiana Central	173,249 24	139,144 32	34,104 92	
9.	Grand Tower and Carbondale	40,583 94			
10.	Gilman, Clinton and Springfield	156,750 09	123,224 53	33,525 56	
11.	Hannibal and Naples	95,397 47	118,613 00		23,215 53
12.	Illinois Central	6,453,585 17	4,439,203 86	2,014,381 31	
13.	Illinois and St. Louis	76,355 82	72,551 24	3,804 58	
14.	Indianapolis, Bloomington and Western	777,128 00	494,740 68	282,387 32	
15.	Indianapolis and St. Louis	1,422,897 00	962,680 46	469,216 54	
16.	Lake Shore and Michigan Southern	224,000 00	148,319 78	75,680 22	
17.	Ohio and Mississippi	1,250,563 01	872,270 21	378,292 80	
18.	Peoria, Pekin and Jacksonville	321,076 36	218,777 91	102,298 45	
19.	Peoria and Rock Island	137,744 25	80,590 10	57,154 15	
20.	Pekin, Lincoln and Decatur	71,316 46	64,585 23	6,731 23	
21.	Pittsburgh, Ft. Wayne and Chicago	437,477 92	229,685 64	207,792 28	
22.	Rockford, Rock Island and St. Louis	1,067,748 69	823,214 35	244,534 34	
23.	St. Louis, Alton and Terra Haute	508,306 96	294,289 66	214,017 30	
24.	St. Louis and Southeastern	357,852 60	270,105 12	87,747 48	
25.	St. Louis, Vandalia and Terra Haute, by T. H. & I. Co.	1,110,450 06	796,149 06	314,301 00	
26.	Toledo, Peoria and Warsaw	1,277,310 46	921,594 59	355,715 87	
27.	Toledo, Wabash and Western	6,006,728 43	3,991,077 53	2,015,650 90	
28.	Western Union	481,172 16	379,018 08	102,154 08	
	Totals,	$43,227,128 04	$28,408,324 31	$14,883,172 97	$104,353 18

LEGAL TRANSPORTATION RATES IN ILLINOIS.

The relations of the Railroad and Warehouse Commissioners to railway charges have been explained. In accordance with law they have set forth a scale of charges for passengers and freight. They have classified the railroads of the state, making a five-fold classification. The schedule given on page 330, and taken from the *Railroad Gazette*, of Sept. 13th, 1873, furnishes a key to the freight schedules prepared for the roads of the first class. The rates for roads of the second class are fixed at 10 per cent. below the first or standard rates. The rates for the third class are fixed at 5 per cent. above the standard. The rates for the fourth class at 10 per cent. above. The rates for the fifth class at 15 per cent. above. The passenger rates for these classes are 3 cents per mile for the first class; 2½ for the second; 3¼ for the third; 3½ for the fourth; 4 for the fifth. These variations are based on the amount of patronage the several roads enjoy, and the relations of gross to net receipts, as shown by the sworn reports to the Board, made by the officers of each company. The classification is as follows:

First Class—Columbus, Chicago and Indiana Central; Indianapolis, Bloomington and Western; Chicago, Alton and St. Louis; Illinois Central; Chicago, Burlington and Quincy; Chicago and Northwestern; Indianapolis and St. Louis; Chicago, Rock Island and Pacific; Toledo, Wabash and Western; Ohio and Mississippi. *Second Class*—Michigan Central; Lake Shore and Michigan Southern; Pittsburgh, Ft. Wayne and Chicago. *Third Class*—Western Union; Chicago, Danville and Vincennes; Toledo, Peoria and Warsaw; St. Louis, Alton and Terre Haute; Illinois and St. Louis. *Fourth Class*—Peoria, Pekin and Jacksonville; Peoria and Rock Island; Rockford, Rock Island and St. Louis. *Fifth Class*—Gilman, Clinton and Springfield; Chicago and Iowa; Hannibal and Naples; Peoria, Lincoln and Decatur; St, Louis and Southeastern; Cairo and Vincennes; and all other organized roads in the State.

The standard rates for one mile and less than two, are 12 cents per hundred for first-class merchandise, 10.67 for second-class, 9.23 for third class, 8 for fourth-class; 10.67 per barrel for flour and meal in car loads; 12.73 for salt, plaster, etc., in lots of 25 barrels; 4.26 cents per hundred for all grains except wheat in car-loads; 4.68 for wheat; $8.27 per car-load for lumber; $9 for horses and mules; $8 for cattle and pigs; $7 for sheep in single deck cars; for classes "A," "B," "C," and "D" respectively, $11.20, $9.60, $8.69 and $7.63 per car-load; and for coal 30 cents per ton in car-loads ($3 per car-load). The method of graduation may be seen by inspecting the rate for first-class goods. An addition of 0.5 cent for each additional mile is made up to 5 miles; then an addition of 0.4 cent per mile up to 20 miles; then of 0.3 cent per mile up to 30 miles; then of 0.2 cent per mile up to 140 miles; then of 0.15 cent up to 247 miles.

SCHEDULE OF RATES FOR FREIGHT.

CLASS OF FREIGHT.	Rate for First Mile.	Addition for Each Additional Mile up to 5 *miles.*	20 *miles.*	30 *miles.*	140 *miles.*	247 *miles.*
First class, ℔ 100 lbs.	12.00 cts.	0.5 cts.	0.4 cts.	0.3 cts.	0.2 cts.	0.15 cts.
Second class, ℔ 100 lbs.	10.67	0.4	0.3	0.23	0.165	0.13
Third class, ℔ 100 lbs.	9.33	0.3	0.21	0.167	0.133	0.10
Fourth class, ℔ 100 lbs.	8.00	0.2	0.12	0.10	0.10	0.075
				Up to 100 *ms.*	*Up to* 155 *ms.*	
Flour and meal, ℔ bbl., in car loads, ℔ bbl.	10.67	----	----	0.22 cts.	0.11 cts.	0.088
Salt, cement, plaster and stucco, in 25 brl. lots, ℔ brl.	12.73	----	----	0.26	0.13	0.105
Grain (exc. wheat) and millstuffs, in car loads, ℔ 100 lbs.	4.26	----	----	0.087	0.044	0.035
Wheat, in car loads, ℔ 100 lbs.	4.68	----	----	0.097	0.05	0.04
Lumber, ℔ car load	$8.27	----	----	17.00	8.60	6.80
				Up to 50 *ms.*	*Up to* 100 *ms.*	
Horses and mules, ℔ car load	9.00	35.0	28.0	20.0 cts.	13.0 cts.	10.00
				Up to 55 *ms.*	*Up to* 200 *ms.*	
Cattle and hogs, ℔ car load	8.00	----	24.0	12.00 cts.	10.0 cts.	9.00
			Up to 30 *ms.*			
Sheep, in single-deck cars, ℔ car load	7.00	20.0	15.0	----	10.0	6.00
		Up to 25 *ms.*		*Up to* 50 *ms.*	*Up to* 100 *ms.*	
Class "A," ℔ car load	11.20	31.0 cts.	----	26.0 cts.	17.6 cts.	11.00
Class "B," ℔ car load	9.60	----	28.0	20.0	16.5	10.30
		Up to 20 *ms.*				
Class "C," ℔ car load	8.68	27.0	----	----	11.6	10.50
Class "D," ℔ car load	7.63	----	16.0	----	----	10.50
		Up to 5 *ms.*	*Up to* 10 *ms.*		*Up to* 200 *ms.*	
Coal, in car loads, ℔ ton	0.30	7.5 cts.	2.0	----	1.0 cts.	0.50

No rate has been, as yet, established for car service; but the law is plain. It requires that all cars shall be hauled at a reasonable and impartial rate. The present uniform arrangement is to allow the car owner $1\frac{1}{2}$ cents per mile for the use of his car, whether loaded or empty. This arrangement gives, on an average, thirty per cent. of the gross receipts on through freight transported in transportation company cars to the transportation companies. Thus the railroads have themselves, without legislation, fixed the thirty per cent. as a fair allowance for car service. It is a more liberal arrangement for the car owner than the Commissioners would probably have fixed had there been no precedent to follow; but since that schedule for car service has been fixed for through freight, by the railroads, they could not complain of its application to way freight. It is worth more both to furnish cars and to do the hauling for a short distance than for a long, and by allowing thirty per cent. to one and seventy per cent. to the other, an equitable division would be made, which would be equally applicable to short and long hauls, to way and through freight, and to all stations. The Railway Law of Illinois, by thus requiring the railroads to allow the competitive system already in vogue, as regards through freight, to be applied universally, has struck the key note of the practical solution of the transportation problem. Where competition is possible monopoly is impossible.

INDEX.

THE FIGURES REFER TO THE SECTIONS.

G.

H.

I.

J.

K.

L.

M.

N.

O.

P.

www.ingramcontent.com/pod-product-compliance
Lightning Source LLC
LaVergne TN
LVHW010203110826
845151LV00002B/596

* 9 7 8 1 4 2 5 5 3 6 1 8 3 *